The Dynamite Club

The Dynamite Club

How a Bombing in Fin-de-Siècle Paris
Ignited the Age of Modern Terror

John Merriman

Houghton Mifflin Harcourt

BOSTON · NEW YORK

2009

For information about permission to reproduce selections from
this book, write to Permissions, Houghton Mifflin Harcourt
Publishing Company, 215 Park Avenue South,
New York, New York 10003.

www.hmhbooks.com.

Library of Congress Cataloging-in Publication Data
Merriman, John M.
The dynamite club : how a bombing in fin-de-siècle Paris
ignited the age of modern terror / John Merriman.
p. cm.
Includes bibliographical references and index.
ISBN 978-0-618-55598-7
1. Bombings—France—Paris—History—19th century. 2. Terrorism—
France—Paris—History—19th century. 3. Anarchism—France—
Paris—History—19th century. 4. Henry, Emile, 1872–1894. I. Title.
HV6433.F7A636 2009 363.3250944'361—dc22 2008049470

Printed in the United States of America

Book design by Robert Overholtzer

DOC 10 9 8 7 6 5 4 3 2 1

2/20/2009

FOR VICTORIA JOHNSON

Contents

PARIS, 1894

Places Where Émile Henry Lived and Worked

1. 101, rue Marcadet
2. 10, boulevard Morland
3. 31, rue Véron
4. Villa Faucheur, 1–3, rue des Envierges
5. 32, rue du Sentier
6. 5, rue de Rocroy

Other Addresses

7. Constant Martin's Shop, 3, rue Joquelet
8. Offices of *La Révolte*, 140, rue Mouffetard
9. Salle du Commerce, 94, rue du Faubourg-du-Temple
10. Home of Élisa Gauthey, 167, boulevard Voltaire
11. Carmaux Mining Company, 11, avenue de l'Opéra
12. Police Station, 22, rue des Bons Enfants
13. Execution site, place de la Roquette
14. Café Terminus, rue Saint-Lazare

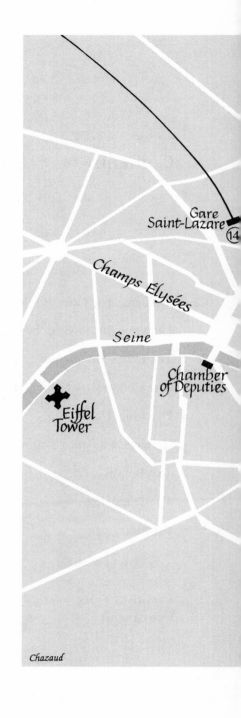

Gare Saint-Lazare

⑭

Champs Élysées

Seine

Chamber of Deputies

Eiffel Tower

Chazaud

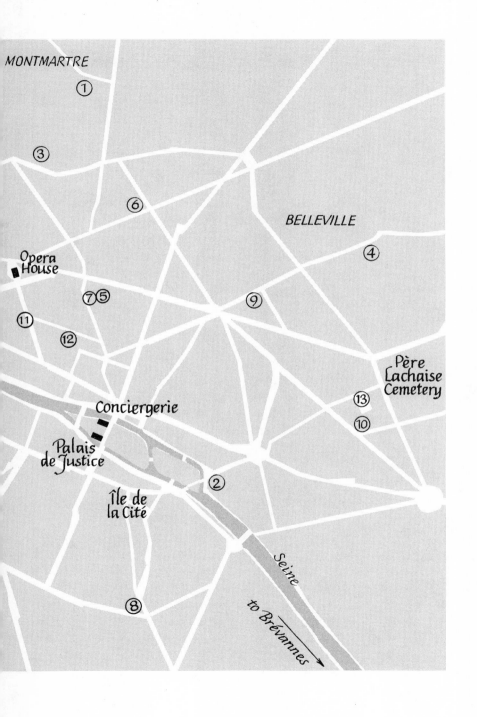

The Dynamite Club

The Café Terminus

IN HIS ROOM on the edge of Paris, Émile Henry was preparing a bomb. He took a worker's metal lunchbox, broke off the handle and lid, and placed a cartridge of dynamite inside. He then filled a zinc tube with 120 pieces of buckshot, adding green powder and picric acid to make a deadly mix. In a small opening in the tube, he put a capsule of mercury fulminate, along with a fuse that would burn for fifteen to eighteen seconds, which he attached with sealing wax. The fuse protruded from the screw hole that had once secured the handle. Having soldered the tin container and wrapped wire around it, Émile put the bomb, which weighed about five pounds, in a deep pocket of his overcoat. He then armed himself with a loaded pistol and a knife, and walked out the door. It was February 12, 1894.

His hand firmly on the bomb, the pale young man headed to the elegant boulevards in the area of the Opera. He wanted to detonate the bomb in this wealthy district, killing as many people as possible. He counted on fifteen dead and twenty wounded at the very least.

At the end of avenue de l'Opéra, Émile Henry stopped in front of the opera house, a giant gilded wedding cake of a building, its scale and rich decoration signifying the monumental ambition and self-indulgence of its founders and patrons. In that twenty-year-old edifice a fancy ball was taking place, and Émile knew that he could not get past the guards to throw his bomb. Upon moving away he mumbled to no one in particular, "Oh, I would have made them dance in there." He checked out the restaurant Bignon and the chic Café de la Paix in the Grand Hôtel, then proceeded to the Café Américain on rue de la Paix. (Had he consulted the Baedeker guide for 1889, he would have noted that it was "less frequented in the evening.") He looked a little like a flâneur, an intellectual who might be something of a dandy, but Émile was in fact an impoverished bourgeois who lived on the margins of urban life. He strolled along the *grands boulevards* not just to observe nightlife in a detached manner, but to hate and to kill. The carriages and wagons that passed as he walked along boulevard des Capucines may have included a black wagon carrying the *"bois de justice"*—the guillotine. An execution was planned for the following morning at place de la Roquette in a working-class neighborhood of Paris.

At about 8 P.M., Émile reached the Café Terminus, around the corner from the busy Gare Saint-Lazare. The Hôtel Terminus was only about twenty years old. The café, which one entered from rue Saint-Lazare, took up the ground floor; the hotel rooms occupied the upper floors. Opposite the entrance stood the counter where waiters collected drinks for patrons and behind which stood the cashiers and bartenders. Beyond that, up several steps, was the grand hall of the adjacent Restaurant Terminus. In the far left corner of the grand hall stood a compact raised stage, set for a small gypsy orchestra scheduled to play that evening.

Although his clothing was hardly elegant, with his dark pants, tie, and black felt hat, Émile Henry seemed like someone who might naturally be present there. At 8 P.M., as the café was slowly filling, he went in and took a small table to the right of the glass door that gave onto rue Saint-Lazare. He ordered a beer, and soon another, along with a cigar, and paid for them as the orchestra played. The musical program began at exactly 8:30, as it did each evening. It was to include seven pieces in the first set, to be followed by five violin solos (among them, pieces by Meyerbeer and Rossini). Several instrumental transcriptions of popular operatic arias were on offer. A short entr'acte, consisting of polkas, and a little Wagner were to follow. By 9 P.M., about 350 people had assembled in the Terminus. At 9:01, the small orchestra had just started to play the fifth piece in the first set, music from Daniel Auber's opera *Les diamants de la couronne.*

Émile found the music annoying, but, in any case, he had other plans. He took the bomb from his overcoat pocket, got up, and walked to the door, which a waiter closed behind him. But after taking a step or two outside, Émile turned back, lit the fuse (on the third try) with his cigar, opened the door, grabbed it with his left hand for support, and threw the bomb into the café, toward the orchestra.

This book is motivated by a very simple question: why did Émile Henry do what he did? Getting inside the mind of a bomber is no easy task, especially when the bombing took place over a century ago and halfway around the world. But for a historian in the early twenty-first century, the temptation is irresistible. Embroiled in our own "war on terror," it may well be instructive to look to the past for insight. The parallel is not a perfect one—the differences between the Islamist fundamentalists and Émile Henry's circle are obvious—but a deeper look reveals a gossamer thread connecting the two. And in that thread lies an important story.

Paris at the end of the nineteenth century was a place of shocking social inequalities. Far from the magnificent cathedral of Notre Dame, the sparkling opera house, the recently constructed Eiffel Tower, then the tallest structure in the world, and indeed far from all the glittering electric lights, department stores, and sprawling cafés of "the capital of Europe," the poor lived in wretched neighborhoods. They had no political or economic recourse to improve their lot and no voice in government. Over the course of the nineteenth century, European states had enormously increased their ability to extract taxes from the people and conscript men into the military, all in the name of national pride. These demands placed a heavy burden on millions of subjects and citizens, from whom the ruling classes required unquestioning allegiance, even as they themselves started wars and crushed political dissidence. The powerful even engaged in state-sponsored terrorism—the terms *terror* and *terrorism* had, after all, been coined to describe state policies during the most radical phase of the French Revolution.

Naturally, this state of affairs fueled outrage among many Parisians. One of them was Émile Henry. He blamed capitalism, religion, the army, and the state for the plight of the underclass, who struggled to get by as the rich lived it up. In the city of lights, Émile Henry felt dislocated, alienated, and angry. It made him a perfect recruit for anarchism.

A historian once said that it "is bitter hard to write the history of remainders." This is certainly the problem facing any chronicler of anarchism, a philosophy that today has very few followers indeed. During its heyday, from 1880 to 1914, anarchist assassinations and bomb attacks occurred, by one count, in sixteen countries, including Australia and others in Europe, North America, and South America. Like many utopian movements, anarchism developed as intolerable social and political conditions led its proponents to imagine and strive for a different, more just world, in which the beleaguered would at last prevail. This vision transcended national boundaries and cultures.

Thus *The Dynamite Club* is a story of Europe at the end of the nineteenth century: of those who held power and others who rose against it, in the name of what they saw as a just cause. But it is also the story of a changing world, in which new networks of communication and transportation connected people around the globe and brought waves of immigrants to countries such as the United States.

Most of all, it is the story of a very unusual terrorist. Armed with a bomb—and not his first—Émile Henry struck out blindly. While earlier anarchist bombers chose, for symbolic reasons, to target heads of states and uniformed officials, Émile was different. He was willing to sacrifice innocent life for what he considered a great cause. Moreover, unlike many anarchists, he was not born into abject misery. His family owned property, and he was an intellectual of academic achievement, with a bright future. The day he threw a bomb into the Café Terminus was a defining moment in modern history. It was the day that ordinary people became the targets of terrorists.

CHAPTER 1

Light and Shadows
in the Capital of Europe

VERY EARLY IN France's Second Empire (1852–70), Emperor Napoleon III summoned Georges Haussmann, prefect of the *département* of the Seine. He instructed him to forge wide boulevards through the tangle of Parisian streets. Ostensibly, the emperor's goal was to help free the flow of goods and commerce and to bring more light, air, and thus better health to France's proud capital. But there was also a more subtle goal. At a time when European monarchs were desperately trying to maintain their authority against rising liberal, nationalist, and socialist movements—this would come to be called "the rebellious century"—Paris was the capital of revolution. Napoleon III wanted Haussmann to plow new boulevards through and around some of the most traditionally revolutionary neighborhoods, *quartiers* that had risen up during the French Revolution of 1789, the Revolution of July 1830, and the Parisian civil war of June 1848. Even more recently, barricades had gone up following the coup d'état on December 2, 1851, orchestrated by Louis Napoleon Bonaparte, then the president of the Second French Republic. After destroying the republic, he proclaimed himself emperor the next year, just as his uncle, Napoleon Bonaparte, had done almost fifty years earlier.

Parisian insurgents had used the narrow streets of plebeian neighborhoods to their advantage in the various insurrections. Now under the careful direction of Haussmann, whose name would eventually become a French verb (to "Haussmann" something means to bulldoze it), 120 miles of new boulevards and streets were constructed. Dubbed subsequently "the Alsatian Attila" by virtue of his family's origins in that eastern province and his penchant for urban demolition, Haussmann carried out the imperialism of the straight line, decimating neighborhoods in the heart of Paris in which tens of thousands of ordinary people lived. The rebuilding, and the soaring rents that followed, forced many to move toward the urban periphery, and for this upheaval they received compensation equivalent to about ten dollars per family. Most could not afford to live in the 34,000 new buildings and their 215,000 apartments along the boulevards. To the impressionist painter Auguste Renoir, the striking new buildings that fronted the boulevards were "cold and lined up like soldiers at review." The term Triumphal Way, sometimes applied to the Champs-Élysées, was well suited to other boulevards too. (A joke from Haussmann's time had an elderly soldier speculating that "the Seine itself would be straightened, 'because its irregular curve is really rather shocking.'")

When insurrection arose again in Paris in 1871, Haussmann's boulevards served one of their principal purposes. In the election following France's crushing defeat in the Franco-Prussian War (1870–71), conservatives prevailed, electing a strongly monarchist assembly. Ordinary Parisians felt betrayed. After all, they had mobilized every resource to defend the capital against the Prussians, and now they were suffering from massive unemployment and soaring prices for scarce food. Landlords were demanding back rent, which could not possibly have been paid during the awful four-month siege of Paris.

On March 18, 1871, Adolphe Thiers, the head of the provisional government, ordered troops to seize the cannons of the National Guard on Montmartre. In response, local people forced two generals against a wall and executed them. On March 26, the people of Paris — at least the men — elected their own government, which they called the Paris Commune. The Commune was in some ways a "festival of the oppressed," allowing many ordinary Parisians to become masters of their own lives for the first time, albeit briefly. Idealism and optimism abounded. The Commune initiated a number of significant social reforms — for example, it abolished night baking (a common grievance of bakers), created nurseries for working mothers, and recognized women's unions. The painter Gustave Courbet, who had shocked some bourgeois critics with his realist paintings of ordinary peasants and workers, embraced socialism and took an active role in the Commune. At his suggestion enormous pulleys were used to bring down the Vendôme column, on which stood a grand statue of Napoleon I. Photos from the period show workers and their families standing near pieces of the fallen imperial monument, in one of the most elegant neighborhoods in western Paris. They had simply walked into the fancy *quartiers* from which economic reality and police prejudice had previously excluded them.

But soon the authorities fought back. The Versailles troops poured through the western walls of Paris on May 22, and the network of broad, recently constructed boulevards allowed them to penetrate the area efficiently and repress the Commune. As many as twenty-five thousand Parisians perished at the hands of government soldiers, both in street fighting and by execution. To the elite, the Commune presented an apocalyptical vision of social revolution. The myth that the Communards consisted of "drunken commoners" and "apostles of absinthe" took hold. The government investigated more than forty thousand Parisians, some of whom were convicted and sent to prison or forced into exile. In the words of one prosecutor, *"À Paris, tout le monde était coupable"* — "In Paris, everyone was guilty."

To staunch Catholics, France's shocking defeat in the war and the subsequent rise of the Paris Commune seemed to be divine punishment meted out to "a nation fallen from grace," set right by a "sword brandished by a vengeful God." In expiation for the country's sins, Montmartre was chosen as a site for "a temple on a sacred mountain towering above the profane," a "point of intersection between heaven and earth." However, to those who rejected the public role of the church in France, the glistening white marble of Sacré-Coeur represented—like Haussmann's boulevards—the architecture of conquest, standing defiantly apart from its working-class environment: a strange "colossal monster."

By the time Émile Henry threw his bomb into the Café Terminus, Paris, the "capital of Europe," really comprised two cities. The boulevards Saint-Michel, de Sébastopol, and Saint-Denis, which joined in a single long stretch cutting through the center of Paris and running north and south, symbolized the distance between the "People's Paris" of the east and the increasingly chic neighborhoods of the west. The latter, particularly after Louis XIV constructed his opulent royal palace and gardens at Versailles in the seventeenth century, had pulled privilege westward, leaving the artisans and ordinary workers to their own devices in the neighborhoods of central and eastern Paris. To the west, the Bois de Boulogne became a destination at which the wealthy could see and be seen, preening in the comfort of carriages on their way to outdoor restaurants and balls. To one critic, "The straight line [of the boulevards] has killed off the picturesque and the unexpected." Rue de Rivoli, "so long, wide, and cold, on which promenade prosperous people as cold as the street on which they walk," formed an apt example.

Viewed from Sacré-Coeur on Montmartre, the electric lights, which had replaced the old gas lamps, glowed far below in the fancy neighborhoods of the boulevards and created a magical but also somewhat unreal spectacle. Some aspects of fin-de-siècle

Paris were so strangely new, they seemed more than a little overwhelming.

In the late nineteenth century, the *grands boulevards* of Paris symbolized urban modernity, their wide sidewalks planted with trees and offering ample space to stroll, window-shop, and dream. The boulevards became the staging ground for the belle époque —the "good old days" or the "gay nineties"—that period of rapid material progress and exhilarating cultural innovation. These grand thoroughfares were dotted with kiosks offering a vast array of newspapers and periodicals, some now available with brightly colored illustrations. Department stores, decked out with new electric lights, carefully arranged shop windows, and a wide range of products, welcomed a constant flow of customers. The novelist Émile Zola referred to these stores, which were built early in Napoleon III's Second Empire, as the Cathedrals of Modernity. Their aisles appeared to be an extension of the *grands boulevards* themselves. Rather than bargaining, the time-honored way to acquire goods in a traditional market, in the new department stores you simply paid the price as marked.

The boulevards of the Right Bank of the Seine featured luxurious hotels and expensive restaurants frequented by foreign tourists and their counterparts from other parts of France. The names of the *grands cafés,* catering to a well-heeled clientele who came to sit, observe the passing scene, and read newspapers, reflected British and American influence: Grill Room, Express Bar, Piano Player. One knowledgeable contemporary insisted that "the bar, the democratic and modern café, has dethroned the old drinking places that were on street corners and are now disappearing . . . What can one say about the innumerable harm brought by the bars, foreign imports all!" Flâneurs observed the never-ending spectacle of the boulevards. Here, crowded, dark, and dirty Paris seemed to disappear into the "city of light."

In front of the recently constructed train station of Saint-Lazare stood the Hôtel Terminus. The widely respected Baedeker guidebook described it as "not quite so well situated" as the other great hotels, just a little beyond the fanciest *quartier*. It provided five hundred rooms, each with electric lighting and a telephone, and its least expensive accommodation cost four francs, a full day's wage for many workers. Lunch, including wine, coffee, and liqueurs, cost five francs; dinner cost seven, and full board could be had for sixteen francs.

The elegant avenue de l'Opéra, along which wagons and carriages, including those of the police, were still pulled by horses, was lined with hotels, cafés—notably, the Café de Paris—and luxury shops. The avenue, almost 650 yards long and 30 yards wide, stretched from place du Théâtre-Français, not far from rue de Rivoli, which runs parallel to the Seine to the opera house. No trees had been planted along the avenue, so the view of the commanding edifice would not be obstructed.

With the inscription ACADÉMIE NATIONALE DE MUSIQUE, the Opera, which opened in 1875, was at the time the largest theater in the world. It covered nearly three acres but seated only 2,156 people, fewer than La Scala in Milan, San Carlo in Naples, or the opera house in Vienna. A prominent guidebook proudly noted that "there is hardly a variety of marble or costly stone that has not been used," green and red granite from Sweden and Scotland, yellow and white marble from Italy, red porphyry from Finland, and marble from other regions of France. The purchase of the site and the construction of the building cost fabulous sums. It took fourteen years to put together the principal façade; its rich ornamentation included a portico with seven arches, whose pillars were embellished with statues representing Music, Idyllic Poetry, Lyric Poetry, Drama, Lyric Drama, Dance, and Song. Inside, the grand staircase led to the boxes and balconies on each floor, from which the lavishly dressed operagoers could observe the magnificent stage, 178 feet wide and 74 feet deep. Monday and Friday evening performances were considered the most fashionable, with evening dress required for the best seats, which cost the equivalent of three or four days' wages for most workers.

In Émile Zola's novel *Paris* (1898), Abbé Pierre Froment arrives at place de l'Opéra and describes it thus:

> The heart of the great city seemed to beat on that spot, in that vast expanse where met so many thoroughfares, as if from every point the blood of distant districts flowed thither along triumphal avenues. Right away to the horizon stretched the great gaps of avenue de l'Opéra, rue du Quatre-Septembre, and rue de la Paix . . . Then there was the detached mass of the opera house, slowly steeped in gloom and rising huge and mysterious like a symbol, its lyre-bearing figure of Apollo, right aloft, showing a last reflection of daylight amid the livid sky. And all the windows of the house fronts began to shine, gaiety sprang from those thousands of lamps which coruscated one by one, a universal longing for ease and free gratification of each desire spread with the growing dusk; while, at long intervals, the large globes of the electric lights shone as brightly as the moons of the city's cloudless nights.

Avenue de l'Opéra and the opera house itself stood as centerpieces of a city caught up in a feast of consumer goods. Across the stage of the Parisian boulevards strolled proud bankers, captains of industry, and successful merchants, wearing dark coats and top hats; their ladies were decked out in elegant long dresses, constricting corsets, and huge stylish hats. Doormen clicked their heels in respect as the well-to-do passed by, and policemen and soldiers stood at attention. The mien of the wealthy told the poor, "I live at your expense."

The term *boulevardiers* came into use to describe men who turned up "at the proper moment in the proper café." According to Jules Claretie's *Life in Paris 1896,* "On the boulevard each day one can gamble on love, money, winning or losing, the *boulevardiers* are like fish in the water of this urban aquarium, residents in this zoo, where it is better to be a young fish or a young lion." For the upper classes, such display was part of urban life, constantly reaffirming and celebrating their social distance from, say, the waiters in the fine restaurants who brought plate after plate of elaborately prepared food, along with wine, which according to the current taste was now coordinated to complement each dish.

Sold in kiosks, hawked by peddlers, and delivered to homes, newspapers flourished as never before in belle époque Paris. Given their low cost, as well as the continued growth of Paris itself, print runs of the twenty daily newspapers doubled in the 1880s, and weekly supplements followed, all this largely due to improvements in printing techniques. The Linotype machine, introduced in the 1880s, made composition easier. Through lithography, photographs and color could appear in print. A wide range of subject matter was on offer: sensational scandals, of which there were no small number in the first decades of the Third Republic, as well as entertaining serials, crimes big and small, and enticing advertisements. Several newspapers featured interviews and investigations.

The press played a decisive role in the mass politicization of this period, and each newspaper had a particular political slant. People got most of their news, as well as discussion of the issues of the day, from the papers, which together powerfully shaped public opinion. The government paid journalists to support its policies, and politicians themselves penned articles in the major papers. Zola described "steam-powered journalism, polished off in twenty minutes, edited on the fly, written at full gallop at a café table." *Le Matin* had begun publication in 1882, and many considered it the first "American-style" newspaper in France. The relatively moderate *Le Petit Parisien* printed nearly a half-million copies of each issue in the early 1890s, and *Le Petit Journal* a million. Posters were plastered all over Paris to advertise the advent of *Le Journal* in September 1892, with an ambitious first print run of 200,000 copies. The wealthy read the right-wing *L'Écho de Paris* and the more moderate republican *Le Temps,* considered a newspaper of quality and more serious (especially about expanding France's colonial empire) than other more flamboyant contenders, along with its rival *Le Figaro.* Monarchists had their own newspapers (*Le Soleil* and *Le Gaulois*), among others on the political right

(*L'Intransigeant, La Presse, La Cocarde, Le Drapeau, L'Éclair, La Patrie,* and the viciously anti-Semitic *La Libre Parole*). The right-wing press dominated Paris and would have its heyday during the campaign, a few years later, against the Jewish army captain Alfred Dreyfus, falsely accused of selling military secrets to Germany.

The modern glories of Paris were on full display during the magnificent Exposition Universelle in 1889, a world's fair that affirmed the triumph of the Third Republic, France's prominent role in Europe, and the expanding French colonial empire in Southeast Asia and Africa. This empire, to be sure, had been constructed at the expense of peoples considered to be the "inferior races," as Jules Ferry, who had served as minister for foreign affairs, termed them. This attitude was reflected in some of the exhibits, including the "Negro Village," which exhibited hundreds of Africans. The exposition, which stretched along both sides of the Seine in western Paris, also celebrated technological progress (with omnipresent reminders of France and Paris as the center of Beaux-Arts). Most of the more than 32 million visitors who strolled through the enormous Gallery of Machines gazed down from a catwalk to view the wonders achieved by science, especially in the form of consumer goods. Thomas Edison himself, "the Wizard of Menlo Park," had a look at the pavilion that celebrated his work, ten years after electricity illuminated a grand Parisian café for the first time.

The Eiffel Tower commemorated the Revolution and France's Third Republic. Nine hundred feet in height, it then stood as the tallest structure in the world. Built of iron, the tower symbolized the glories of engineering as well as the industrial age in general.

But the progress celebrated at the exposition and the fruits of capitalism on display in the boulevards, department stores, hotels, and cafés brought unforeseen economic and social consequences. Even as the middle classes embraced Paris's elegant cafés, the horseraces at Longchamps, and rides through the Bois de Boulogne. Some bourgeois came to feel disconnected, even isolated, anonymous, and helpless, as they sought new urban pleasures. The work of the early impressionists, particularly Gustave Caillebotte, reflects this sense of dislocation. Bourgeois couples or individuals share space, but nothing else, or gaze down on the street from the isolated safety of an apartment. The Catholic poet and writer Charles Péguy would famously exclaim that "the World has changed less since Jesus Christ than it has in the past thirty years," and the pace of innovation was hard to adjust to.

But if one was to be a victim of this trend, it was certainly better to be a rich one, or at least a middle-class one, than truly poor. The seemingly endless wonders of modern times had brought precious little to the indigent. Augustin Léger, an anarchist, described the place of the Opera in the imagination of the poor:

> What I saw in the evening when I wandered through the wealthy neighborhoods! The other day, I was walking near the opera. There was some sort of nighttime occasion going on . . . I saw luxurious carriages, men and women covered with jewelry, dressed in their finery, carrying rare flowers, and I noted scandalous scenes, as well! I was shocked. What a beautiful society when the budget of the state spends four million francs on the opera each year as a subsidy, with the goal of making even it ever more beautiful . . . while poor people try to get by in the streets and public places, without anywhere to live . . . What kind of society is this when the rich drink full glasses of champagne with women to whom they give fistfuls of money, while their brothers in the lower classes die of misery, the cold, and hunger!

A visitor who glanced away from the centers of flamboyant Parisian prosperity observed that "away in the distance, on the horizon, across light violet mists, lay uncertain outlines of smoky suburbs, behind which, nothing being visible, we still fancied Paris. On another side, other enormous suburbs, crowded upon the heights like armies ready to descend, full of sadness and menace." The guest was looking toward the north and northeast. Paris, after all, was still predominantly a city of workers, the privileged neighborhoods in western Paris notwithstanding. Handicraft production was still important in the capital of luxury but had declined in relative terms. The second industrial revolution brought factories producing rubber, steel, and machines to the outskirts of Paris, an area that offered more space, proximity to rail and canal transport, and a way to avoid the customs barriers that taxed goods entering Paris's city limits, thereby making raw materials somewhat cheaper. The northern and eastern faubourgs—peripheral settlements once beyond the city limits but now well within them—gave way to increasingly industrialized suburbs, where many of the workers lived. These included skilled workers such as ironsmiths, foundry workers, and mechanics; semiskilled laborers such as machine tenders; unskilled proletarians, among them thousands of women; and service workers who lived on the outskirts of Paris but often worked in the fancier neighborhoods of the center and west. "Dirty" industries, such as manufacturers of soaps and chemicals, were relegated to the outskirts; they involved activities and people unwanted by those in the center. Beyond the city limits, wine and other drinks were cheaper, and modest bars thrived.

In the second half of the nineteenth century, the lives of most workers had marginally improved, at least if one considers wages and the cost of living. Their diet was more varied, and the relative price of food had declined. Yet economic instability, physical exhaustion, and frequent unemployment still defined working-class existence. The contrast between the relatively prosperous west and the proletarian east was gradually matched by the disparity between center and periphery, a development hastened by Haussmann's construction. In the mid-1880s, in twelve of these poorer neighborhoods, ordinary workers made up more than 70 percent of the population. Other neighborhoods boasted an even larger proportion of them.

In fact, the population of Paris had risen from about 1.8 million people in 1872 to almost 2.5 million by 1891. Impoverished people from the provinces arrived and accelerated the development of working-class suburbs on the margins of urban life. This immigration swelled the ranks of Parisians—many, if not most, driven to urban life by the monumental difficulty of making ends meet in rural France. Falling prices for farm products meant that what farmers raised brought in little money. Moreover, the grape phylloxera epidemic attacked the country's vineyards. In Paris, craft production became saturated. These new workers found jobs in recently established industries, such as metallurgy, which by 1898 occupied over two thousand factories, employing more than twenty workers each. The exterior districts (arrondissements) grew far more rapidly than did the central city. These heavily populated industrial suburbs subsumed land that had only recently presented a bucolic scene of villages and farms.

If wages and conditions of life had improved for Parisian workers during the 1870s, unemployment kept about half of the working population on the edge of economic disaster. During years of recession, notably 1883–87, 1889, and 1892, between a quarter and a half of all workers in major occupations were unemployed. And in most years, perhaps half of all industrial workers lived in poverty, particularly as wages in some sectors declined. Getting enough to eat was a constant preoccupation for ordinary working people.

Within the limits of the city itself, tens of thousands of workers were piled into old houses, basements, attics, and even stables that had been divided and then subdivided into small rooms. Many were only a few square yards in size, some with ceilings of less than two yards in height. Extra floors were maladroitly added where possible, and the tiny, unsanitary apartments often lacked running water or heat. Thousands of workers lived in rooming houses, which offered little more than a bed in a tiny room or in a dormitory, where beds were laid out side by side. Because of these conditions, landlords were a target of popular wrath.

"People's Paris" remained in many ways a very unhealthful place to live, its hovels notorious. Rates of infant mortality and death from tuberculosis were both much higher on the periphery—for TB, five times greater in the impoverished twentieth district in the far northeast than in the district of the Opera. Moreover, in the industrial suburbs, with their chemical and metallurgical factories, tanneries, freight railway stations, and canals, shacks of all sorts formed nascent shantytowns, standing amid mud and raw sewage. If drinkable water was now available in the center of Paris, this was by no means the case in the industrial suburbs such as Saint-Ouen, where women lined up early in the morning with buckets to get filtered water when the faucets were opened for the street sweepers. In the suburbs more than thirty thousand wells stood near cesspools that were hardly ever emptied.

People of means got around in Paris by horse-drawn omnibus, tramway, taxi, or private carriage. Thirty-four lines of omnibuses—rectangular, closed carriages with windows, drawn by two or three horses—crisscrossed Paris from seven in the morning until shortly after midnight. An omnibus could be expected to pass about every five minutes. They complemented the tramways, even larger carriages pulled by horses along tracks, which could accommodate up to fifty people. The poor, however, had to walk, because they lacked the money for a fare.

In the mid-1880s the tramway lines radiated to a number of suburbs, including Saint-Denis, Gennevilliers, and Vitry, as well as Versailles, a rather different kind of suburb. But their cost—fifty centimes for the tramway—was prohibitive for most people. Riverboats (*bateaux-mouches*) had begun their journeys through Paris in 1867, depositing passengers on both sides of the Seine. There were now more than a hundred of them—but, again, it cost ten to twenty centimes to take them. Private carriages, much more expensive, were simply out the question for ordinary people. Thus each day, from the heights of the eighteenth, nineteenth, and twentieth arrondissements, thousands of workers and domestics of every conceivable variety walked down to work, returning on foot that night. Most anyone having to go from one suburb to another walked, because there was no other way: public transportation lines in Paris radiated like spokes on a wheel, just as the railroads did, to and from the capital.

In short, the belle époque was not *belle* for most French men and women, who had little reason for optimism and great concern for the future. Millions still lived in abject misery. The gap between the wealthy and the poor had, if anything, increased. The *livret,* a booklet that workers were obliged to carry in which was inscribed past work experience (and made it easy to blacklist militants), disappeared only in 1890. In the best of circumstances a working-class family of four all had jobs, and the father who worked three hundred days a year could bring home about 450 francs. His spouse could earn about 180 francs, and two children each about 65, for a total of 760 francs. Unfortunately, a family of four required about 860 francs just to get by.*

The elite residents of the center and the western districts considered Paris's periphery dangerous, even if they actually knew little about these neighborhoods. Conservative supporters of the republic associated loss of religion, crime, and political radicalism with these outlying urban areas, especially those districts that lay beyond the now obsolete fortifications ("it is a completely red area, exuding death and blood"). Indeed, most of the exterior arrondissements, with the exception of western Paris, supported socialist candidates in national and municipal elections. Beginning with May 1, 1890, when workers marched for the eight-hour day in a country that lagged behind other nation-states in legislative reform, each May Day seemed to raise the possibility of Armageddon in Paris, despite the fact that the marches were invariably peaceful.

The numerous bars of the working-class neighborhoods—about twenty-five thousand such places were licensed to sell alcohol in Paris in the 1890s—aroused apprehension, even fear, among the

---

* This assumes lodging cost 130 francs, food 570 francs, clothes and shoes about 140 francs, and at least 20 francs, absolute minimum, for other expenses—transportation, doctor, and so on.

upper classes. Henry Leyret, a journalist, bought a shabby estaminet, Le Déluge, in Belleville, to observe for himself the life of ordinary people in Paris. It was in such places, "barely furnished with basic necessary objects, extremely modest with several wooden tables covered by waxed cloth, where the worker can feel at home, and can be as he is. He feels at ease there, he talks, gossips, relating his little stories, elbows on the table . . ." For the price of a small cup of coffee in a central Parisian café, here a glass of absinthe, or several glasses of wine, could be had. Leyret counted twenty-five drinking spots within two hundred yards of his bar, a world of popular slang and boisterous celebration as well as heartbreaking despair.

Leyret observed the solidarity of ordinary people, their constant need for short-term loans, and their conscious hatred of the police and the petty bourgeois, many of whom had conveniently forgotten their working-class origins as they rose in society and now considered workers with contempt, if not complete revulsion. For the petty bourgeois, it was "everyone for himself."

Workers chronically feared not being able to make ends meet. As Leyret put it, "Life is not just a bowl of cherries. One has to eat, that ultimate necessity that dominates all other feelings." There were 200,000 unemployed workers in Paris. When their children complained, "Papa, I'm hungry!" some workers were forced to steal and some women became part-time prostitutes in order to pay the bills. In the opinion of the fledgling barman, ordinary workers might not tolerate such misery for much longer. They were bitterly disappointed by the Third Republic, rife as it was with financial scandals. Yet only a minority of these workers had joined unions. Some were suspicious of them, and others were not employed long enough in a unionized trade. Still others were indifferent, or demoralized. Most ignored elections, which had done virtually nothing to improve their lives. Utter disgust for parliament was rampant, particularly the Chamber of Deputies, scorned as "The Aquarium."

Leyret recalled a discussion with a muscular worker, who exclaimed, "Goddammit, there are real men in Paris, who could take up their rifles, tools, pickaxes, and other things. To give a real thrashing to the government and its fat cat deputies, there had been the Revolution! . . . But then they spent their time yowling and jabbering, and that was the end of it . . . !" When the government shut down the Paris Labor Exchange in a typical act of repression, Leyret was struck by how fast the working-class initially mobilized, as the word "spread from the Latin Quarter to place de la Bastille, from place Maubert to Ménilmontant, reaching the heights of Belleville, awakening the old instincts of the old Parisian fighters who work hard and who suffer." But that was all. The partisans of violence had missed "a wonderful occasion!" There were no chiefs ready to lead. Yet study groups and political organizations had proliferated. Public meetings and debates filled the halls of the periphery. The socialists, who now had organized political parties, were profiting from all this, swelling their ranks. To some, they at least seemed to offer some hope.

But then there were those who sank into despair. They hated the wealthy, who danced about, seemingly oblivious and indifferent to the misery of much of the working population. From his hospital bed, M.L., a porcelain worker, wrote a letter that spoke for many. The disease of consumption was killing him, and there was nothing left for the doctors to do. He did not know how much time he had left, perhaps a year at best. He felt himself dying. His chest burned. "Accursed society," he wrote, "you are responsible for my illness." Before he died, he wanted to "spit out again his hatred." It was the organization of French society that was killing him: "it is because of you that the unfortunate die of misery, if they do not first take their own lives in a cowardly and useless way." A worker and the son of workers, he had married "an unhealthy job," entering the factory at too young an age. When he had become ill, he was let go and told to head for the sidewalk, "old broken-down machine!" Bourgeois politicians and social reformers would only talk on and on about improving the situation of workers and leading the battle against misery, encouraging "savings."

But the only remedy, according to M.L., was destruction, violent if necessary, of the existing order, so as to replace it with a society "free of bourgeois lies, laws, judges, police, and executioners. Ironically, the ruling classes had succeeded in persuading the masses that property is immutable and that authority is indispensable, and that one has to wait for improvements. They had emasculated the masses, annihilated its healthy feelings, proclaiming that these are the way things have always been, and will always be." Did not bourgeois society understand the evil that someone like him could do — someone who would not in any case live much longer? The comfortably off should not doubt "the power of a single man, fully resolved, master of himself . . . Thoughtless and cruel bourgeois, do you not sense that I can transform myself into someone who can right wrongs, an avenger of the innumerable existences that your society has massacred, an avenger of all those who have revolted and live as outlaws, and those who have been tortured or eliminated?" He would soon die, to be sure, but not alone. "Bourgeois . . . I want to take with me at least some of those who are responsible for my death."

In Émile Zola's novel *Germinal,* published in 1885, the Russian anarchist Souvarine blows up a mine. Zola warns "the masters of society to take heed . . . Take care, look beneath the earth, see these wretches who work and suffer. There is perhaps still time to avoid the ultimate catastrophe . . . [Yet] here is the peril: the earth will open up and nations will be engulfed in one of the most appalling cataclysms in history." In the Paris where Émile Henry lived, this prophecy seemed to be coming true.

CHAPTER 2

The Exile's Second Son

ÉMILE HENRY WAS BORN into political militancy but not into terrorism. His father, Sixte-Casse Henry (always called Fortuné), the son of a furrier, was born in Nîmes in 1821. When he was about nine, his teacher, a priest, accused him of stealing a loaf of bread, calling him a "little thief." The boy grabbed the loaf of bread back and smacked the priest in the face with it. At age sixteen, he left his family to seek adventure, which he found on the barricades in Paris during the Revolution of 1848, an uprising of republicans and some socialists that led to the Second French Republic (1848–51). That regime was swept away in a wave of reaction and repression orchestrated by Louis Napoleon Bonaparte, its first and only president. During the Second Empire, Fortuné was a republican and then a socialist. He joined the First International Workingmen's Association, a socialist organization founded by trade unionists and political militants in London in 1864. In 1857 Fortuné married Rose Caubet, who also came from the Midi, from French Catalonia, the Pyrénées-Orientales. Both retained a strong southern accent. Elegant and proper, with a rosy face and a shock of white hair, Fortuné was intelligent and educated. He wrote poetry and edited a radical newspaper in Carcassonne, where he was arrested for outrages "against the Catholic religion" and "against public morality" in 1861, as well as in Montpellier, for similar charges, that same year. He then moved to Brévannes, a village southeast of Paris, where he labored in quarries. In 1863 he was again arrested for political militancy, spending several months in prison then, and once more in 1867.

Fortuné Henry became a prominent figure in the Commune. Elected to its leadership, representing the plebeian tenth arrondissement (including the Gare du Nord and the Gare de l'Est), Fortuné signed authorizations for sending machine-gunners and munitions to the western suburb of Neuilly, a "certificate of indigence" for a very poor person, a requisition for one hundred Chassepot rifles for the Committee of Public Safety, an order to "put into effect the decree concerning the hostages," and another ordering the railroad stations of western Paris "to not let anyone leave for Versailles." Fortuné also put his name to an order that three hostages drawn from the clergy, the judicial authorities, the army, or the bourgeoisie "be executed for each Parisian civilian killed by shellfire from the attackers."

As troops from Versailles gunned down Parisians, Fortuné managed to escape, disguised as a painter. He made it to Zaragosa in Spain, and then to Barcelona, where his wife had already found refuge. The Versailles government condemned him to death in absentia for "insurrection."

At first the Henry family prospered in Spain. Fortuné worked in a copper mine in Catalonia, and then a coal mine in Bayarque, near Cartagena. He rose to the position of manager in one of them. Life was difficult in a new place, though, with a new language, Catalan, to learn (at least for Fortuné—Rose Caubet Henry probably already knew some Catalan because of her place of origin). Fortuné Henry faced the challenge of earning enough money to take care of his family, while dreaming of returning to France, where his first son, Jean Charles Fortuné—he too was always known as Fortuné—had been born in 1869. Émile (Joseph-Émile-Félix), Fortuné's second son, was born in 1872 in Sant-Marti-de-

Provensals, part of Poble Nou, on the edge of Barcelona, which was then becoming industrialized. The official witnesses at the baby's baptism were a welder and a locksmith. The expansion of Barcelona made Poble Nou essentially part of the Catalan city, adding its textile and chemical plants to the increasingly industrial landscape. A third son, Jules, would be born in 1879.

When Émile was six, he did so well on the obligatory examination given in the primary school of Sant-Marti-de-Provensals that he was awarded a certificate of merit, proclaiming that the boy had demonstrated "a great proof of his hard work and talent." The citation was presented in the name of King Alphonso XII by the governor of Barcelona on June 1, 1878.

But things began to fall apart for the Henry family. "Several reverses overtook us," Madame Henry would later recall. Anarchism was finding an increasing number of adepts in Spain, particularly in Catalonia, where the Italian anarchist Giuseppe Fanelli had arrived to propagate his creed. The elder Henry stood accused of involvement in the Catalan anarchist movement, as one of the troublemakers in Cartagena and Murcia. The Spanish government confiscated the family's possessions.

Following the amnesty of the Communards in 1879, the Henry family returned to France, settling in Brévannes, where they owned a small piece of property. During the Commune, in order to prevent the government from seizing Henry's property, an uncle, Jean Bordenave, arranged its transfer to Fortuné's sister-in-law, a diminutive hunchback who lived with Fortuné's older sister, the marquise de Chamborant, in elegant Passy on the western edge of Paris. The Henrys were able to reclaim the property, though they had to threaten legal action against their relatives before doing so.

Brévannes was part of the commune of Limeil-Brévannes, two villages less than two miles apart, located nine miles southeast of Paris. From the crest of Limeil, Paris could be seen in the distance. The view from lower-lying Brévannes was blocked by a big hill.

Limeil had a thirteenth-century church, but Brévannes only a small chapel, served by a chaplain. Brévannes had no public school until 1867. In September 1870, as Prussian troops began their siege of the capital in the war of 1870–71, virtually all the inhabitants of Brévannes fled to Paris. When they returned, following France's capitulation in late January 1871, they found their houses pillaged.

Late in 1881, Fortuné Henry published the first volume of a collection of songs and dances for children. (There would be no sequel.) He dedicated the book to mothers and teachers. The song "Peasants and Workers" celebrated the riches of France's fields and workshops, ending with "It is work that brings us together / work that tomorrow can / bring happiness to the entire human race!" Fortuné's radical politics and contempt for the army—which had, after all, massacred thousands of Communards—is clear in another composition, "The Two Malbrough" (a misspelling of Marlborough), sung to the tune of a song written by French soldiers to mock the English general John Churchill, duke of Marlborough (an ancestor of Winston Churchill), against whom they had fought.

Fortuné Henry had returned from Spain with mercury poisoning, which he contracted either from vapors from veins of mercury discovered in the copper mines or from a hat factory, where he had also worked. He began to suffer "attacks of brain fever." He met up with an old acquaintance, a doctor and former Communard named Goupil. The latter found him poor but hardworking and hired him as his secretary. Yet Fortuné died in 1882, when Émile was just ten. Two years later, Émile contracted typhoid fever. He could not see for several months, though he eventually recovered.

Madame Henry struggled to make ends meet, at first working as a dressmaker. Dr. Goupil offered to seek public contributions in order to help the family. Madame Henry's sister-in-law, the marquise de Chamborant, convinced her not to agree to this, fearing public humiliation. But things got worse, and the widow and her three sons had neither food nor heat in Brévannes. Through the intercession of someone on the Paris municipal council, a former Communard, the Henry family received one hundred francs as public assistance.

At times, Rose Caubet Henry had little good to say about her more well heeled relatives, most of whom had turned their back on her family. Her sons had been "abandoned by those in our family who could have helped them. There was no humiliation that they were not made to suffer." However, relations with her husband's family improved, and overall her children could not complain about their relatives. The marquise took an interest in her nephews; she indulged and even spoiled them. Émile, in particular, often spent his school vacations with his aunt's family.

A village of fewer than a thousand people, with small tile and cotton factories, Brévannes remained very much a country place. Fields of potatoes stretched along the central avenue de la Planchette, although phylloxera had killed the village's grapevines. Rose Henry, whose gray hair, enveloped in wool cloth, gave her the look of a peasant, built a small house on the land she owned on the main road. She turned the house into an auberge, which she named À l'Espérance (Hope). The sign informed passersby that there was goat's milk for sale. Behind the auberge was a small garden enclosed by a fence, a clothesline, and a few chickens and a goat scratching for something to eat. The auberge itself consisted of three rooms. Furnishings were sparse: a counter, a table made of white wood with the ubiquitous checked tablecloth, and several chairs. Workers sat around the table, or, when the weather permitted, in the garden. The second room served as a small store offering a few grocery items and drinks. The third room was the kitchen. In the back, at the end of the garden, stood a small building with rooms that Madame Henry rented to workers. Mainly these were builders working on a hospice for the elderly and the terminally ill, the front gate of which stood across the street, on the grounds of an old château that had seen better days.

At the age of ten, Émile received a small scholarship to a school in Fontenay-sous-Bois, east of Paris. Émile began his studies there during the 1882–83 academic year, remaining for two years. He received excellent marks. A teacher there noted Émile's superior intelligence and excellent disposition. At the suggestion of school administrators, he took the entrance exam for one of the upper-level schools in Paris. In 1884 he received a half scholarship to the École primaire supérieure Jean-Baptiste Say in Auteuil, on the western edge of Paris, where he studied for four years. The marquise paid the rest of his annual fees. The other pupils playfully called Émile "Microbe" because of his small size. He ranked third in his class after the first semester, and his report praised his excellent conduct, good judgment, and lively imagination. Émile had done extremely well in all subjects except chemistry. His second report was even more glowing, saluting "perfect" conduct, "an excellent pupil in every way, very intelligent, hardworking, and docile. Certainly will do well." He received a grade of three out of five for his responses to questions on Caesar's *Commentaries* in Latin, a textual reading of a passage from a classical play, the history of the Treaty of the Pyrénées in 1659 (which fixed the border with Spain), the geography of the French coasts, and finally, syllogisms. Moreover, Émile's progress in chemistry, which had been his weakest subject, had been remarkable. His professor added, "I can only sing the praises of this pupil so far as his character, conduct, and performance." Monsieur Philippe, another of his teachers, remembered that he never had to reproach or punish Émile. Émile was the most talented pupil he had ever known. A fellow student remembered him as brilliant, while yet another considered him "a perfect youth, the most honest that one could ever meet."

Over the next years, Émile continued to shine. He earned a second prize for excellence in 1885–86, first prize for excellence in the same year, a second prize the following year, and honorable mention in 1887–88. Émile received his *baccalauréat* in science, with honors, four days before his sixteenth birthday, passing examinations in physics, math, and chemistry. His examiners asked him about the detonating properties of chlorine. Émile demonstrated uncommon promise.

At J.-B. Say, Émile was a member of the "moles," students preparing for possible admission to one of the *grandes écoles,* highly competitive institutions of higher education. The moles paid a small membership fee and occasional fines (sometimes given in jest), and at the end of the year the money was pooled for a banquet honoring those admitted to the prestigious École polytechnique, a school for future engineers. On some Sundays, he invited his friends from Paris to go with him to Brévannes for a day in the country.

Émile was eligible, by virtue of his good schoolwork, to apply to the École polytechnique, which had been founded by Napoleon. Graduating from that *grande école* could earn him a place in the army, as an officer or an engineer. However, after passing the written exam, Émile failed the oral one. During this part of the test, another student threw some sort of stink bomb into the hall. Émile later claimed that the professor had taken revenge on him for the incident by giving him an extraordinarily difficult question or an unjustifiably low grade. The comte Ogier d'Ivry, son-in-law of the marquise de Chamborant, an *homme de lettres* and an army officer who considered Émile "a charming boy, something of a dreamer," urged his distant relative to try again for the École polytechnique. His own excellent situation in the army might later assist Émile. But the young man refused any help.

At seventeen, Émile needed a job, since the auberge in Brévannes brought in barely enough money to keep the Henry family afloat. In 1889, Émile's uncle Jean Bordenave, a civil engineer, employed Émile, who worked hard and took on difficult tasks, sometimes even stepping in for his uncle. Bordenave soon gave him a raise, then proposed that Émile accompany him to Venice. With several new patents, the engineer had signed a contract to provide a new water system for the city. Émile accepted the offer.

On December 28, 1889, Émile wrote his chemistry professor at

J.-B. Say, Monsieur Philippe, from Venice, to apologize for having left school so abruptly in November without saying goodbye. All was going well for him in Italy. He was doing a bit of everything, sketching proposed projects, penning correspondence, and calculating the resistance of building materials. He was extremely happy working for his uncle, confidently adding, "I hope to build a good future, if not a brilliant one at least something sure, working on such new, wonderful projects, which will surely be part of great developments in the future." His uncle had received offers of contracts in Cayenne in French Guiana as well as Algeria, Belgium, Switzerland, and Russia to build canals or reservoirs for petroleum. Émile hoped that soon he would be in one of "these diverse countries" and that he would be most happy to see himself ultimately working in a branch of the civil engineering corps (Ponts-et-Chaussées), which looked after the national road system.

The possibility of reapplying to the École polytechnique remained, but Émile confessed to Monsieur Philippe that he was worried about what kind of future this could offer him, even if he was admitted. Now he added, "My tastes and my too limited financial situation keep me from any kind of military career. I found myself after leaving school without a position, with considerable general knowledge, but without really having a profession." He thanked Philippe for all his "good lessons" and frank conversations and asked him to promise his friends at the school that he would never forget them and would visit them upon his return.

In September 1890 the postman brought three letters from Émile to Brévannes. They had been penned on August 24 and September 1 at the Albergo della Luna in Mestre, outside Venice. He was happy to have received letters from both of his brothers four days earlier, bringing welcome news of good health, his older brother Fortuné's new job, and the "dazzling successes of our *picciolo* Jules" in school. After so long without word from his family, Émile was relieved. Émile had written a letter of birthday greetings to Fortuné in care of his "political friends" (Fortuné had adopted the left-wing politics of their father), but he suspected that it had never arrived. He hoped to return to France very soon and surprise his family. In September they would see what "passes for my head" on the train, or on the road near his mother's auberge.

In his letter to Jules, after trying to imagine the surprise of the mailman delivering a letter from so far away, he congratulated his younger brother on having passed the general exam following primary school. If he won any more prizes, would not the auberge risk collapsing under the enthusiastic bravos of the people saluting his success? He hoped that his younger brother would soon write him back "without making too many spelling errors and in a style that would surpass those of all the Madames de Sévigné of the past, present, and future." He described the canals of Venice, the Piazza of Saint Mark with the famous winged lion to its side, and the palace of the Doge, "really as old as time itself, all in marble with its first steps bathing in the sea." These had been well worth seeing, but he worked most of the time and had very little leisure. He asked Jules to tell their mother that he would send some money soon, though it was difficult to find a way to do so. In the meantime, he should give her a kiss for him, tell her that he thought of her often, and give his greetings to their older brother and all their friends. After asking him to send news of the family to "Signor Emmilio Henry" in Mestre, he signed the letter "Your brother who loves you and will watch over you."

On September 1 Émile was still in Italy, writing to his mother as a good son to wish her a happy feast day, that of Saint Rose. He promised that he and his brothers would do all that they could to make her happier and try to repay her for some of what she had done for them. He implored her not to worry about his health, although his face, neck, and hands had been so much in the sun that they now appeared the color of baked bricks. He also sent along one hundred francs.

And then, Émile suddenly left Venice. The precipitating event may have been Bordenave's asking him to undertake secret surveillance of the workers. The two had argued about the assignment on the way to Venice. Bordenave later explained that a misunderstanding had occurred. His nephew was naive, "absolutely new to life and believed the word of a man to have the same exactitude as the sciences." The engineer had drawn an analogy to help Émile understand the rationale behind the assignment: if he was a finance inspector, would he consider it unacceptable to monitor the money under his responsibility? But from Émile's perspective, supervising—and perhaps spying on—the workers would have put him in the unpopular role of foreman, something he was unwilling to do. He departed for Paris, leaving his disappointed uncle behind.

Back in Paris, Émile lived briefly with an aunt before moving in with his brother near the quai Valmy on the canal Saint-Martin, close to place de la République. He briefly considered taking more preparatory courses for the entrance exam to the École polytechnique. He went to see the former director of J.-B. Say, who knew him and thought well of him. But that was the end of it, perhaps because he lacked funds to continue his studies. After several months without work, late in September 1890 Émile found a position with a store selling special fabrics from the town of Roubaix, at a salary of eight hundred francs a year. He came recommended by the father of a former classmate, and the manager, Monsieur Veillon, created a position for him as a clerk. As expected, Émile did very well.

Now nineteen years of age, Émile was short, about five feet, four inches in height. He was thin and invariably pale, and had dark chestnut-colored hair; he sported the beginnings of a reddish blond beard. Rather elegant in appearance, he liked being well dressed. Without appearing haughty, he nonetheless gave the impression of being a rather cold and somewhat aloof intellectual.

It was during this time that Émile began to wrestle with the great questions, "the most perplexing philosophic speculations. What is matter? What is mind? Are psychic phenomena regulated by universal laws in the same way as physical phenomena? Is death the annihilation of the Ego?" He had begun to dabble in Spiritism (the French name for the movement known in America as spiritualism), trying to contact the soul of his father. Indeed, his friend Charles Malato later claimed that Émile "lost his footing and fell into the abyss of Spiritism, even became [a medium] and wasted his health unhesitatingly in exhausting experiments, because he longed for knowledge."

Given Émile's strong attachment to the memory of his deceased father, one can understand his desire to communicate with dead souls. Émile's flirtation with Spiritism was perfectly in tune with the fin-de-siècle bohemian idealism of many young intellectuals in Paris. The increased number of private and formally organized Spiritist groups reflected contemporary critiques of modernity in an age when scientific materialism seemed to triumph. Their quest drew upon tensions between faith and reason—and attempts to reconcile the two. New ideas about psychology, for example, emphasized hyponotic trances. Spiritists believed that they could provide proof of metaphysical concepts in the realm of philosophical speculation.

Yet, rebelling against "the frauds," as he discovered them to be, Émile soon abandoned the quest, which lacked the certainty and precision of the science he had studied. Later he dismissed this period, suggesting that it had been extremely brief: "Me, a Spiritist! Well, it is true that . . . a friend who was absorbed by occult science invited me to take part in a certain number of experiments. I saw right away that this was just another form of charlatanism and I did not continue with it. Mathematics gave me the taste for things both positive and precise."

Émile's life became something of a mystery to Rose Henry. He had changed. Whenever he did appear in Brévannes, he was eager to return to the capital. Once his mother chastised him for how he looked, and he replied, "You know, Mother, that I love you dearly, but I can't escape my destiny, which is stronger than even my feelings for you. Let me do as I see fit." Books, which he had always loved, no longer interested him. No amusements could distract him. He appeared sad, pensive. And he had been overtaken, in her words, by "an unfortunate passion."

In 1891, Émile fell in love with a woman named Élisa Gauthey. She was the wife of an anarchist who lived in eastern Paris on boulevard Voltaire. Émile's brother Fortuné, who had become an anarchist, was often present at the Gautheys' attic apartment. He introduced his younger brother to the couple. Élisa remembered "a quiet and shy boy, a dreamer who did not seem to see or hear anything that was going on around him."

Élisa was a tall, striking woman with long curly hair, a "strong Byzantine nose," large black eyes, and a rounded mouth with "sensual lips" resting above a solid chin. Overall, her face offered "more strength than grace" but, at the same time, appeared both "reticent and teasing." This, along with the "amplitude of her bosom," gave the appearance, at least to Émile, of "a reposing creature of love."

One day when the brothers were visiting, Élisa, on a "woman's whim," asked Fortuné, who had a reputation in anarchist circles for writing poetry, if he would write a couple of verses for her. Émile overheard this, and when they got up to leave later in the evening, asked if she also wanted *him* to write a poem for her. Surprised, she looked at him. He looked back, staring intently into her eyes. Élisa, stifling a burst of laughter, told him, "Well, why not? Go ahead, write me some verses!"

And he did, for he was in love. One long, rambling poem reflected his Spiritist phase, suggesting cosmological vision. The concluding verse, with its idea of a "reign of attraction" and a spirit able to purify itself, reflects the influence of Allan Kardec (the pen name of the educator and philosopher H. Léon Rivail), who had created the Spiritist Society in Paris in 1869 and dominated the movement for many years.

Another was more directly addressed to Élisa:

> I see around me the angels
> And goddesses of love

All running up and, each in turn,
Coming to sing me their praises.

But they all murmur: "Hope"
And I, who know they are liars
Feel my sorrows revive
Because they laugh at my misery.

I cannot have hope
After these verses I will be quiet;
But always I will love you
And I will consecrate my suffering.

I will suffer silently
And you will always be my lady
The beautiful ideal of my soul
Dreaming of love under the high heavens.

Émile's poems "amused" Élisa, but she did not attach any significance to them. Shortly thereafter, she and her husband spent
several weeks in the country at Brévannes. Fortuné and Élisa's
husband shared a commitment to anarchism, and such a visit
seemed perfectly normal. During their stay, the smitten Émile
stayed at Élisa's side, constantly looking for opportunities to talk
to her, and more. A friend remembered "how many afternoons he
spent in the garden, lying on the grass at the foot of the coquette
he loved, gazing at her in silence, like a true believer on his idol."
On one occasion, he tried to kiss her neck when her husband was
not around. Among the "thousand" incidents she would later recall, one day in the garden Élisa kissed her husband, who offered
her his arm. Émile became quite pale and left suddenly. Shortly
thereafter, he went to bed with a fever. His mother did not know
what to think. Élisa went to see him, asking him what was wrong.
Émile expressed astonishment that she did not understand. She
had kissed her husband right in front of him. This hurt him very
deeply, and he confessed that he loved her "desperately." The ob-

ject of his thoroughly unrequited passion now began to laugh. Émile reproached her for treating him like a child, telling her, "You will learn later how much I love you."

In September 1891, Émile sent Élisa several letters. In clear, elegant script he asked her to excuse the incoherence of his words. So many ideas were swirling about in his head. Sadly, he wrote, she did not understand "the extent of my love . . . I have so much need for affection, consolation, and loving caresses that I see myself alone and isolated, lost in this vast morass of human egotism." Sometimes life itself filled him with horror. At such times, "I would like simply to disappear, to annihilate myself, in order to escape the perpetual anguish that strangles and breaks heart and soul. To love someone so much and not to be loved!"

However, a vestige of good sense now allowed Émile to see the absurdity of his current state. He begged Élisa to be patient with him and excuse his "painful ruminations." What exactly was "this mysterious affinity" that can push one person toward another, "throwing him without any compulsion at the feet of his conqueror?" He was trying to understand "this accursed passion, which annihilates all of a person's faculties, which takes over the entire brain, which can turn even the most resilient person into a toy in the hands of someone he adores." He hated this passion because it "caused so much harm, suffering, tears, disillusionment, and discouragement." He wanted to flee far from her, in the hope of curing his heart and mind, because for now he could do nothing but sleep, inert, "like an animal without any conscience!" However, such a separation would compromise his very existence. He would conclude the letter, because the more he wrote, the less reasonable he became, "such that madness would take me over if I followed along with my thoughts."

Yet Émile's thoughts had already begun to turn away from Élisa Gauthey. In Paris, he was increasingly appalled by the omnipresence of grinding poverty. Every day he encountered the miserably poor, the jobless, the hungry, the desperate. They became his passion. A friend remembered that when "he saw a poor wretch wasting away of hunger and had nothing of his own to share with him, he stole"—including, on one occasion, a cow, which he took to a starving woman. A worker who lived on boulevard Voltaire recalled Émile giving money and sometimes shelter to "unfortunate people" and his particular love for children. On one occasion, he invited a friend who had been evicted by his landlord to stay in his room until he could find another place.

Until the middle of 1891, Émile Henry had always respected what he called "the present morality," including the principles "of country, family, authority, and property." However, his teachers had forgotten to teach him one thing, "that life, with its struggles and disappointments, with its injustices and inequalities, opens the eyes of the ignorant . . . to reality." This had happened to him. He had been told that life was "open to the intelligent and the energetic," but what he saw in the Paris of the Third Republic clearly demonstrated otherwise. He began to realize "that only the cynics and grovelers can get a place at the banquet." He had believed that social institutions were based on justice and equality but had found only "lies and treachery," a republic rife with sleazy financial scandals and massive corruption, amid shocking poverty. The upper class "has appropriated everything, robbing the other class not just of the sustenance of the body but also of the sustenance of the mind."

In 1887, it emerged that Daniel Wilson, the son-in-law of the president of France (Jules Grévy), had sold the Legion of Honor, a medal signifying France's highest honor, to those who could afford it, making a tidy profit. He and other members of the Chamber of Deputies had also taken large bribes in exchange for their support of a company that had begun construction of the Panama Canal and then run into daunting difficulties before going broke in 1889. Such sums paid for fine dinners in the restaurants and hotels of the *grands boulevards* on which Émile walked. Without a hint of shame, Wilson, who used the stationery of the president of France to drum up business, proclaimed that he had done nothing more than any politician worthy of the name. Many criticized the blatant corruption, along with the wasteful colonial adventures, of the current government, questioning its legitimacy.

The injustice plagued Émile, an extremely sensitive young man. Every hour of every day, the bourgeois state ignored or even abused the weak. The contrasts between rich and poor in Paris were indeed astonishing. According to those on the upper rungs of society, the factory owner who accumulated a colossal fortune from the labor of his pitifully poor workers was an honest man, and the politician and the minister who took bribes were "devoted to the public good." Army officers who experimented with new rifles by shooting African children understood that they were doing their duty to their country; one of them had received congratulations in the Chamber of Deputies from its president. Émile felt profoundly dislocated and alienated by this state of affairs. He loved humanity but hated what he saw around him.

At first, briefly, Émile considered himself a socialist. Then, late in 1891—or at the latest, the beginning of 1892—Émile became an anarchist. A primary influence was his older brother, Fortuné, who had left school in 1885 to take a job at the Central Pharmacy. Even shorter than Émile, Fortuné was stocky and dark-complexioned, with brown hair, a mustache, and sideburns. Excused from military service because of an ankylotic arm, Fortuné left the pharmacy after a "discussion" with his boss, probably about politics. Fortuné was then a socialist and briefly worked on a socialist newspaper. By 1889, he was known to the police, turning up at various socialist meetings, including one determined to achieve "the union of all proletarians" in view of "the decisive struggle" that would end the bourgeois republic. Early in 1891, Fortuné broke with the socialists and embraced anarchism. He believed that the state could not be transformed by socialist votes or even a socialist revolution; rather it had to be destroyed so that mankind could begin again. Fortuné emerged as a prominent, eloquent orator at anarchist meetings and debates. He spoke at gatherings of the League of the Anti-Patriots in Saint-Quentin, Bourges, and in the Loire mining basin. In the Ardennes on the Belgian border, a union leader, Jean-Baptiste Clément, had denounced the anarchist newspaper that was sponsoring a speech by Fortuné. The evening of the talk, Fortuné carried a pistol and a knife with him, fearing that Clément or one of his supporters might attack him.

As is often the case, Émile's relationship with his older brother was complex. They often disagreed. Émile resented the fact that Fortuné, as the eldest, insisted on exercising authority. Émile later said that at one point he had even wanted to kill him. But after some difficult times, they had become close friends. Anarchism reconciled the Henry brothers, giving them something they could both believe in.

Émile was now at the age for possible military conscription. A gendarme had come to the auberge in Brévannes with a letter summoning him to the military lottery. Émile's mother showed the gendarme a letter she had received from her son, who claimed to be working in Berlin for a wholesale merchant. The police could not find him in Paris. Émile's mother believed that he had gone to Berlin to sell merchandise purchased in Paris. But Émile was never in Germany. The letter to his mother was probably posted in Berlin by a German anarchist. In it Émile made clear that he had no intention of serving in the army and did not plan to return to France in the near future: "You know that if I fled France, it was because I will never be in the army." At the lottery, the mayor drew the number fifty-one for Émile. This meant that he was to serve in the 148th Infantry Division, beginning in September 1893. Émile would be officially declared a deserter in February 1892.

At about the same time, Émile left socialism behind, believing that its intrinsically hierarchical nature (there were party leaders, for one) rendered it incapable of changing the existing order of things. His study of science had gradually led him to materialism and atheism. Structure and authority, inherent in all religions and political philosophies, had to disappear. How else could one reconcile morality with the laws of nature, in order to "regenerate the old world and give birth to a happy humanity"? He considered the anarchists whom he had met in Paris the finest people he had ever known because of their integrity, sincerity, straightforward nature, and contempt for prejudice. An anarchist environment, in which "individual ownership" would be replaced with communism, and "authority with liberty . . . will raise humanity's moral standards. Man will grasp that he has no rights over a woman who gives herself to someone else, because that woman is simply acting in conformity with her nature." The "selfish bourgeois family" would be eliminated.

When Émile went to Brévannes, he took his anarchist theories with him. A family friend, Madame Denaples, who worked in a restaurant in Paris, tried in vain to dissuade him from his newfound passion. Jules, the younger Henry brother, was quickly taken with his brother's new ideas and began reading anarchist tracts. In 1892, when he received a prize for his schoolwork, he shouted, "Long live the Commune!"

A half-century earlier, in 1840, a printer from Besançon in the mountainous Franche-Comté in eastern France had been the first to call himself an anarchist. The bookish Pierre-Joseph Proudhon started his studies wearing wooden sabots, lacking enough money to purchase books. A painfully shy man who preferred solitude, Proudhon was horrified by what he had seen in Lyon and Paris, those centers of luxury that represented the "royal rule of gold." And he hated the state. "Whoever lays a hand on me to govern me is a usurper and a tyrant. I declare him to be my enemy," he insisted. According to Proudhon,

> To be governed is to be watched, inspected, spied upon, directed, law-driven, numbered, regulated, enrolled, indoctrinated, preached at, controlled, checked, estimated, valued, censured, commanded by creatures who have neither the right nor the wisdom nor the virtue to do so. To be governed is to be at every operation, at every transaction noted, registered, counted, taxed, stamped, measured, numbered, assessed, licensed, authorized, admonished, prevented, forbidden, reformed, corrected, punished.

It is, under pretext of public utility, and in the name of the general interest, to be placed under contribution, drilled, fleeced, exploited, monopolized, extorted, squeezed, hoaxed, hunted down, abused, clubbed, disarmed, bound, choked, imprisoned, judged, condemned, shot, deported, sold, betrayed, and to crown all, mocked, ridiculed, derided, outraged, dishonored. That is government; that is its justice; that is its morality.

Proudhon became well known for his 1840 pamphlet called "Property Is Theft." (He was being provocative — what he actually believed was that *too much* property was theft.) Proudhon and his followers saw universal manhood suffrage as a constitutional tyranny in which the people nominally ruled but did not really govern, a sham perpetuated by the powerful. The seeming "disorder" of anarchism would in reality lead to a natural economic order based on equal social relationships, organized into cooperating mutual associations without the hindrance of the state. And because people were basically good, a truly just society could then be constructed, permitting individuals to reach their full potential. As Proudhon put it, "Anarchy is order; government is civil war."

The influence of the Enlightenment can be seen here, particularly the writings of the philosophe Jean-Jacques Rousseau, who had celebrated the primitive as something of an ideal. He imagined that people learned from each other by embracing nature, cooperating freely, and living happily ever after. Proudhon insisted that anarchy was an "organized, living society," offering "the highest degree of liberty and order to which humanity can aspire." Everybody would have enough to get along.

In part, anarchism was a reaction to the rapidly expanding power of governments following the creation of nation-states in the nineteenth century. On one hand, the nation had become an object of allegiance for an increasing number of ordinary people in France, one of the consequences of the French Revolution and the Napoleonic period. Primary schools taught French in regions in which other languages, dialects, or patois had long dominated.

Maps of France, and of its colonies, took on a symbolic role. At the same time, states extracted more taxes and military conscripts from the people. Expanding bureaucracies, police forces, and armies manifested state power. Like France, Prussia, Russia, and Austria had crushed the revolutions of 1848, which had broken out in these conservative states on behalf of nationalism, political liberalism, and the rights of workers.

To be sure, there was a decidedly millenarian (as well as utopian) quality to anarchism, which resembled certain political movements of previous centuries. Anarchists were confident that a new, improved society could exist one day, but they believed that violent revolution was a prerequisite. The French Revolution (1789–99) had offered a similar hope. Ordinary people had overthrown the monarchy. Moreover, several radicals (including Jacques Roux and Gracchus Babeuf) had then called for social revolution, including the redistribution of property. Despite their relatively short lives (the former committed suicide, the latter was executed), they left the legacy that revolution could be fomented by conspiracy.

Proudhon's followers maintained considerable influence among artisans in France during the Second Empire and the Commune. When a laborer asserted to an anarchist during the Commune that this time, unlike 1848, the workers would not be cheated of their victory, the anarchist replied, "They have already robbed you of your victory. Have they not named a government?" The fierce repression that followed the Commune made it very difficult for anarchists (or for that matter, socialists) in France.

The cause to which Émile now pledged himself was dominated by two Russian figures, Mikhail Bakunin and Peter Kropotkin. And they would affect events on the world stage for years to come. Both were of noble origin, examples of the "conscience-stricken" Russian gentry aware of the fact that they were well-off because others were poor. Born in 1814, Bakunin, the consummate rebel, was an enormous man with a huge beard and a hearty appetite for food, drink, and cigars, which he smoked incessantly. After leaving Russia in 1840, he traveled, a mobile revolutionary, to the German states, Switzerland, and then France, from which he was expelled when the Russian ambassador complained about his activities. He went to Paris after the Revolution of February 1848 drove King Louis-Philippe from the throne. Borrowing money from the new provisional republican government, he headed toward Russian Poland to try to foment revolution there. During the "Springtime of the Peoples," a period of optimism for many ordinary people following the liberal and nationalist revolutions that took place in 1848 in the German states, the Habsburg Empire, the Italian states, and France, he led police in several countries on a merry chase. He set up various anarchist groups, some real, some imaginary, before ending up in a Russian prison for six difficult years. Undaunted, he then resumed his career as a professional revolutionary.

Bakunin believed in the revolutionary instincts of the masses but held that they would not rise up spontaneously against the state. A single spark, or several, were needed to bring about the revolution. The Commune gave him hope, as anarchists had been among its exponents, and his vision of the eventual abolition of the state found resonance among Russian as well as western European disciples. Even if unsuccessful, terrorist attacks—which he did not specifically advocate—would inevitably be followed by massive state repression. This in turn would increase dissatisfaction among the people, bringing revolution closer.

Unlike Karl Marx and other revolutionary socialists, Bakunin looked not to an enlightened working class, but to the peasantry, to bring about revolution. He viewed peasants as revolutionaries who did not yet know it. The village (*mir*) provided a natural, harmonious setting, but it was beset by avaricious landlords and by soldiers defending the interests of the state. In earlier centuries, after all, Russian peasants had risen up against tsars, or on behalf of false tsars. Revolutionaries should work feverishly to prepare for an even greater revolution: "The revolutionary is a man under vow. He ought to occupy himself entirely with one exclusive passion: the Revolution . . . He has only one aim, one science: destruction . . . Between him and society, there is war to the death, incessant, irreconcilable." Bakunin defined freedom as "the absolute right of every human being to seek no other sanction for his actions but his own conscience, to determine these actions solely by his own will, and consequently to owe his first responsibility to himself alone . . . I become free only through the freedom of others." Thus destruction became "a creative passion."

Bakunin distrusted and quarreled loudly with Karl Marx, who he felt did not go far enough. After all, Marx was not interested in destroying the state but in replacing it with another one, socialist in character. Bitter divisions between anarchists and socialists helped bring an effective end to Marx's International Working-men's Association in 1876, following its meeting in Philadelphia—a site Marx had selected because he knew that European anarchists could not afford the passage across the Atlantic. "Let us not become the leaders of a new religion," Bakunin warned his rival, not long before Bakunin died that same year. The Russian who once said that to be a true revolutionary, one had to have the devil in the flesh, continued to influence the development of anarchism from the grave, above all in Spain and Italy. In France, the break between anarchists and socialists became final in 1881. The anarchists defiantly went their own way, rejecting electoral politics because they saw it as a means of propping up the bourgeois state. They adopted the black flag as their symbol and in France rejected the "Marseillaise," which represented the bourgeois republic.

A different kind of anarchist led the charge after Bakunin's death. Peter Kropotkin was a geographer and a prince, the son of a Russian army officer of the nobility. Convicted of sedition because he had written a manifesto describing the structure of a future anarchist society, Kropotkin spent two years in prison before escaping Russia in 1876. After first going to London, he spent time living in Switzerland in the Jura Mountains, where watchmakers seemed to live in perfect harmony without the intrusion of the state. Moreover, Switzerland was federalist, and the original home of the

Red Cross, the kind of voluntary association that the anarchists believed would spontaneously emerge following the destruction of the state. Kropotkin became convinced that local organizations were both a means to a better life and an end in themselves, infused with the morality of individuals left to their own devices. In the end, ownership of property would become superfluous: everyone would have enough to get along. This was the basis of Kropotkin's anarchist communism. (Proudhon, on the other hand, believed that the revolution would not eliminate all private property.) Kropotkin's optimism was contagious, respect for him enormous, even among those who did not agree with him, and his influence, like his vision, was international. The British writer Oscar Wilde once said that Kropotkin lived one of the only two perfect lives he had ever seen.

How was the revolution to be made? Bakunin believed that the rebellious passion of the peasants would bring about the revolution. Kropotkin believed in the necessity of a vanguard of heroic anarchists who would spread the word and lead the downtrodden masses toward revolution. In *Catechism of the Revolutionary* (1869), the Russian nihilist Sergei Nechaev described the revolutionary as "a doomed man," without even an identity: "he has no personal interests, no affairs, no sentiments, attachments, property, not even a name of his own. Everything in him is absorbed by one exclusive interest, one thought, one passion — the revolution . . . To him whatever aids the triumph of the revolution is ethical; all that hinders it is unethical and criminal." Although he was not an anarchist, Nechaev helped shape the future image of the anarchist, anonymously putting together his bombs and depositing them before disappearing into the night. Nechaev founded a terrorist organization: People's Will (Narodnaya Volya). But it was not an anarchist group. People's Will was a socialist organization that was hierarchically organized and demanded universal suffrage and political liberties, as well as land for all people. Its members planned the assassinations of state officials and political personages in the hope of increasing public awareness of the plight of the masses. Bakunin, as well as other revolutionaries, eventually turned against Nechaev, concluding that he was a murderer and a disreputable fanatic who could not be trusted.

Martyrdom played an important part in the struggle of these Russian revolutionaries. It became part of revolutionary lore that as Vera Figner, a leader of People's Will, awaited execution (the sentence was commuted at the last minute), she imagined her martyrdom, thinking of revolutionaries who had perished before: "Pictures of people who had died long ago awoke in my memory, my imagination worked as never before." Even if this account could never be verified, the execution scene itself became an important part of the collective memory of anarchists.

The imperial Russian police crushed People's Will, but its tactics came to be adopted by some anarchists worldwide. And in western Europe, events during the 1880s encouraged anarchists, particularly in wretchedly poor rural regions in southern Spain and Italy. Errico Malatesta was among the optimistic, active, and influential. Born into a landowning family in southern Italy, Malatesta was expelled from medical school in Naples for taking part in a demonstration. He became an anarchist, eventually learned the trade of electrician, and gave away property he had inherited from his parents to the tenants who lived there. Anarchism appealed to poor rural laborers in southern Italy, who retained a strong sense of injustice and suffering at the hands of policemen. Malatesta led armed Calabrian peasants in Benevento, northeast of Naples, in April 1877 as they burned parish and tax records, distributed rifles seized from the national guard and money taken from the safe of a tax collector, and called for the seizure and collectivization of land. The insurgents received some support from nearby villages in a revolt that lasted ten days before being put down.

In 1883, police in Paris broke up an anarchist-inspired march of unemployed people; some of the demonstrators pillaged a bakery, and arrests followed. In Andalusia in southern Spain that same year, peasants murdered an innkeeper they believed to be a police spy. The Civil Guard moved in, using perhaps fabricated evidence of a secret society plot to kill the rich in order to crush anarchism in Andalusia. And in Montceau-les-Mines in Burgundy in 1884, striking workers organized a group called the Black Band and went on a rampage, pillaging the French town.

Several other small-scale events gave French authorities further pause. About the same time, a gardener called Louis Chavès shot to death the mother superior of the convent that employed him, and then fired at police, who killed him. He had already sent a letter to an anarchist newspaper, "You start with one to reach a hundred, as the saying goes. So I would like the glory of being the first to start. It is not with words or paper that we shall change existing conditions. The last advice I have for true anarchists, for active anarchists, is to arm themselves according to my example with a good revolver, a good dagger, and a box of matches." An anarchist newspaper began to raise money to purchase a pistol to avenge Chavès. That same year, a man claiming to be an anarchist tossed a bottle full of explosive chemicals into the Paris Bourse. It exploded, although no one was hurt. He then fired three random shots, without effect. A burglar named Clément Duval, who stole from a wealthy Parisian residence, was transformed into Comrade Duval. His explanation: "The policeman arrested me in the name of the law; I hit [the policeman] in the name of liberty! When society refuses you the right to existence, you must take it." In the eyes of some anarchists—though hardly all—any act that might hasten "social disorganization" and ultimately the revolution was legitimate, including theft and the destruction of private property. An Italian thief called Vittorio Pini announced during his trial in Paris that he was not a thief but had merely taken riches that the bourgeoisie had taken before.

Émile Henry could not help but soak up the charged atmosphere of fin-de-siècle Paris. The plight of ordinary people was growing ever more serious. Someone would have to carry the mantle of visionaries like Proudhon and Bakunin.

CHAPTER 3

"Love Engenders Hate"

DURING THE LATE 1870s and early 1880s, groups of anarchists began to organize in and around Émile Henry's Paris. In 1882, approximately thirteen anarchist groups existed, with at least 200 members in all. Eleven years later, the police counted more than 2,400 anarchists and considered 852 of them dangerous. Most French anarchists were average workers—metalworkers, bricklayers, printers, and others drawn from myriad occupations in late-nineteenth-century France.

In Paris, such groups were based in specific neighborhoods, in keeping with the anarchist view that the revolution would be achieved through local insurrections. Usually groups of anarchists organized street by street. They communicated through the anarchist press, meetings, debates, and brightly colored posters advertising such events. Anarchists opened soup kitchens to feed the hungry and started several anarchist libraries—really just book collections in the homes of certain anarchists. The subculture of ordinary people, including the slang (argot) of the streets and bars, infused the movement with dynamism.

Anarchists did not have to work hard to win recruits in northeastern Paris. For example, in plebeian Belleville, a neighborhood of artisans (particularly brass workers and jewelers) and laborers on the edge of the capital, had more than its share of disaffected poor people. In a place that Maurice Chevalier and Édith Piaf would make famous four decades later, a strong local identity had been forged, in part through the knowledge that the fancy central and western neighborhoods of Paris spurned and feared Belleville's poor while using their labor to maximize their own wealth and comfort. Belleville had suffered disproportionately in the violent repression that followed the Commune, in part because of the leftist political tendencies of its residents. The salient role of the neighborhood in the Commune reinforced the association — at least in the minds of Parisian elites and government authorities — between Belleville and the "dangerous classes," cementing its unjustified reputation as a place of rampant crime.

The anarchist groups in Belleville and the twentieth arrondissement in the mid-1880s sported colorful names such as the Libertarians, the Black Flag, the Tiger, the Deserters of Charonne, the Anarchist Group of Belleville, and the Anarchist Group of Père Lachaise (Cemetery). The Anarchist Group of Belleville and the Anarchist Group of the Twentieth Arrondissement had existed for years. Dynamite, Revolver in the Hand, the Starving, Hatred, Social War, and the Indigent also sprang up. In the Marais district on the Right Bank, a good many immigrants brought their anarchism with them from Russia, reading Yiddish publications dedicated to the cause.

Anarchism was also particularly attractive in the growing industrial suburbs. Indeed, one short-lived anarchist newspaper that appeared in 1891 was called simply *The Suburb (Le Faubourg)*. In overcrowded Saint-Denis (the population had more than doubled there from 1861 to 1891, to fifty thousand) fewer than a third of the houses had running water. Thousands of people lived in shanties that were literally thrown together, made of bricks or any other material that could be found and covered with sheet metal or asphalt-reinforced cardboard.

Anarchists held their usually modest gatherings in bars or cafés, sometimes in a backroom or upstairs room that was rented, sometimes not (it was understood that the group would at least purchase drinks). Or they would rent a small hall in the neighborhood for the evening. When it was time to pay for the hall rental and drinks, those with money paid up, and the place for the next gathering was decided. Larger halls were rented for meetings that brought together various groups of anarchists to discuss abstaining from elections, propaganda encouraging conscripts to refuse to report for military service, or plans for demonstrations or events to mark the anniversary of the Commune—an enduring source of inspiration as well as a practical guide for the movement. Two of the most important venues were Belleville's Salle Favié and the Salle du Commerce on rue du Faubourg-du-Temple. On Friday, March 30, 1883, for example, posters announced a grand public meeting, organized by the group Vengeance of Anarchist Youth and located on rue de Charenton in eastern Paris. The topic for discussion: "the workers' crisis, revisionist agitation, and revolutionary movements." The small entry fee went toward the rental of the hall and other related expenses.

Yet finding rooms or even bars in which anarchist groups could meet was extremely difficult, particularly once the police started pressuring owners. Neighbors tired of the shouting and singing that emanated from the meetings also took a stand. For example, in November 1893 the group known as the Lads of the Butte (Montmartre) met in a bar. But when the gathering was over, the owner of the establishment told them that they could not return. They had recently been evicted from another bar on the same street because their presence terrified local shopkeepers.

The meetings of most anarchist groups were relatively small but swelled in size when speakers from other groups were invited, or debates, sometimes with socialists, were planned. When the Père Lachaise group met in June 1886, eleven members showed up. The same number attended a meeting in the Salle Bourdel, rue de Belleville, in late June 1888 to discuss opposition to the celebration of Bastille Day at a time when about 200,000 workers in the capital were unemployed. Unlike the format of socialist gatherings, presiding officers did not lead meetings of anarchists. The idea of having officers, even for one gathering, was totally antithetical to the anarchist principle of "individual initiative."

Anarchists organized "family evenings" and "popular discussions," usually on Sunday. At times they offered soup or something else to eat in exchange for listening to speeches. Amid boisterous singing, they put small coins in a passed hat to help anarchists and their families who were struggling to make ends meet, such as those whose husband or father had been jailed. On these occasions, crowds of one hundred, four hundred, or even more were not uncommon. In December 1892, more than two thousand bowls of soup, along with anarchist newspapers, were distributed at a *soupe-conférence* in the Salle Favié, amid occasional shouts of "Death to the cops!" and "Death to the pigs!"

Anarchist songs reached an ever larger popular audience. Adrienne Chailley was one of the better-known anarchist singers. Twenty-six years old, she went by the name "Marie Puget," a poor soul who sang in various Left Bank brasseries while living in an attic room in a cheap hotel on the Left Bank near the Seine. This "hysterical madwoman" was denigrated by a conservative newspaper as a "priestess of anarchy" who, with short brown hair and a snub nose, sang rough, vulgar anti-bourgeois tunes, "her blouse open, hair blowing in the wind, eyes lit up by alcohol . . . while wiggling in the middle of the hall, wearing herself out amid a chaotic uproar which often concludes with some major act of imprudence."

Henry Leyret, the Belleville bar owner, did not believe that "the people" were anarchist, even if most occasionally read anarchist newspapers. Yet Leyret remembered in particular two workers standing at the counter, drinking their absinthe and coolly, with considerable perception, discussing and comparing the literary talents, merits, and weaknesses of two anarchist journalists. Leyret's customers in general did not like anyone associated with the authorities and resented the uneven application of the law. They hated the police, who, they perceived, had it in for them. So the enemies of the police, whoever they might be, automatically became their friends. Even if these customers did not know much about anarchism, they approved in principle of the anarchist struggle, often forgiving the deeds of the anarchists, whom they viewed as the righters of wrongs.

Émile Henry plunged into the world of Parisian anarchism. It soon became clear to him, and to others, that despite the movement's emphasis on individual autonomy, anarchists would have to work together to build the revolution. Thus anarchists were part of an informal corporation (*compagnonnage*), which provided moral and sometimes material assistance for *compagnons* — the word itself stemming from the idea of sharing bread. Some anarchists served as "midnight movers," helping poor families move in silence from their apartments without paying the rent while their landlord or concierge slept. The anarchist Augustin Léger described one very rapid move in the dark of night. At the agreed-upon time, his anarchist pals showed up, hauling a little wagon, which they parked in an alley to avoid attracting attention. Then they quietly went upstairs, carrying their friend's belongings back down. On at least one occasion, a property owner or concierge was gagged, tied up, and left on his bed. Midnight moves could be enacted swiftly, since most anarchists owned very little.

Newspapers provided some cohesion to the anarchist cause, underlining its international character while solidifying anarchism's informal network and keeping *compagnons* informed of debates concerning theory and tactics. At the base of rue Mouffetard behind and below the Panthéon, near the misery of the faubourg Saint-Marcel, Jean Grave published *La Révolte*. Grave, whose father was a miller and then a farmer in central France, had become a shoemaker before turning full-time to the anarchist cause. He had taken over publication of the newspaper's predecessor, *Le Révolté*, in Geneva in 1883, after its founder, Peter Kropotkin, was permanently expelled from Switzerland. In the wake of harassment from Swiss authorities, Grave moved the newspaper to Paris. With a slight change in its title, *La Révolte* became a weekly in May 1886. From the workshop of "the Pope of rue Mouffe-tard" also appeared anarchist pamphlets, sold in anarchist book-shops, particularly in Montmartre, but also in the Latin Quarter, where the first group of student anarchists was formed in 1890.

Grave's office was in the attic of a four-story building. Four flights of stairs and a narrow ladder led there. A small sign on the door indicated the newspaper's presence, but since there was no bell, a visitor had to knock. A large room that had once served as a place to dry laundry now accommodated piles of papers and newspapers. Grave's desk consisted of a board resting on two sup-ports, next to which lay his shoes. Four pages long and printed on good-quality paper, *La Révolte* included a literary supplement and appeared each Saturday.

Grave struggled to keep the publication going. Raising money from a generally impoverished clientele was not easy; printing 6,500 to 7,000 copies each week cost 320 francs. A few intellectuals and artists helped Grave along with small gifts of cash. The paper provided a forum for the philosophy of anarchism, with articles on "property," "anarchism and terrorism," "the noxious influence of industrialization," "anarchy and order," and so on. Other pieces described incidents of state repression in France, crackdowns on demonstrations, or other actions against anarchists, including raids that began with the sudden arrival of jail wagons in working-class neighborhoods.

For all this, *La Révolte* was relatively staid compared to Émile Pouget's *Père Peinard*. Père Peinard was the name of a fictitious cobbler, a straight-talking soul who exuded common sense and in the name of justice went after corrupt politicians, officials, and magistrates, with the imposing leather strap of his trade. After try-ing to organize department store employees, the well-educated, twenty-two-year-old Pouget, the son of a notary in Dordogne in the southwest, was sentenced to prison for "provocation to pil-lage." (This followed the incident in the Parisian bakery in 1883.) After his release three years later, he joined an anarchist group, the

Revolutionary Sentinel, in Montmartre. In 1889, he began to publish *Père Peinard*.

Defiantly vulgar and profane, Pouget appealed to the emotions of ordinary people, using familiar slang—some of which was virtually unintelligible to outsiders—to considerable advantage. That the speech of ordinary workers differed so markedly from that of the elite reinforced the distance, both cultural and geographic, that separated rich and poor in the City of Light. Some popular argot was borrowed from the language of criminals at a time when court convictions seemed to be reaching new heights. *Père Peinard* helped convince many upper-class Parisians that the "dangerous classes" were perched on the edge of the capital, ready to strike. At the same time, Pouget's newspaper reinforced popular solidarity and the sense of being separate from and opposed to the state and its urban elite. At a cost of *cinq ronds* ("five round ones," or coins, still common parlance), *Père Peinard* grew to eight pages. About eight thousand copies, and sometimes even more, were printed each week in 1892. Police estimated that each copy reached an average of five people.

If Pouget himself was soft-spoken, his pen was not. Considering "militarism . . . a school for crime," *Père Peinard* noted that despite the nominal goal of "civilizing" the Vietnamese, French troops had committed five times more atrocities on that southeast Asian land than had their Prussian counterparts during the war of 1870–71. Factories were almost always referred to as prisons—and the Palais de Justice became the "Palais d'Injustice," the clergy became "clerical-pigs," the rich *"les richards"* (a term still in use), supporters of the Republic *"la républicanaille,"* and so on. These coinages were interspersed with salty phrases such as "goddammit," "be damned," or *"kif-kif"*—meaning "it makes no difference" or "it is all the same." The latter was the caption for an illustration showing a poor peasant in 1789 and a late-nineteenth-century worker standing in front of a statue that depicted the republic, suggesting that this form of government had done absolutely nothing for the poor of either era.

A constant theme of *Père Peinard* was that ordinary people needed to act for themselves. The Communards had missed an opportunity to "burn down all the old residences where the bandits live who govern us, as well as the edifices of mindlessness: churches, prisons, ministries—the whole mess . . . It's easy, a thousand bombs! . . . We await *la Belle*," the beautiful days that would surely follow revolution and the destruction of the state. During a miners' strike in Decazeville, *Père Peinard* proclaimed, "First of all, goddammit, it is never a bad thing to attack the good-for-nothings when one gets the opportunity, as did the good chaps of Decazeville with Watrin" (a foreman in the mines of that town who was killed and castrated). After a worker murdered a boss who had been giving him a hard time, Pouget commented, in a piece titled "One Less," that this murder demonstrated what goodwill could accomplish. It all came down to this: "It will be by the force of a violent Revolution that we will expropriate the rich and we will throw the old society onto the trash heap . . . The land to peasants! The factory to workers!! Lodging, clothing, and food for all!" Pouget's newspaper suffered seven judicial condemnations from April 1890 to November 1892.

The third major anarchist publication was *L'Endehors*, a cerebral, literary, and artistic weekly newspaper. It was the inspiration of "Zo d'Axa," born Alphonse Gallaud in Paris in 1864, the son of a railroad official of the Orléans Railroad Company. Looking like "a gentleman buccaneer," he turned to anarchism after deserting the army in Algeria. He fled to Jerusalem, was extradited to France, and took refuge in Belgium. Zo d'Axa then became a journalist. The meaning of the name *L'Endehors* reflected the anarchist story: "on the outside." Zo d'Axa sought converts to anarchism with irony and sarcasm, defending strikes and aggressively chronicling stories of army officers who brutalized soldiers. Such articles brought him repeated court convictions, leading one wag to comment that he went to prison "as one goes to the telephone, when it rings."

Sold on the boulevards by some of the editors themselves,

L'Endehors published as many as six thousand copies per issue. Each had an editorial, "First Shout," on the first page, which announced the latest injustice: "It is rare that M. Carnot goes a fortnight without guillotining someone." Or "Riols, the head of the police in Saint-Nazaire, was gravely wounded by a rock thrown by a likable sailor. The night before, the policeman in charge of the neighborhood of Marceau was equally badly treated by seamen. The navy is obviously improving."

One day during the spring of 1892, Émile Henry showed up in the cellar offices of *L'Endehors* near Montmartre, saying simply that he wanted to work for anarchism. The newspaper office was a gathering place, of sorts, for artists, intellectuals, and bohemians. It was there that Émile met the art and literary critic and anarchist Félix Fénéon, a dandy sporting a greatcoat, a full cape, dark red gloves, and black patent-leather shoes. Fénéon became attached to the young anarchist, seven years his junior, with his wide eyes, pale complexion, and close-cropped hair. Quite taken with Émile's youthful intelligence, "the mathematical precision of his thinking, and the intense way he identified with the suffering of the people while maintaining a cool and detached exterior," Fénéon lodged Émile on several occasions in his apartment in Montmartre.

Émile's friendship with Charles Malato, another anarchist, developed during this same period. Malato's father, Antoine (called Cornetto), had been born in Sicily and fought with the Italian patriot Garibaldi and in the Commune, after which he had been exiled to New Caledonia in the South Pacific. His son had worked for the French government there, remaining at his post even after several of his colleagues had been massacred by the indigenous Kanaks (Canaques). The clever Malato offered the reassuring aspect of an Anglican clergyman, careful not to alienate anyone. A wonderful orator and writer, Malato spoke four or five languages.

Malato introduced Émile to a small, recently formed group of anarchists, whose members had tired of "the noisy, vapid, and often dubious individuals who invade the larger groups, paralyzing all activity." The young Émile became one of the most active and enthusiastic members of the group. Malato remembered that Émile would stay up virtually all night with his new anarchist friends, and then despite the lack of sleep, go off to work. During this period of feverish initiation, Émile rarely went to Brévannes. His mother did not really know what he was doing. All she could see was that he no longer seemed to enjoy himself, or even smile.

Malato too saw a transformation in Émile and believed that it was caused by the appalling social injustices he saw every day. Despite his rather frail appearance, Émile's "indomitable will" seemed even more prominent than his "superior abilities and a burning enthusiasm for lofty ideals." The American anarchist Emma Goldman asserted that it was not anarchist theory that created terrorists but rather the shocking inequalities they saw around them, which could overwhelm a sensitive nature and indeed, a person's very soul. This rang true for Émile, who once said, "To those who say: hate does not give birth to love, I reply that it is love, human love, that often engenders hate."

Émile became obsessed with the power of the state, embodied by the French army and by the police, so detested by the poor. The slaughter of more than twenty-five thousand ordinary people in the Paris Commune hung over French politics during the first three decades of the Third Republic. For Émile, the tragedy was deeply personal: his father, a good man who had escaped death "thanks to his coolness under pressure and his courage," was forced to flee to Spain, where he had contracted the mercury poisoning that ultimately killed him.

After Émile had worked for several months at the Roubaix cloth company, his boss found in Émile's desk a manual for practical anarchism, along with a translation he had begun of an article in an Italian newspaper, whose headline read "Long Live Theft!" The newspaper also explained the advantage of "reversal bombs," which would explode when turned over or jarred, mixing the chemicals, if all went well, in the hands of a policeman. Émile lost his job.

In January 1892, Émile found a position as an accountant for a small firm owned by Félix Vanoutryne, who produced cloth covers for furniture on rue du Sentier in Paris's garment district. The budding anarchist sent a third of his wages to his mother. He could not afford to eat lunch on many days, and may for a time have stayed with the singer Adrienne Chailley.

Nine months later, Émile moved into a room on the third floor of a building beneath Montmartre on the extremely plebeian rue Marcadet. At least twenty-five different anarchist groups were based on Montmartre from 1889 to 1896, and they included some Spanish and Italian refugees. These groups shared space on the butte with painters, writers, and other artists and bohemians who frequented café-concerts in cabarets whose owners sympathized with the anarchists. The singer Aristide Bruant's famous, festive cabaret Le Chat Noir on boulevard de Rochechouart attracted anarchists, who were often shadowed by police spies and informants. Police also censored and antagonized artists, which, if anything, made them more daring, leading to the temporary shutdown of a few cabarets.

The neo-impressionist painter Paul Signac was one of many artists with anarchist leanings. He had begun to paint peasants in the 1880s before becoming impassioned about urban poverty, and his work appeared in Grave's *La Révolte*. Henri Toulouse-Lautrec knew anarchists living in Montmartre as he brought to life its cabarets and café-concerts in paintings, lithographs, and posters. The impressionist Camille Pissarro joined the short-lived Club of Social Art in 1890, expressing the view that even if anarchism was strongly idealistic and utopian, one had to admit "it is a beautiful dream." Some utopian dreams in the past had, moreover, become realities, and thus there seemed to be reason for optimism, unless mankind returned to "complete barbarism." Pissarro, who had been forced into exile after the Commune, twice put up money so that *Père Peinard* could be printed when the newspaper's coffers were empty. Believing that art could be revolutionary, he also contributed drawings, as did Henri Ibels and Maximilien Luce.

The symbolist poet Adolphe Retté was an anarchist, and so was, at least for a time, the naturalist and symbolist writer Paul Adam. The poet Laurent Tailhade's play *Enemy of the People* announced "that genius, beauty, and virtue are antisocial facts of the first order." A member of the audience, age seventeen at the time, recalled, "What dynamism and what dynamite! What bombs did we not intend to explode, charged with new explosives, a new art . . . bombs that would be fireworks, bouquets of light." The writer Édmond de Goncourt made exactly the same connection in March 1892: "Oh, the songs of Bruant in the salons and dynamite under the coach doors! These two facts are very symptomatic of the end of the bourgeois era!" The anarchist critic Fénéon, one of the "midwives" of symbolism, considered colorful posters to be as "lively as dynamite."

With memories still vivid of the brutal repression of the Paris Commune, Montmartre represented the informal alliance between anarchism and avant-garde art. "We were all anarchists without throwing bombs," the Dutch fauvist painter Kees van Dongen reflected. "We had those kinds of ideas." Symbolists in particular, impressionists, and postimpressionists—the term was first used by Félix Fénéon—spurned the conventions of the salons, which they considered bourgeois; they insisted on expressing themselves aesthetically in any way they wanted, in total revolt. Like ordinary members of anarchist groups, they sought complete freedom to express their individuality. Shocking the reactionary bourgeoisie was part of their art. They also cared about the plight of the poor. Some of them were ambivalent about bombs, even though dynamite seemed to offer the potential of putting an end to horrific social inequalities. Idealists, they dreamed of a sparkling future society. Émile soaked up the anarchism of Montmartre. But unlike others, he would not be content with art as a weapon.

In about 1876, Peter Kropotkin, Paul Brousse (a former Communard also living in exile in Geneva), and Malatesta began to speak of "propaganda by the deed." Kropotkin included the phrase in a program that he proposed in August 1878 to a congress of anarchists. The Russian terrorist Nechaev had viewed propagandists who sought to communicate to the masses with written propaganda as "idle word-spillers." To make the revolution, acts, or deeds, were required. A "deed" was to be a violent, even murderous act, a single initiative worth much more than a thousand pamphlets. Deeds could awaken "the spirit of revolt" in the masses by demonstrating that the state did not really have the strength it projected. Deeds would offer hope to the downtrodden: "Permanent revolt in speech, writing, by the dagger and the gun, or by dynamite . . . anything suits us that is alien to legality." Such propaganda would reach the rural destitute as well as urban workers. Moreover, deeds like the assassinations of heads of state could incite a terrifying government reaction that might swell the ranks of anarchists and thus advance the revolution. A placard posted in Paris proclaimed, "Yes, we are guilty of proceeding with the practice of our theories by all means, by the word, by the pen, BY THE DEED—that is to say by revolutionary acts whatever they may be . . . Yes, we acknowledge them loudly. We claim them as ours. We glory in them." The anarchist London Congress of 1881 formally adopted the strategy of "propaganda by the deed."

In January 1883 a bomb exploded in a seedy music hall in Lyon. Kropotkin had nothing to do with it but was among the anarchists arrested. Accused of membership in the First International Workingmen's Association—which he denied—and denounced for his editorials published in Geneva, he was sentenced to prison. After his release early in 1886, Kropotkin returned to England, where he was active in anarchist circles and a frequent visitor to Paris. However, in 1890 he began to have second thoughts about "deeds," genuinely troubled by the deaths of innocent victims in such attacks. In March 1891 he came out against terrorist acts and denounced a deadly bomb attack in 1892 in Barcelona, a center of European anarchism. Isolated acts of violence were not enough, Kropotkin wrote. Indeed, they seemed counterproductive. But he added, "We who . . . seclude ourselves from the cry and sight of human sufferings, we are no judges of those who live in the midst of all this suffering . . . Personally I hate those explosions, but I cannot stand as a judge to condemn those who are driven to despair." Malatesta was also against terrorism, saying that it brought out the beast in human beings and it was better to kill a chicken than a king, for one could eat the former.

Terrorism became a European, then a worldwide, phenomenon beginning in the 1880s. After assassinating Tsar Alexander II, who had eliminated serfdom in Russia twenty years earlier, the group People's Will was itself eliminated in a wave of repression in 1882 carried out by a powerful national police force established to defend the Russian autocracy. Subsequently, spectacular anarchist assassinations struck down the Spanish prime minister Cánovas de Castillo in 1897, Empress Elizabeth of Austria-Hungary in 1898 (despite the fact that she could not stand her husband, Emperor Franz Joseph, from whom she lived apart), and the American president William McKinley in 1901. King Umberto I of Italy, who survived an attempt on his life made by an anarchist in 1878, remarked that he considered assassination a "professional risk." He was murdered twenty-two years later by Gaetano Bresci, an Italian silk worker who was part of an active group of anarchists in Paterson, New Jersey. Bresci bought a pistol for seven dollars, practiced using it, and returned to Italy to kill the monarch he called "King Machine Gun" because the army had gunned down demonstrators in Milan in 1898.

In western Europe, anarchists wanted to remake the world through revolution. To Kropotkin, this required "men of courage, not satisfied with words, but ever seeking to transform them into action, men of integrity for whom the act is one with the idea, for whom prison, exile, and death are preferable to a life contrary to their principles . . . these are the lonely sentinels who enter the battle long before the masses are sufficiently ready to raise the banner of insurrection." In Joseph Conrad's novel *The Secret Agent,* the anarchist Karl Yundt ruminates, "I have always dreamed . . . of a band of men absolute in their resolve to discard all scruples in the choice of means, strong enough to give themselves frankly the name of destroyers, and free from the taint of that resigned pessimism which rots the world. No pity for anything on earth, including themselves, and death enlisted for good and all in the service of humanity—that's what I would have liked to see."

Émile became part of an increasingly strident group of anarchists in Paris. Their targets were private property and authority, "two vicious germs" that formed the basis of contemporary society. Both had "to be destroyed, eradicated from social life" in order to bring about "absolute equality." Émile had lost all faith in the socialists, rejecting the claims of Marxists that the destruction of capitalism was inevitable once workers became sufficiently conscious of themselves as a class. With his anarchist friends, he distrusted the hierarchy of socialist organizations, which he felt compromised individual initiative.

To Émile, the repressive power of the state was clearly becoming greater amid the poverty in "People's Paris." An English newspaper later had it right, affirming that "no anarchist forgot the savage repression . . . Henry is the son of a man who has seen thousands of working men, women, and children shot down in heaps, while well-dressed men and dainty ladies struck the bound prisoners with canes and parasols, shrieking 'Shoot them all!'" Only a new kind of revolution could save humanity.

Émile read Kropotkin's popular pamphlet "The Anarchist Morality" and his book *The Conquest of Bread,* in which the anarchist argues that a minority of humanity had succeeded in controlling the majority of resources, despite the fact that "all belongs to all." Two French anarchist theorists also influenced Émile's intellectual development. On several occasions, Émile brought the anarchist propagandist Sébastien Faure, whose work he had also read, to Brévannes. Born into a prosperous commercial family in Saint-Étienne, Faure emerged as a tireless and effective anarchist orator and propagandist. Virtually all *compagnons* revered Faure, except the many husbands whose wives he seduced. Essentially a propagandist unwilling to participate in any illegal or violent activities, he nonetheless accepted in principle any act that could ultimately serve the cause of anarchist revolution.

Émile also acknowledged the influence of Élisée Reclus in his development as an anarchist. Like Kropotkin, Reclus was a respected geographer, a theoretician admired by many for his spirit of solidarity and his kindness to other anarchists who needed assistance. The son of a Protestant pastor in the southwest, he had first become a democrat-socialist. Banished from France after Louis Napoleon Bonaparte's coup d'état in 1851, Reclus traveled for the next six years in England, Ireland, the United States, and Senegal, where he married a Senagalese woman with whom he had two children. Early in the 1870s he became an anarchist, founding a group with Bakunin. He was expelled from France again in 1871 following the Commune. Upon his return Reclus wrote for a number of major journals and published a guide to London and a book about towns on the Riviera. Reclus argued that revolutions were a natural part of human development. Society would eventually reach a state of perfection, making governments and nations unnecessary. Anarchy thus stood as "the highest expression of order." Émile was among his many followers.

Émile remained an intellectual, somewhat detached from most of the people who crowded into the anarchist meetings. Unlike Fortuné, a gifted speaker, Émile stayed out of the limelight and was introspective, taciturn, and resolutely individualist. Only occasionally attending anarchist meetings and never giving a speech in public, Émile was a loner. However, at one gathering in central Paris he had a violent altercation with an anarchist (who later killed himself); Émile accused the man of being insufficiently militant.

Late in February 1892, Émile become one of several anarchists who signed a letter, published in *La Révolte,* stating that anarchists should participate in the May Day demonstrations. In principle, anarchists believed that such events, which called for reforms like the eight-hour workday, merely helped prop up the bourgeois state and kept workers from the real business of revolution. But if anarchists refused to become involved in a real working-class movement, might they not cut themselves off from the proletariat, losing the occasion to make converts to their cause?

The letter in *La Révolte* laid out four reasons for supporting the demonstrations planned for May 1: (1) on any occasion that workers left their workshops and factories to demonstrate in the street, anarchists should be there to win them over to the cause of social revolution; (2) May 1 was no more important than any other date, but because "people have a tendency to think about revolution on that day, it would be strange and even pitiful if anarchists advised them to stay at home to rest"; (3) even if May 1 was to be a political demonstration in which socialist leaders sought to make the masses follow them, proletarians had the capacity to go further than their "so-called representatives" would like; and (4) the fears of several *compagnons* that periodic demonstrations could ultimately prevent more serious action on other days were not well founded. Malato and "Jacques Prolo" (the alias of Jean Pansader, one of the most effective organizers of anarchist groups in the suburbs, with contacts in Spain, Italy, and especially Chicago) were among the eight other anarchists who signed with Émile.

The letter raised suspicion among the police, who were eager to prevent armed confrontation on May 1. They believed that Émile was living with his close friend Constant Martin, who ran a small shop selling milk and cheese near the Bourse in central Paris. Like Émile's father, Martin had gone into exile following the Commune and likewise returned when amnesty was offered. He had converted quickly to anarchism, becoming something of a patriarch to a small group of militant anarchists suspected of thefts. Martin was a complex personality, selfless, devoted, and ready to make any sacrifice for the cause, which rendered him suspicious, and thus he was constantly on guard. The police considered him dangerous. In some ways he was Émile's mentor. Martin sympathized with the "right of theft," a topic anarchists hotly debated and which some practiced. Jean Grave's *Le Révolté* had condemned "the right to theft" in 1885. Malatesta in 1889 understood that anarchists who stole from the bourgeoisie were merely "robbing the robber" if they were hungry, but he did not support thefts merely to get more money. In any case, advocating the "right to theft" was unusual for a shopkeeper, as Martin presumably did not want even anarchists stealing his goods.

Like his brother Fortuné, the younger Henry now made it onto the police's watch list because of his new anarchist sympathies and his embrace of "propaganda by the deed."

Another person whom the police took a strong interest in was François-Claudius Ravachol, a poor dyer's assistant turned anarchist. He would come to have a great deal of influence on Émile —and events in Paris.

CHAPTER 4

Dynamite Deeds

FRANÇOIS-CLAUDIUS RAVACHOL, whose name would become synonymous with terrorism, was born in 1859 into gnawing poverty in the small town of Saint-Chamond near the burgeoning industrial city of Saint-Étienne in the *département* of the Loire. His father was a Dutch mill worker who beat and then abandoned his French wife and their four children. Ravachol's mother worked, at least when employment was available, in a factory that prepared raw silk. When Ravachol was a young boy, she often sent him out to beg for money. The boy was handed over to a farmer whose animals he was to help care for, but he was sent back to his mother the following year. Until he was eleven, Ravachol attended primary school, where he was mocked for his shabby clothes. One winter he herded cows and sheep in the mountains, but lacking proper shoes, his feet were always freezing. It was at this time that his youngest sister died of fever.

As a boy and then a young man, Ravachol worked in a mine and in various textile workshops, once joining other workers on strike. He quit one job because the pressure to work constantly left him no time to eat or to go to the bathroom. In Saint-Chamond, he was fired from a job because he was a few minutes late, despite the fact that he had often been forced to work overtime for nothing. After three years of an unpleasant apprenticeship as a dyer, during which his master refused to reveal the secrets of the trade, he left for Lyon in search of work. There, Ravachol joined a study group that read socialist and anarchist newspapers and hosted a small lecture series. Periods of unemployment became longer. By age eighteen, he had a reputation as a brawler. He read Eugène Sue's *The Wandering Jew,* a popular novel evoking the poor neighborhoods of Paris in the 1840s. Ravachol later claimed that by revealing the "odious conduct" of priests, the novel had turned him against religion. This process was completed by attending a socialist lecture, where he learned about the massacres that had followed the Paris Commune. After listening to several anarchist speakers, Ravachol embraced this new philosophy. He tried without success to make explosive devices. Then he was arrested for having provided a young woman with sulfuric acid, which she claimed to have needed to remove a corn from her foot. Instead, she had thrown it into the eyes of a lover who had cheated on her.

Unable to feed his mother and his younger siblings, Ravachol turned to stealing chickens, while his brother stole coal. He played the accordion at a few small festivals to earn a little money. When his mother rebuked him for having a relationship with a married woman, he severed ties with his mother. Ravachol subsequently broke into the grave of a baroness in search of jewelry (finding only a decomposing body and rancid flowers) and turned to counterfeiting, the illegal sale of alcohol, and, finally, murder.

In 1891 Ravachol suffocated an elderly hermit monk who had a good deal of cash hidden in his house in a hilltop village. After Ravachol made five or six trips back to the house to find more money, while the monk's lifeless body remained in bed, the police arrested him. But he managed to escape when the officers transporting him to jail were momentarily distracted.

Ravachol fled to Paris, living in the northern industrial suburb of Saint-Denis under the alias "Léon Léger." He stayed with a couple named Chaumartin, who introduced him to militant anarchists, exponents of "propaganda by the deed," who had made the capital their own. These included Charles Simon *dit* Biscuit (known as "Cookie"), eighteen years old, also from the Loire. The four were soon swept up in the furor surrounding two separate May Day incidents that would send shock waves through France.

For several months in 1891, in Fourmies, a wool-producing town of fifteen thousand people in northern France, a crisis had been looming. Salaries in textile mills had fallen by as much as 20 percent over recent years, and a strike seemed imminent. On the morning of May 1, 1891, a confrontation occurred between those who wanted to continue to work and those who wanted to strike. A year earlier, French workers had chosen May 1 to commemorate the Haymarket affair in Chicago and to demonstrate for improved wages and conditions. Now, a year later, at about 6 P.M., several hundred young people and children marched through town. They were led by Maria Blondeau, eighteen years old, who danced along while holding a mayflower. Arriving at the small square in front of the church where troops had assembled, she taunted the soldiers, who were determined to stop the march. A few demonstrators hurled stones, hitting two soldiers. The commander ordered the troops to fire. Maria Blondeau fell dead, the top of her head torn off by bullets. A priest ran out, taking in his arms Félicie Pennelier, seventeen years old and also mortally wounded, and carrying her to the presbytery. He then returned with other clergy to implore the commandant to stop the shooting. Nine demonstrators lay dead, and more than thirty people had been wounded, some of whom were then shot dead by soldiers.

That same May Day, a small group of anarchists marched toward Clichy on the northwestern edge of Paris. Four policemen tried to block their way, and a brief scuffle ensued. A few of the anarchists stopped to get something to drink in a bar, and the police entered, supposedly to seize a "seditious" symbol, a red flag. Shots rang out, apparently from both sides—the police insisted that an anarchist fired first. Four gendarmes arrived as all but three of the demonstrators hurriedly departed. Three workers, Decamps, Dardare, and Léveillé, continued to resist in the bar but were subdued after suffering saber wounds and then were dragged off to the police station. There policemen kicked, punched, and pistol-whipped them, put them into cells for at least half an hour, and then went at them again. The prisoners were left without water or treatment for their wounds, which included a bullet lodged in Léveillé's leg.

In August the men went on trial, accused of violence toward "agents of public order." The prosecuting attorney, Bulot, demanded the death penalty. Decamps defended himself by saying that he had merely tried to fend off the police, who were drunk. He had four children to feed. When Léveillé had his turn to speak, he sketched the anarchist position on modern society:

> At the top there are priests engaged in the traffic of sacraments and religious ceremonies, soldiers selling secrets of a so-called national defense, writers glorifying injustice, poets idealizing ugliness, shopkeepers measuring produce with false scales, industrialists faking their products, and speculators fishing for millions in the insatiable sea of human stupidity. At the bottom there are building workers without homes, tailors without clients, bakers without bread, millions of workers beaten down by unemployment and hunger, families heaped in slums, and young girls, age fifteen, forced to earn money by enduring the sweaty embrace of old men or the rapacious assaults of young bourgeois.

Decamps and Dardare received exceptionally harsh sentences of five and three years in prison, whereas Léveillé was acquitted.

The events at both Clichy and Fourmies mobilized anarchists in Paris, notably Ravachol and his new friends. A group in the fifteenth arrondissement began to call itself Revenge for Fourmies. In *L'Endehors*, Zo d'Axa described the "martyrdom" of Decamps, Dardare, and Léveillé in the Clichy police station. To anarchists like Ravachol, the three names echoed like a battle cry.

In early August, even before the trial of the Clichy three, an anarchist meeting in the Salle du Commerce in northeastern Paris attracted about seven hundred people. A speaker sang the praises of the arrested anarchists, adding provocatively that "the life of a policeman is not worth that of a dog." There were rumors that a bomb would blow apart the Clichy police station. Indeed, in December, three small bombs were discovered there, leading Zo d'Axa to note in *L'Endehors* that "all seemed to point to better things, in terms of cleaning up the place!"

Ravachol, aided by his young friend Cookie, set out to avenge the "martyrs" of Clichy. He would do so with an explosive that was leveling the playing field for terrorists intent on striking against the state: dynamite.

In 1863, Alfred Nobel, a Swedish chemist and manufacturer, experimented with nitroglycerin, in an attempt to invent a more powerful industrial explosive. A year later, a shed used for the production of nitroglycerin exploded, and Nobel's brother and four other people were killed. Nobel then experimented with mixing nitroglycerin with a fine, porous black powder. In 1867 he took out a patent for dynamite. He developed a detonator, or blasting cap, made up of a copper casing filled with a charge of mercury fulminate. Dynamite immediately found a market, particularly among mining and construction companies, which used Nobel's invention to blow apart rock or anything else that stood in their way. Armies also quickly found uses for dynamite. Nobel became a very rich man. With some of the proceeds from his discovery, he later set up a fund to award people deemed to have furthered the "good of humanity."

In France, Nobel's writings were translated and made available by 1870. Dynamite quickly entered French mines and factories. The president of the state Committee on Fortifications produced a study of the theory and practice of dynamite use, and the French navy began to explore the possibility of creating dynamite-loaded torpedoes.

The dangers of dynamite became clear almost immediately. Inadvertent and sometimes premature explosions of this substance killed workers. Soon, legal guidelines were established to define how it might be produced and used. In 1875 a law authorized the production and sale of dynamite and "eventually new explosives, that science could discover." It set some restrictions on its manufacture and transport, at least for civilian uses, specifying the places where it could be stored. Railroad companies, worried about the dangers associated with the explosive product, were extremely reluctant to transport it, despite being obliged to do so by a law in 1879. Annual reports tallied the number of accidents for the Ministry of Commerce and Industry, which oversaw the production, transport, and use of explosives; also, a parliamentary commission, preparing possible new legislation, listed terrible explosions that had occurred over the previous three centuries before dynamite had been invented. Other government officials published a separate history of the ways in which assassins, or would-be assassins, had made use of gunpowder, beginning with a failed attack in 1605 against James I of England. New regulations in 1882 further tightened conditions of transport, storage, and use. Other countries began to enact laws against the criminal use of explosives.

Then reports reached the Ministry of Foreign Affairs concerning deadly new "infernal machines," powerful bombs being produced in the United States. It was believed that a Philadelphia inventor had manufactured one such combustible called the "Ticker," which packed the equivalent of nine hundred pounds of powder and came with a clock that could be set thirty-six hours before the intended explosion. Elsewhere, a wicked "eight-day machine" had been created, and it could blow up three thousand pounds of powder with the help of a similar clock mechanism. Stories arose about other awful inventions: the "Little Exterminator," a mere two inches high, which could spread deadly vapors; the "Bottle Machine," filled with acidic powder; and the newest threat, "That Explodir" [sic]. Within French circles of power, rumors abounded that orders for these deadly devices were pouring in from Mexico, Italy, Austria, Germany, and Russia.

And indeed, governments had cause for fear; dyamite's potential for destruction was not lost on the anarchists. The "apostle of dynamite" was a German bookbinder named Johann Most. Born in 1846, Most was elected to the Reichstag as a Social Democrat, but then quit socialism after Chancellor Otto von Bismarck's anti-socialist legislation in 1878 forced him and others to flee. He moved toward anarchism, publishing in London the newspaper *Freiheit (Freedom)*. Most was the first to realize that the mass press could greatly enhance the appeal of anarchism across the globe. In 1880, Most contended that "it was within the power of dynamite to destroy the capitalist regime just as it had been within the power of gunpowder and the rifle to wipe feudalism from the face of the earth." Dynamite thus developed a mystique. Johann Most saluted the destruction wrought by the Fenians in Ireland, who blew up a prison in 1867, killing twelve and wounding more than one hundred in their bid for independence from Britain. In Russia, the anarchist group People's Will made dynamite their weapon of choice, helped by a member who was a scientist. Most celebrated the assassination of Tsar Alexander II, in which dynamite had done its part. After being jailed in London, Most moved to the United States.

Most preached direct, violent action against the agents of the state, admitting that some "innocents" might get hurt in the process, which had in fact happened when Irish bombs, though not made with dynamite, had been detonated. Revolutionary groups welcomed him as a hero when he arrived in the United States as a political refugee. He continued to publish *Freiheit* in New York, lectured widely, and greatly influenced American anarchists. He worked for a time in an explosives factory in New Jersey, the right man in the right place. Imagining new uses for these substances, such as letter bombs (although the first one was not sent until 1895) and bombs dropping from the sky, Most wrote, "Let us rely upon the unquenchable spirit of destruction and annihilation which is the perpetual spring of new life." Most then published "The Science of Revolutionary Warfare—A Manual of Instruction in the Use and Preparation of Nitroglycerine, Dynamite, Gun-Cotton, Fulminating Mercury, Bombs, Fuses, Poisons, etc., etc.," which was printed in Chicago and Cleveland in 1885 and 1886. What better way to prepare for revolution than with the "thunder" of dynamite? The explosive could "be carried in the pocket without danger . . . a formidable weapon against any force of militia, police, or detectives that may want to stifle the cry for justice that goes forth from the plundered slaves . . . It is a genuine boon for the disinherited, while it brings terror and fear to the robbers . . . Our lawmakers might as well try to sit down on the crater of a volcano or on the point of a bayonet as to endeavor to stop the manufacture and use of dynamite." An anarchist newspaper in 1885 praised dynamite, "the good stuff! Stuff several pounds of this sublime stuff into an inch pipe . . . plug up both ends, insert a cap with a fuse attached, place this in the vicinity of a lot of rich loafers who live by the sweat of other people's brows, and light the fuse . . . A pound of this good stuff beats a bushel of ballots—and don't you forget it!" The newspaper *La Révolution Sociale* included a column called "Scientific Studies," which described how to make dynamite, as well as other explosives.

Poems sang the praises of dynamite:

> At last a toast to Science
> To dynamite that is the force
> The force in our own hands
> The world gets better day by day.

In Paris, *Père Peinard* did its part to perpetuate the cult of dynamite among the anarchist faithful. It seemed so simple. "Do you want some dynamite?" the newspaper asked. "For a little money . . . you can buy a liter of it." An international anarchist gathering in London called for "the study of the new technical and chemical sciences from the point of view of their revolutionary value." Several anarchist groups during the 1880s in Paris enthusiastically took names invoking dynamite, such as the Dynamitards. In the

Dordogne in southwest France, a liquor called Dynamite went on sale in 1888. At Montmartre's Cabaret du Chat Rouge, "Dame Dynamite" was high on the list of favorite songs. One could even dance to the "Dynamite Polka."

Dynamite played a part in the Haymarket affair in Chicago in 1886. During the 1880s, the influence of anarchism had grown in Chicago's labor movement, finding adherents particularly among the large number of German and Bohemian workers there. A wave of labor militancy, marked by increased organization, brought massive strikes followed by some major victories that affected workers of many trades, skilled and unskilled. Notably "The Great Upheaval" of 1886 led to a shorter workday. The lords of finance and industry launched a counteroffensive, targeting militants such as Albert Parsons.

A Texas-born former employee of the Internal Revenue Service, Parsons had married Lucy Gonzalez, a black woman with Mexican and Indian antecedents. He edited an anarchist newspaper, *Alarm,* which contended that one man with dynamite was the equivalent of an entire military regiment. According to Lucy Parsons, "The voice of dynamite is the voice of force, the only voice which tyranny has ever been able to understand." Other anarchists joined this chorus. During a speech, the German-born labor leader August Spies, who edited a German-language anarchist newspaper, held up an empty piece of tube and implied how it could be used: "Take it to your boss, and tell him we have 9,000 more like it—only loaded." Rumors spread quickly that anarchists planned to blow up the Board of Trade building.

On May 3, 1886, Chicago policemen attacked strikers outside the McCormick Reaper Works, shooting six men dead and beating others with their clubs. Such acts were fairly typical of the way bosses and police, cheered on by people of means, dealt with labor militancy at the time. Anarchist leaders prepared an armed retort.

The next day, a mass meeting began at 7:30 in the evening on Desplaines Street, adjacent to Haymarket Square. As armed police moved in amid fiery speeches by Spies and others, someone — probably a German anarchist — threw a small dynamite bomb in their general direction. A policeman lay dead, probably killed by the explosion. Subsequent shots resulted in the death of four other policemen, almost certainly killed by "friendly fire." Businessmen and newspapers screamed for revenge. Albert Parsons, who had gone into hiding in Wisconsin, returned (foolishly) to stand trial with seven others. The prosecution proved no conspiracy of any kind to start a social revolution or to bomb the police, nor any connection between the men and the bomb, but that made little difference to the jury. It found seven of the defendants guilty of murder as charged, giving them the death penalty. The penalties of three were commuted, but Louis Lingg, a violent German anarchist, somehow managed to get a dynamite cartridge into his cell and committed suicide by blowing himself up. Despite petitions calling on the Supreme Court and the governor of Illinois for clemency, Albert Parsons, Spies, and two others were hanged in Cook County Jail in November 1887.

The Haymarket riot was a touchstone for anarchists in Europe and in the United States, where the trials and subsequent executions pushed Emma Goldman, an immigrant from Russia, to anarchist militancy. The events in Chicago demonstrated three things to anarchists: that anarchism had international appeal, that anarchists could mobilize workers, and that the repressive power of the state, serving the interests of high finance and big business, remained strong. The image of the bodies of four men hanging in the Windy City in the United States, supposedly a progressive republic, became etched in the anarchist collective memory. Like the Paris Commune, Haymarket made clear that given the strength and resolution of the bourgeois state, the revolution would have to be bloody.

And François-Claudius Ravachol was prepared to take action. He wanted to avenge the three anarchists mistreated by the Clichy police, two of whom had been sent to prison in 1891. During the night of February 14–15, 1892, Ravachol and several other anarchists stole a considerable amount of dynamite, called "La Camelote" (or "junk"), from a quarry in Soisy-sous-Étiolles, southeast of Paris and not too far from Brévannes. In all, thirty kilograms of dynamite, 1,400 to 1,500 capsules, and two hundred yards of fuse disappeared in the night. The *compagnons* left the site with pockets "full of firecrackers." On February 29, a bomb exploded at an elite residence on elegant rue Saint-Dominique, doing little damage but frightening the city.

On March 7, with the help of Cookie and a cooking pot, Ravachol put together a bomb in a warehouse in Saint-Denis. It consisted of fifty dynamite cartridges and pieces of iron. His target was the Clichy police station, to avenge the three anarchists severely beaten there. But since police stations tend to be surrounded by police officers, Ravachol could not get close enough to place the bomb. He decided instead to kill Judge Benoît, who had presided over the trial of the Clichy three. On March 11, after Cookie had checked out the magistrate's house on boulevard Saint-Germain on the Left Bank, he, Ravachol, and two others took the tramway into Paris. After a few nervous moments at the customs barrier surrounding the capital—with the bomb hidden under the skirt of Rosalie Soubère (known as Mariette)—they entered Paris, after which the woman, her work accomplished, got off the tramway and returned home, the three men continuing on their route. On boulevard Saint-Germain, Ravachol entered the building, carrying two loaded pistols. Because he did not know which apartment was Benoît's, he placed the bomb on the second floor in the center of the building. He lit the fuse and sneaked out without being seen. The bomb detonated as he reached the sidewalk—a huge, terrifying explosion. But it killed no one and injured only one person slightly. Judge Benoît, who lived on the fifth floor, was unhurt.

Four days later, a dynamite cartridge exploded in front of the Lobau barracks near the town hall, shattering windows in Saint-Gervais church. The man responsible was Théodule Meunier, a cabinetmaker who had managed to escape to London after serving jail time for another crime. Charles Malato described him as "the most remarkable type of revolutionary visionary illuminist, an ascetic, as passionate in his search for the ideal society as [the French revolutionary] Saint-Just, and as merciless in seeking his way towards it." Many anarchists celebrated what *L'Endehors* called a "nicely symbolic" bomb.

The team of Ravachol and Cookie went to work again, preparing another bomb, this one with 120 cartridges of dynamite. The target would be Bulot, the prosecuting attorney in the Clichy case. On March 17, thanks to a police informer, Chaumartin (Ravachol's host) and Cookie were arrested. But Ravachol had already left for the suburb of Saint-Mandé. On March 27, he placed the bomb in Bulot's building on rue de Clichy, taking off down the street as it exploded. Seven people were injured, but not the magistrate and his family, who were away at the time. Ravachol climbed onto a bus that would take him down rue de Clichy so that he could see the great damage his bomb had inflicted. Soon thereafter, he stopped in a restaurant called Le Véry, on boulevard de Magenta. He engaged a waiter called Lhérot in conversation. When the latter complained about military service, Ravachol held forth on anarchism. The waiter remembered a scar the diner had on his left hand. Three days later, Ravachol returned to dine in the same place. The waiter by then had seen a newspaper description of Ravachol, and instead of going to get the first course, he went to see the *patron,* who returned with the police. Ravachol was arrested, but not without a fight. It took ten policemen to subdue him.

Ravachol's arrest became the talk of anarchist circles—a policeman observed that the anarchists "hoped for and counted on at least some sort of violent response." Some bemoaned Ravachol's extreme imprudence. They felt it would have been better if he had been gunned down after shooting a policeman, not taken because he had talked too much. The police knew that Lhérot, the waiter, needed to look out for himself. At a gathering of about fifty anarchists on March 12, a speaker advised the faithful that the time had come to attack the "great exploiters"—banks, the Bourse, and elegant private residences. Foreign tourists began to flee the City of Dynamite. The fact that some anarchist publications brazenly described how to assemble bombs and even recommended the use of chemical weapons or poison heightened mass anxiety.

On April 22, 1892, at 5 A.M., twelve policemen banged on the door of the journalist Zo d'Axa and searched his apartment for dynamite. After fifteen days in custody, he managed to leave the tribunal before his sentencing on charges of insulting a magistrate and provocation to murder (condemned to eighteen months in prison and a fine of two thousand francs). He headed for London, first staying with Charles Malato near Regent's Park. Émile Pouget and Errico Malatesta were now also in the British capital, along with other anarchist exiles.

Just before Ravachol's trial was to begin in Paris, on April 25, a bomb blew up the restaurant Le Véry. It had been placed in a small suitcase recently purchased for the occasion. The explosion killed two men, including Monsieur Véry himself, giving rise to the savage pun of *Père Peinard: "Vérification."* With Ravachol in jail, two principal suspects remained, both members of a group of anarchist cabinetmakers called the Flat Feet: Meunier and Jean-Pierre François, known to friends and police simply as Francis—a powerful man, with a black beard and mustache and a look of sullen resignation etched on his face. Francis accompanied Meunier to the restaurant, and the latter placed the bomb in its case next to the counter. A French police agent working in London noted that as far as he knew, Francis had not previously killed anyone, and he spent most of his time drinking. In and out of jail for years, Francis had the typical itinerary of many a militant anarchist, as he dodged policemen and landlords alike.

On April 26, Ravachol's trial took place in the Assize Court in the Palace of Justice on the Île de la Cité. Soldiers guarded the courtroom, and police even stood between the accused and the judge and jury. Bulot, the prosecuting attorney, the same man Ravachol had tried to kill a month earlier, contemptuously called the anarchist "a mere knight of the dynamite club," which the anarchist took as a compliment. Four other anarchists, all workers, were also tried, including Cookie, Ravachol's faithful, dangerous assistant. When asked specifically if he had helped Ravachol, Cookie coolly replied, "Absolutely." The jury condemned Ravachol as well as Cookie to life in prison with hard labor. (Cookie would be killed two years later during a prison riot on Devil's Island, French Guiana.)

In June, Ravachol again went on trial in the town of Montbrison, near Saint-Étienne. Amid rumors that anarchists would strike a blow there, security measures were extremely tight. In the Palace of Justice, a former convent, Ravachol addressed horrified magistrates and jurors. "See this hand?" he asked the courtroom. "It has killed as many bourgeois as it has fingers." As for the murder of the hermit monk, Ravachol explained, "If I killed, it was first of all to satisfy my personal needs, then to come to the aid of the anarchist cause, for we work for the happiness of the people." His only regret was the society he saw around him. Condemned to death for the murder of the hermit and two women near the small industrial town Saint-Chamond, as well as for several other killings that he probably did not commit, Ravachol went to the guillotine on July 11, 1892. Smiling, confident, insolent, with his "jaw of a wolf" set firmly forward, he told the priest who approached him with a crucifix, "I don't give a damn about your Christ. Don't show him to me; I'll spit in his face." On the way to the guillotine, which was guarded by a cordon of troops, he sang,

> To be happy, goddammit,
> You have got to kill those who own property,
> To be happy, goddammit,
> You must cut the priests in two,
> To be happy, goddammit,
> Put the good Lord into the shit . . .

The guillotine's blade, operated skillfully by the chief executioner, Antoine-Louis Deibler, cut short Ravachol's attempt to shout *"Vive la révolution!"*

In his "Eulogy for Ravachol," the anarchist critic Paul Adam warned that "the murder of Ravachol will open an era." He had been impressed with the way that Ravachol had propagated "the great idea that the ancient religions advocated the quest for death for the good of the world, the abnegation of oneself . . . for the exaltation of the poor and the humble." Ravachol became "the peal of thunder to which succeeds the joy of sunlight and of peaceful skies." Adam portrayed Ravachol as "a redeemer" and compared his "sacrifice and suffering" to those of Jesus Christ: Both were nonconformists, both expressed contempt for the values of contemporary society, and both represented high ideals. Both were executed at age thirty-three. Christ had been betrayed by Judas, and Ravachol, a "violent Christ," as described by Victor Barrucand in *L'Endehors,* had been betrayed by the waiter in Le Véry (as well as by his former friend, Chaumartin, who had provided magistrates with important evidence). A woodprint by the artist Charles Maurin, reproduced frequently in the anarchist press, portrayed Ravachol as a martyr, his defiant, heroic visage set within the frame of a guillotine.

Ordinary criminals might appear downtrodden, colorful, or wretched, victims of fate or poor choices. Ravachol had been different. His almost "noble bearing" before death and his determined defense of anarchism until the very end stood out for all to see. He seemed to mock the guillotine, confident that ultimately his cause would win out. *Père Peinard* taunted,

> Ravachol's head has rolled at their feet; they fear it will explode, just like a bomb! . . . And for Christ sake's shut up about your whore of a society; it has no need of being defended—it's at its death rattle . . . You claim that his death at the guillotine is an expiation. Well, why did you hide like bandits to do the trick? Why encircle the prison with thousands of troops, rifle in hand, bayonets fixed? Why only one little spot left free: the one where Ravachol would be assassinated? . . . And the guillotine-lickers are there surrounding him, never taking their eyes off him. If only he would have a

moment of weakness. If only his eyes had become misty for a moment or two and they could have bleated to their whorespapers: "Ravachol trembled."

Ravachol had wanted to keep speaking, but Deibler's assistants had thrown him down on the plank and, holding him by his ears, forced his head into the guillotine's glassless window, even as he continued to shout.

The "Song of Père Duchesne," which Ravachol had sung during his last steps to the guillotine, was reprinted by *La Révolte,* and the lyrics were widely circulated. Anarchist publications saluted his "greatness of character." Pouget's almanac in 1893 reproduced his portrait and saluted Ravachol's "dandy adaptation of cooking pots to the solution of the social question." Five thousand copies of a brief commentary titled "Ravachol, an Anarchist? Absolutely!" were circulated, echoing Cookie; it was attributed to Fortuné Henry. Fénéon proclaimed that the anarchist "deeds" had done more for propaganda than two decades of brochures by Kropotkin or Reclus. Anarchist newspapers and arguably the coverage given to such attacks by the mainstream press publicized "propaganda by the deed." Thus emerged the stereotype of the dark-coated, elusive anarchist lurking in the shadows with a bomb hidden under his coat, an image that Joseph Conrad would later capture in *The Secret Agent.*

The anarchist press called for vengeance, saluting the memory of the martyr Ravachol. According to *L'Endehors,* when dynamite spoke, people listened, and "the conspiracy of silence [was] vanquished." It was sheer delusion to imagine a peaceful revolution "in face of the blind oppression of Capital"; this was the dream of those who had never been hungry. Anarchists sang "La Ravachole" to the tune of a leftist song from the days of the French Revolution, the "Carmagnole":

In the Great City of Paris
Live the well-fed bourgeois

And the destitute who have empty stomachs
But they have long teeth.
Let's dance the Ravachole, Long live the sound,
Let's dance the Ravachole, long live the sound of the explosion!
It will be, it will be,
All the bourgeois will taste the bomb,
It will be, it will be,
These bourgeois, these bourgeois, we'll blow them up!

A tailor penned a song in honor of "Dame Dynamite":

Our fathers once danced
To the sound of the cannons of the past!
Now this tragic dance
Requires stronger music.
Let's dynamite, let's dynamite!
    Refrain
Lady Dynamite, let's dance fast!
Let's dance and sing!
Lady Dynamite, let's dance fast!
Let's dance and sing, and dynamite!

The spectacular and seemingly unprecedented attacks generated a veritable psychosis that took hold of Paris. Everyone knew that a considerable stock of dynamite had been hidden somewhere. Ravachol had proudly refused to account for the remaining cartridges that had been in his possession. Moreover, Ravachol himself had promised that he would be avenged. This was hardly reassuring. The factories that produced explosives and chemicals were located in the industrial suburbs, right in the hotbed of anarchy. Authorities suspected that workers were stealing dynamite and cartridges from factories, workshops, and mines, and stored them in secret places. Miners, in particular, could easily procure dynamite.

Dynamite and the fear of anarchist attacks became lodged in

the upper-class imagination, contributing to the sense that Parisians were living in a whole new era. As one bombing followed another, it became possible to imagine an organized plot—a dynamite club—against society of unprecedented destructive power. Newspaper headlines stoked Parisians' anxieties. The dailies dramatized each anarchist attack, competing for eager, if apprehensive, readers. This coverage pushed the Third Republic's financial scandals off the front pages, to the relief of compromised politicians. People of means were afraid to frequent elegant restaurants or attend the theater, and many planned to send their families to the provinces if the government did not act decisively against what seemed to be a rapidly increasing threat. Some owners of apartments in fancy neighborhoods now hesitated to rent to magistrates, for fear of the *"dynamitards."* Bulot, who had prosecuted the Clichy three and Ravachol, noted that magistrates were becoming targets: "Really!" he complained, "the profession of judge is becoming impossible because of the anarchists!" Jean Grave replied in *La Révolte* that it was surprising that a functionary who earned his living calling for executions did not realize that there might eventually be some danger in it for him. Ravachol so terrified his upper-class contemporaries that for a time his name was used as a French verb: *ravacholiser* meant "to kill someone, preferably by blowing up the person with dynamite."

In the meantime, hundreds of scrawled messages left in mailboxes or sent by regular mail gave ravenous landlords and unfair concierges something to worry about. Such missives were signed by "the avengers of Ravachol," "the *compagnons* of Ravachol," or "an anarchist from the *quartier.*" An "exploiter of the proletarian" received a message telling him that "Next Sunday, May 1, you will be blown up!" It was signed "Dynamite." A group of anarchists had sworn to eliminate the bourgeois who exploited them. How would this be accomplished? Nothing could be simpler—"a little dynamite and you can kiss goodbye the riches you have accumulated, thanks to the sweat of workers." A certain Madame Boubonneaud, a property owner of some means, received her warning from those who followed "the school of Ravachol . . . We are going to Ravachol you."

In the Chamber of Deputies, one deputy accused anarchists of working "to wipe out the work of six thousand years and take the world back to the age of cavemen, without seeing that humanity would again assume the painful burden of centuries of barbarism . . . Their savage hatred and furious rage aim at nothing less than the destruction of all that exists."

The police moved against anarchists, whether or not they espoused "propaganda by the deed"—and the vast majority of anarchists did not. The authorities used existing laws to expel foreigners, including Germans, Austrians, Belgians, Italians (among them Malatesta), and at least one Spaniard. One day late in April, the police arrested sixty-six anarchists, most of whom were considered propagandists. The prefecture of police increased the number of undercover police and paid informants. The police undertook searches, seized newspapers and correspondence, made arrests for little or no reason, and intimidated employers into firing workers suspected of being anarchists. The government gave the police in Paris free rein, with virtually no constraints. The "dynamite psychosis" seemed to justify countless violations of individual rights.

At first Émile Henry rejected the deeds of Ravachol. "Such acts," he said, "can only do great damage to our cause . . . A true anarchist strikes his enemy, but he does not dynamite houses where there are women, children, workers, and domestics." But Émile soon came to embrace Ravachol's tactics for carrying out the revolution. Indeed, police suspected that Émile and his older brother had gone to Montbrison with the goal of blowing up the house of the prosecuting attorney. Police met virtually every train, but neither brother was actually seen in Montbrison or Saint-Étienne.

As Émile now saw at close range, the state was becoming ever more powerful, fully capable of defending the privileges of the rich while the destitute struggled to survive. The repressive police campaign in the wake of Ravachol's bombs was a reflection of this. Revolution seemed to require strong, violent acts in order to impress ordinary people.

The neighborhoods in which Émile lived help turn his love for humanity into a steely hatred for people of means. With the exception of a short stint in a tiny room at 10, boulevard Morland, between the Bastille and the Seine (he left without paying his rent after a month), his time in Paris was spent in plebeian Montmartre and then in Belleville. From November 25, 1891, to October 8, 1892, he lived in a room on the third floor at 101, rue Marcadet, in the eighteenth arrondissement. Every day, Émile encountered the ravages of poverty and misery.

The building in which Émile lived stood within the shadow of Montmartre, dominated by the basilica of Sacré-Coeur, still under construction at that time. As Émile walked through the streets of his neighborhood, he caught occasional glimpses of the looming structure.

Sacré-Coeur's very presence on Montmartre gnawed at the anarchists, along with other groups of disadvantaged people. The anarchist lithographer Théophile-Alexandre Steinlen depicted an imaginary revolutionary attack on the basilica. At Montmartre's café Le Chat Noir, the audience sang: "Since a temple has burdened it, our old Montmartre is much changed, because of the construction on our butte." It was rumored that more than a hundred dynamite cartridges were ready to go, stocked in Saint-Denis. In July, several *compagnons* let it be known in a meeting that dynamite would be distributed by the anarchist group The Miners' Revenge, with the goal of destroying Sacré-Coeur. A year later, an anarchist meeting protested the "provocations" of the clergy, an occupying force on Montmartre. In 1893, a man known only as "Captain Boulogne" proposed to a meeting of anarchists that they vote to blow up Sacré-Coeur.

In Zola's novel *Paris* (1898), Guillaume Froment wants to strike a blow for anarchism. He first considers blowing up the Opera. But he concludes that this would "in the whirlwind of anger and justice [only] destroy a little set of enjoyers." Why not the Bourse? But such "a blow at money, the great agent of corruption," would also have limited impact. Nor would he target the "Palais d'Injustice," or the Arc de Triomphe, the latter symbolizing warfare and the "sanguineous glory of conquerors." He decides to blow up Sacré-Coeur. He hates the basilica, which haunts him. Guillaume Froment could savor its destruction: "And all at once came thunder and earthquake, and a volcano opening and belching forth fire and smoke, and swallowing up the whole church and its multitude of worshippers . . . And how fearful would be the avalanche: a broken forest of scaffoldings, a hail of stonework, rushing and bounding through the dust and smoke onto the roofs below."

From the heights of the Montmartre butte, stairs still lead down rue des Abbesses to rue Véron, a narrow street of cobblestones beneath Sacré-Coeur. Early in October 1892, Émile moved into a small room on the top floor of number 31, then a shabby building like the others nearby. Today an old sign on that building proclaims GAS AVAILABLE ON EVERY FLOOR, but that was not the case when Émile lived there. A shop stood to the left of the door, with the concierge's apartment to the right. Émile's only known visitor in those months was a certain Lambert, a provincial law student and friend who stayed with him from time to time. But he knew anarchists on nearby rue Lepic, including Félix Fénéon and Léon Ortiz. A tall, elegant, well-spoken anarchist-burglar known to his friends as Trognon ("Cutie"), Ortiz was Mexican-born of a Polish mother. He espoused the right to steal. He lived with his girlfriend (who was thus known as La Trognette). These men shared a hatred of Sacré-Coeur and what it represented.

On May 28, 1892, a large crowd squeezed into the Salle du Commerce, 94, faubourg du Temple. The shadow of the martyred Ravachol was very much present. Trouble had arisen in the hall a month earlier, when anarchists disrupted a meeting held before an election, shouting that workers should abstain from electoral politics. Hundreds of people managed to get into the building. Two glass doors shattered in the tumult, while a crowd outside howled. One speaker set the tone: "Let's steal, kill, and dynamite—all means are good in order to get rid of this scum." Then it was Fortuné's turn. He saluted the theories of Ravachol and denounced "the governmental and bourgeois class." Ravachol had done the right thing. Everybody had seen "the general panic" caused by "two or three rocks" that he had left in apartment buildings. If that could have continued for fifteen days, "we would have been masters of the situation." In the meantime, the bosses were letting the poor die of hunger, while sleazy financial scandals continued. Resistance was difficult when ordinary people faced the rifles that had killed marchers in Fourmies. Then Fortuné shouted, "We have something even better, and you know the results . . . Death to those who govern! Death to the bourgeoisie!" He appeared to wave a dynamite cartridge, pulled from his pocket. "Here are our weapons, what we need to blow up the bourgeoisie! Death to those bandits."

A police informer jotted down Fortuné's words, making note of the cartridge. Two days later, on the evening of May 30, 1892, four policemen pounded on the door of Émile's room on rue Marcadet, where he was living at the time. They were armed with a warrant signed by the prefect of police, noting the presence of "suspect chemistry." Police believed Fortuné could be hiding there, but neither brother was found. In fact, the Henry brothers were attending another meeting on boulevard Montmartre. A locksmith had to be called to open Émile's door. The police seized twenty items from a table and an envelope that had been half consumed by flames in a small fireplace. An eight-caliber revolver, with five of the six slots loaded, rested on the mantel, with a box of twenty-five bullets nearby, as well as a leaded cane (sometimes used in fights). They took a ring engraved with the initials T.M. and the word REVOLUTION, and they pocketed a photo of Louis Matha, part of Émile's circle. A former barber, Matha was fearless and loyal; anarchists could count on him to do his share, even if he did not thoroughly understand the theoretical basis of anarchism. The police also carried away five anarchist newspapers, including a copy of *L'Endehors,* and various brochures. The reading material also included a fragment of an Italian newspaper containing instructions for making a bomb.

Émile was arrested the following day when he returned to his room, charged with the "detention of explosive devices," although nothing suspicious had been found. He gave his occupation as a "commercial employee," working for Félix Vanouytre since January 8, 1892, on rue du Sentier. He affirmed, with some pride, that he was an anarchist but would not tell them anything about his *compagnons.* As for his brother, Émile said that he was in Paris, adding that he hoped they would understand that he could not reveal his whereabouts. But the policemen had uncovered the address of Fortuné in the correspondence they had seized.

The police went to Fortuné's room early the same day. Fortuné lived on the quai de Valmy along the canal Saint-Martin, near place de la République. Fortuné claimed that he was staying with a friend, but a rent receipt indicated that the room was his. The police search turned up only newspapers and letters. Fortuné explained to the investigating magistrate that what had been taken by some to be a cartouche of dynamite was only a small leather case for pencils, which was similar in shape to a cartridge. He insisted that he had not said, "Here is our weapon, dynamite," but rather "Here are our arms . . . the pen, [with which we] write down our thoughts."

After some interrogation, the police released the younger Henry the same day (although he later remembered being in custody "several days"). Fortuné had been charged with "inciting murder and pillage" but was also released. That evening, the Henry brothers went with other *compagnons* to the commemorative Wall of the Fédérés in Père Lachaise Cemetery, where Communards had been executed in May 1871. Despite what they had seized from his room, the police had to admit, after interviewing his concierge and his employer, that the information they had gathered on Émile's "conduct and morality" was favorable.

The next day, June 1, *Le Temps*, one of Paris's most respectable newspapers, carried a brief report on the arrest of the Henry brothers. The arrest cost Émile his job the next day. His boss, Vanoutryne, discovered in his desk a manual "for the production and use of dynamite" and a translation from an Italian newspaper detailing how to make a bomb. Other employees said that they had learned, about two months before, that their colleague was an anarchist. Émile had tried to convert them to anarchism, but Vanoutryne had overlooked this, as he had no complaints at all about Émile's work as an accountant. However, Vanoutryne (and his mother) had decided then to fire him at the first sign of trouble. After the arrest, he was dismissed. That night, Émile went out to Brévannes, walking the several miles from the nearest train station. He told his mother that he was guilty of nothing and that society had condemned him to misery.

Émile soon attended another anarchist meeting in the Salle du Commerce, at which he briefly held forth on a proposed law concerning the press and public meetings. These measures, he insisted, were "dictated by fear and the fact that the representatives of the people only know how to terrify anarchists." The deputies wanted to still "the voice of those who demand their rights."

At the time of his arrest and release, Émile was serving temporarily as the managing director of *L'Endehors*. Zo d'Axa, the editor, had been extremely impressed with the young intellectual "whose constant obsession was to work for anarchism." After Zo d'Axa's sudden departure for London, Émile willingly took over the tedious administrative responsibilities of publishing the newspaper, including correspondence with those distributing it. Despite some differences of opinion, which Zo d'Axa considered an inevitable part of anarchist individualism, Émile had been a good colleague. In some ways Émile still seemed like a child, although rather solemn, even obsessed, "as are those who are no longer troubled by religious faith, those who see—and are even hypnotized by—a goal, and then reason, judge, and make decisions with a mathematical certainty." Émile was convinced that a rationally constructed, wonderful society lay ahead. Yet he seemed anything but happy himself, and often expressed astonishment that any joy could be found in modern life.

The day after his arrest, Émile wrote to Zo d'Axa from the offices of *L'Endehors*. He had received the news that Zo had made it safely to London with Matha. He promised to do all he could to help *L'Endehors*. The letter contained some details about the status of the publication and asked that Zo write him directly. He signed with "a cordial handshake." On June 24, he penned another short letter, sending Zo d'Axa fifteen francs. He would work on the problem of bringing in some income for the paper. In closing, he sent along the good wishes of everybody, including Fortuné.

However, shortly thereafter, Émile suddenly quit *L'Endehors*, without explanation. He wrote to Zo d'Axa, asking him to choose someone take over the paper. Émile had gone to see Félix Fénéon the day before and explained that he could no longer serve as manager and did not want to accept any money, because he had not completed even five weeks of work. Fénéon took over.

For his part, Fortuné continued to be a regular speaker at anarchist meetings. A giant red poster listed him with the other orators to be heard for a contribution of twenty-five centimes at the Salle du Commerce on July 3. During the three-hour meeting, amid shouts of *"Vive Ravachol!"* Fortuné discussed proposed new restrictions on the press. But he warned that those who suffered had another means of making themselves heard. In response, shouts of "Yes, dynamite!" cascaded down on the podium. At one point, Fortuné said that if blowing up ten houses was not enough, then one thousand, and if necessary, ten thousand houses would be fine. There would certainly be deaths, but this was unavoidable. States at war killed lots of people. Anarchists should not be afraid to avenge Ravachol. Even after this, the elder Henry excused himself for not being able to say all that he wanted—to be sure, he had already said a great deal—because police spies were taking down what he said. Over the next couple of months, he gave several more incendiary speeches—on one occasion, if the police are to be believed, interpreting the "propaganda of the deed" as giving anarchists the right and even the duty to assassinate heads of state.

Émile too remained active, but in different ways. One day someone who knew him noticed acid stains on his hands and mentioned it. He replied that he had not put enough nitroglycerin in his preparation, and it had been a waste. He added that he would try again with a little more acid and promised to let his friend know how it went.

Émile spent much of July looking for work, while trying to help raise enough money to assist Meunier and Francis, the two anarchists implicated in the explosion at the restaurant Le Véry. In the meantime, Émile took many of his meals with Constant Martin, who seemed to host nightly gatherings of anarchists at his shop. In September, Émile worked as an unpaid apprentice to a watchmaker whom his friend Matha knew on the elegant rue Saint-Honoré, west of the Opera. Émile even offered to pay the watchmaker fifteen francs a month if he could work in the shop but finally left after a month because he needed a paying job. Watchmaking skills, of course, were useful in putting together bombs that explode with a timing device. A policeman reported that this was precisely what Émile was up to. Another undercover agent insisted he was working secretly in his room on such things, having borrowed an alarm clock that could detonate explosives.

A spirited debate continued in anarchist circles concerning the efficacy of terrorist attacks. After all, one of the originators of the concept of "propaganda by the deed"—Kropotkin himself—had turned away from the idea, repelled by its violence. Émile had already concluded that words and speeches were not enough—that the way to anarchism lay in bombs. He was now obsessed with Ravachol and his courage before the guillotine. Émile told his friend Malato, "We should finish with these people who dishonor our party." Those who wanted to use the pen instead of the bomb aimed to live comfortably in "the bourgeois style," unwilling to sacrifice their lives for anarchism. His departure from *L'Endehors* was likely related to this shift in thinking.

In *L'Endehors* on August 21, 1892, Errico Malatesta expressed his views on "propaganda by the deed" in an article titled "A Little Theory." Clearly, the mood of revolt was becoming greater and greater, in some places the result of anarchist ideas, in other places simply the result of the miserable circumstances of the poor. Malatesta believed that in principle, the end—revolution and a new society—justified any means. He reiterated the familiar notion that all anarchist acts were good if they served to facilitate the revolution. But then he came to a controversial point. Anarchists, in Malatesta's view, should never go beyond "the limit determined by necessity." They should operate like a surgeon who cuts where necessary but avoids inflicting needless suffering. Anarchists should continue to be inspired by love, which remained at the heart of their project: to serve the future of humanity. "Brutal revolt" would indeed come and could put an end to the way society was organized, but revolutionaries had to have a more effective tool than violence to prepare the way. Malatesta warned that "hate does not produce love, and by hate one cannot remake the world." A revolution fueled only by hate—and thus murder—would completely fail, or lead to new repression. In the wake of Ravachol's attacks, Malatesta was issuing a stern warning to the exponents of "propaganda by the deed." His letter reflected the split in anarchist ranks between the "associationalists" like him, who no longer believed in "deeds," and the "individualists," who fully approved of Ravachol's strategy of violence.

Malatesta's letter angered Émile, who had embraced deeds. He considered individual initiative the most effective way of striking at bourgeois society, and held that organizations espoused by the assocationalists risked imposing arbitrary hierarchies on their members, a principle that anarchism was supposed to reject. Moreover, operating independent of a group would make it more difficult for the police to effect a mass roundup of anarchists. Hatred for the ruling classes that was based on noble sentiments rather than envy was "a healthy and powerful energetic passion . . . To those who say, 'hate does not generate love,' I respond that it is love, a burning love, which often generates hate." The "right of insurrection" trumped all other rights. Ravachol had thought long and hard about placing his bombs. It was "for him alone to be the judge if he was right in having such hate and acting in what seemed to be such a ferocious way."

Émile countered Malatesta's views in a long letter published in *L'Endehors* on August 28, 1892. Addressing his letter to the "Comrades of *L'Endehors*," he recalled that Malatesta had long underlined the necessity and imminence of a violent revolution, indicating that all acts "of propaganda or concrete acts" were good when they served to expedite the revolution. Yet by now cautioning anarchists to never go beyond "the limit determined by necessity," he was contradicting a central tenet of anarchism: the development of the individual by his own initiative. This alone ensured happiness. Malatesta wanted to restrain the very autonomy that was so central to the movement. Who should decide if a certain act was useful in bringing about revolution? Émile asked, "Will future Ravachols have to submit their projects for the acceptance by some sort of Grand Tribunal at which sits Malatesta or someone else, which will pass judgment on whether acts are appropriate or not?" It was up to the individual, and anarchists should welcome with pleasure "every energetic act against bourgeois society."

Émile had left rue Marcadet for rue Véron in early October 1892, leaving no forwarding address and telling the concierge that she should refuse any letters or packages arriving for him. The police were trying to keep an eye on him yet did not know that he had moved to rue Véron. A police report noted that Émile was unknown in the slumlike rooming houses, with their shabby attic dormitories, where poor transient workers often perched. It seemed something of a point of pride to the young bourgeois that he was not to be found there, although he frequently shared space and presumably a bed with working-class anarchists he barely knew.

Émile's anarchist friend Ortiz, the burglar, had been working for Dupuy, a decorative sculptor, at 5, rue de Rocroy, in the tenth arrondissement, not far from the Gare du Nord. When he quit his job, he recommended Émile, who began to work for Dupuy in the fall. Émile's new employer was very pleased with his work. Émile seemed "a model employee." His boss was "immediately enchanted by his prodigious abilities and the speed with which the young man learned." He was "a charmer," impressing with his lively intelligence and gentle and obliging nature. He did not hide his anarchism at the office, and Dupuy later said that Émile could probably have converted even him to anarchism.

CHAPTER 5

Carnage at a Police Station

IN AUGUST 1892, Émile Henry's attention, like that of many people in France, turned to a bitter strike in the south. In the small coal-mining and glass-making town of Carmaux, north of Toulouse and near Albi, miners pitted themselves against the Carmaux Mining Company. Many of these men had previously worked as farmers or farm hands, but as it became nearly impossible to make a decent living from agriculture, they found part-time and eventually full-time work in the mines. Now their survival almost totally depended on the low wages they earned there. When the demand for coal fell, unemployment in the mines brought extreme hardship. Even in relatively good times, their work was exceedingly dangerous. Thirty-six men were killed in the mines of Carmaux alone from 1880 to 1892.

Carmaux's glass workers too had gone on strike the previous fall, demanding a unified pay scale for their trade throughout France because their wages were falling (in part because of the mechanization of production). The miners' union had contributed funds to support the glass workers' walkout, but the strike eventually failed. The next spring, Jean-Baptiste Calvignac, a machine fitter in the mines and the secretary of the miners' union, was elected to the municipal council, thanks to the support of workers. The council then elected him mayor. But the powerful mining company fired Calvignac on August 2, 1892, after refusing to give him time off to fulfill his duties as the town's chief administrator.

The miners went on strike the following day, both to protest Calvignac's dismissal and to demand pay increases. This did not sit well with company management. Moreover, on several occasions the unions had challenged the management about disciplinary measures taken against workers. This resistance led to an aggressive counteroffensive against the miners' union. Some labor leaders working in the mines were suspended or fined, and others were fired as Baron Reille, president of the board of directors, reasserted the company's complete authority over the miners.

The Carmaux strike became a polarizing event in France. Collections were taken up in support of the striking miners, who were widely recognized as poorly paid workers in an extraordinarily dangerous industry. The socialist politician Jean Jaurès used the popular press to carry the strike, and the issues it raised about workers and employers, to a national audience. The miners' determination, solidarity, discipline, and political engagement gained the admiration of ordinary people, while the arrogance of the Carmaux Mining Company earned castigation. After three bitter months, with soldiers camped outside Carmaux, innumerable confrontations, and attempts at arbitration and compromise, on November 3, 1892, the miners capitulated.

The Carmaux situation was widely discussed at anarchist gatherings that October. Émile was moved by the strike and impressed by the miners' resolve. His father, after all, had worked in mines in Spain. In Émile's opinion, the strike had been co-opted by socialist leaders, "the fancy speakers," who feared that if a violent struggle began, thousands of men would no longer obey their orders. And then hunger—"their habitual companion"—began to eat away at what meager funds their little union had in reserve. They had been forced to return to the mines, even more miserable than before. And so "order" returned to Carmaux, and the company continued to exploit miners. Company profits rose once again.

Émile was shaken by events in Carmaux, and his anarchism took an even more violent turn. He proudly admitted "a deep hate, each day revived by the revolting spectacle of this society . . . where everything prevents the fulfillment of human passions and the generous tendencies of the heart, and the unimpeded growth of the human spirit." The extremely sensitive Émile had evolved into a fanatic who believed that only terrorism could solve the deep problems of society. Émile wanted to "strike as hard" as he could. He had been particularly impressed by the Russian anarchist Souvarine in Émile Zola's great novel *Germinal*. Souvarine declares: "All the reasonings about the future are criminal, because they stand in the way of pure and simple destruction and thus of the march of the revolution . . . Don't talk to me about evolution! Raise fires in the four corners of cities, mow people down, wipe everything out, and when nothing whatever is left in this rotten world perhaps a better one will spring up!" To Émile, striking out was a perfectly rational decision, based on a sense of both impatience for the revolution to begin and optimism about its eventual outcome. With political scandals rampant, the Third Republic seemed particularly vulnerable. Police repression had increased the indignation of the poor.

Émile decided "to add to the concert . . . a voice that the bourgeoisie has already heard, but which they believed stilled with the death of Ravachol, that of dynamite." The "insolent triumphs" of the bourgeoisie would be shattered, "its golden calf would shake violently on its pedestal, until the final blow knocks it into the gutter and pools of blood." And he wanted to show the miners that only the anarchists truly understood their suffering and stood ready to avenge them.

Émile had told friends that the workers should have attacked the company immediately. They should have burned the stocks of coal, broken the machines, and demolished the pumps necessary for extracting coal. Then the mining company would have quickly capitulated. He blamed "the great popes of socialism," such as Jaurès, for ignoring the anarchists' advice.

Émile decided to take action himself. In a phone book, he found the company's Paris headquarters, located in the elegant building at 11, avenue de l'Opéra. He purchased potassium chlorate on rue de la Sorbonne in the Latin Quarter, receiving a 10 percent discount because he claimed to be an assistant to a professor at a school in Saint-Denis. He picked up an iron pot for 3.30 francs from a hardware store, and back in his room he put ten dynamite cartridges into it. Lacking decent fuses, he put together a "reversal bomb," one that would explode when turned over or jarred. He added potassium chloride and some sodium, which he had locked in a cupboard in his room. When the canister was "reversed," the chemicals would mix and come into contact with water, igniting a fire and producing an immediate explosion. On November 4, he went to a paper store on rue La Fayette to purchase a metal pen case, which he transformed into a detonator by filling it with mercury fulminate.

Émile then went to scrutinize the building on avenue de l'Opéra, to make sure that he would not be blowing up "unfortunates." The company offices were located on the mezzanine. And the rest of the building was populated with the rich: "a wealthy milliner, a banker, and so on." There would be no innocent victims: "The entire bourgeoisie lives from the exploitation of the unfortunate, and all of it should pay for its crimes." If someone found the bomb before it exploded, perhaps they would take it to a police station, and thus, there too serve the purpose of "striking at my enemies." And if someone saw the bomb and called the police to the scene? In the event, Émile told himself, "either I will kill the rich or I will kill the police!" It was all the same to him.

On the morning of November 8, 1892, Émile went to his job at 5, rue de Rocroy, not too far from the Gare du Nord. His employer, Dupuy, gave him two errands to do, handing him a little cash for public transportation. Émile left at about 10 A.M., catching an omnibus on rue La Fayette en route to place de la Madeleine. He walked quickly to the office of a judicial administrator on rue Tronchet, staying only a couple of seconds to drop off a document. Then, instead of proceeding to his second assigned point of call, an architect's office on boulevard de Courcelles, he took one of the capital's twenty-five thousand horse-drawn carriages to place Blanche. From there he walked to rue Véron and bounded up several flights of stairs to his room on the top floor. Reaching into the cupboard, he pulled out his bomb, which he wrapped in a copy of *Le Temps* dated June 1, 1892. Putting the bomb under his coat, he hurried back to place Blanche, where he hailed another carriage. Taking great care not to jar the "reversal bomb," he asked the driver to take him to avenue de l'Opéra. Émile stepped out of the cab at 10:57 in front of a store, Du Gagne-Petit. He then walked a block to number 11. Entering the building, he caught a glimpse of the concierge, who was wearing a short-sleeved shirt. He also saw a woman carrying a basket, as well as a young man on the stairway.

Émile walked up the stairs to the first floor, or the mezzanine level, and placed his gift to the Carmaux Mining Company in front of the door to its offices. It was now between 11 and 11:05. Émile ran down the stairs, left the building, and walked quickly back to place de la Madeleine and then to boulevard des Capucines. There he took another carriage to the office of the architect on boulevard de Courcelles, thus completing the second errand for his boss. He then returned to work on rue de Rocroy, arriving shortly after noon. He had been gone for about two hours and fifteen minutes.

Monsieur Bernich, an employee of the Carmaux Mining Company, had an appointment that day with the chief accountant. Outside the main office door on the first floor, he found a package propped against the door. It was 11:10. He went to get Bellois, the cashier, and Émile-Raymond Garin, the twenty-seven-year-old office boy. Bellois picked up the package and removed the paper. Inside he found a brand-new pot of gray cast iron, resting on its handle. The lid was held on by a cloth strip tied to the handle. It seemed somewhat suspicious—given the recent explosions in Paris—so Bellois asked the concierge, Garnier, to carry it downstairs. He placed the half-opened package on the sidewalk outside the entrance on the back street. A small crowd formed. Several people noticed that white powder seemed to be seeping through the cracks of the cover. Jean-Nicolas Gung'l, the secretary of *Le Matin*, happened by, curious about the group of people clustered around a strange object. Later he remembered seeing the price of the pot written in chalk.

The office boy, Garin, called out to a retired policeman, who was helping children cross avenue de l'Opéra. Although the crossing guard could not leave his post, he alerted two officers—Étienne Fomorin and Marc-Michel Réaux—who went to examine the object on the sidewalk. They decided that the package should be taken to the nearest police station, on rue des Bons-Enfants, not far from the Palais-Royal. Garin and Fomorin hoisted the package, which was now wrapped in a towel supplied by the building concierge. Arriving at 22, rue des Bons-Enfants at 11:35, they entered the courtyard, which separated the two wings of the building. As they crossed the courtyard, Garin asked another policeman to help because the object was heavy. The three carried the package up the stairs into the police office, placing it on a table.

Two minutes later, the bomb exploded. Unimaginable horror followed. In the vestibule, the body of Sergeant Fomorin, a forty-three-year-old former gendarme with a wife and a ten-year-old child, lay face down, still shaking in the middle of debris, his uniform almost completely shredded, his exposed flesh turning an awful gray. Officer Réaux's legs had been blown off below the knee, his thighs crushed, his face and hands charred. Beyond the vestibule, the waiting room was completely destroyed by the explosion; the floor had caved in, and pieces of wood, clothing, and flesh were scattered here and there. Human remains hung from a gaslight attached to the ceiling. Blood splattered the walls. The office boy Garin and Henri Pousset, the secretary of the police station, had been killed. Inspector Troutot lay gravely wounded, his face shattered and one of his legs crushed. He died later that day, leaving a wife and four children.

Several days after the explosion, a funeral Mass was held at Notre Dame de Paris, following a solemn procession that had begun at the prefecture of police on the Île de la Cité. Prime Minister Émile Loubet denounced "the cowardly assassins . . . men, rejected by all parties, blinded by savage hatred, thinking that by such means they can carry out shameful vengeances in order to reform society." Such men were not working to improve society, but to destroy it. The five victims of the explosion were buried in Montparnasse Cemetery. The public contributed money for the families of the victims. In the meantime, prominent socialists and the miners of Carmaux quickly disavowed the attack, the latter affirming that the emancipation of the working class should be achieved through collective action, not dynamite.

When Émile returned to work shortly after noon on February 12, having accomplished the two errands, the other employees did not sense anything out of the ordinary. Dupuy was satisfied with Émile, as always. Indeed, he was considering raising the young man's salary. Before leaving earlier that morning, Émile had been working on a long and complicated report, to which he returned without the slightest hesitation. His letters penned that afternoon were nicely composed, even after news of the bomb had reached the office. Émile appeared sincerely moved, like everyone else, by what had occurred at the police station.

That evening Émile probably met five or six friends at the shop of Constant Martin, who gave him some money. The next day, November 9, Émile left work at about four in the afternoon, telling Madame Dupuy that he had fallen ill. He would be going to Brévannes for a day or two to get well. In a letter to Dupuy, he described his plans to recuperate and told his concierge on rue Véron the same thing. But instead, on the following day he took a train through Rouen to Dieppe and then boarded a boat to London via Newhaven, to avoid the more heavily policed Calais-Dover line. From London Émile wrote Dupuy, sending the letter to a *compagnon* and asking him to mail it from Orléans. He said that he had really left Paris because he "was worried about the consequences of the police investigations that were bound to follow the most recent anarchist events." He hoped that Monsieur Dupuy would not think badly of him because he was an anarchist. He recounted his arrest in late May, insisting that it had been totally unjustified. This had given him "the remarkable honor" of spending a night in a holding cell provided by the prefecture of police, a brief imprisonment that had cost him his job in the garment district just because he had "subversive ideas." He related these details to his boss in order to show that he had reason to dread the police, "who would strike immediately every known revolutionary, whether active or not." He did not want to spend weeks, or perhaps even months, in jail until the police discovered who was really responsible for the bomb that exploded in the police station. A couple of anarchists were languishing in jail six months after being taken into custody, though they had still been charged with no crime. Émile apologized for having left so precipitously, especially as he hoped Dupuy would agree that he had done excellent work. He portrayed himself as a "victim of events" and hoped that his employer would understand. In a flourish of bourgeois convention, he offered "his most profound esteem," sending Madame Dupuy his respects.

Even before Émile's bomb had gone off in Paris, rumors had surfaced concerning a planned attack against the Carmaux Mining Company. But the police had focused their attention on the mining town itself. They were caught off guard by the explosion in Paris. Émile's bomb surprised anarchists too. In London, Kropotkin, Malato, and Malatesta seemed genuinely astonished by the news of the terrorist attack. In Paris, Émile's friend Martin told a policeman that he did not know who had left the bomb but was happy to see the anarchists credited in the press. Jacques Prolo, a well-connected anarchist, told an undercover policeman that the attack had not been planned by any group. Some anarchists expressed concern that the event could hurt the chances of Francis, who was facing extradition from Britain so that he could be put on trial in Paris for blowing up the restaurant Le Véry. The police, however, faced certain challenges that made it difficult to arrest dangerous anarchists: the ease with which they could leave the country and the information provided in the newspapers, which alerted suspects that the police were on their trail.

The police had no idea who had placed the bomb in the offices of the Carmaux Mining Company and received conflicting reports from witnesses. The concierge had noticed no one ascending the stairs to the landing late that morning and remembered seeing only one young man between twenty-five and thirty years of age, with a blond mustache and a dark coat and hat. This visitor had asked to see a seamstress called Lucie, who lived in the building. But when questioned, this young man, a law student named Frapper, mentioned that he had encountered a woman on the staircase, and she was carrying a basket with a large object in it. Was she a patient of one of the doctors whose offices were located in the building? When the police checked into this possibility, they found that no woman had scheduled an appointment for that morning. If the woman was a domestic employed in the building, she would not use the main staircase, but rather the service entrance, which ruled out that line of inquiry. The woman Frapper described was small, with a black shawl over her head. The object, or objects, in the basket was covered with newspaper. When Frapper left the building, between 11 and 11:10, he saw such an object placed against the door. Two men had been seen standing outside the building fifteen or twenty minutes before the bomb was found, but no other man had been seen in the building at that time.

The prefecture of police compiled a list of 180 possible suspects, including Malatesta, who was in London, and the Henry brothers. The June 1 edition of Le Temps, in which the bomb had been wrapped, carried a short article about the arrest of Fortuné and

Émile Henry on May 30–31. Moreover, someone who knew Émile had written a letter to the prefect of police, denouncing him.

Fortuné had an alibi. He had been sitting in a courtroom in Bourges in central France on November 8 (this was his fifth court appearance within a few years). He was scratched from the list of suspects.

Police broke into Émile's room on rue Véron, with the help of a neighboring locksmith, but they found nothing to implicate the occupant in the crime. The renter had lived there only since October 8 and had paid in advance. Police found few furnishings and possessions: a shabby iron bed, a chair, and odds and ends of no value—nothing suspicious. The concierge informed the police that on the day after Émile's precipitous departure, she had received a letter from him, mailed in London and asking her to give an accompanying missive to Lambert, the law student who had slept in Émile's room a couple of times.

The police interviewed Émile's boss, Dupuy, on rue de Rocroy. He described the two errands that Émile had completed on the morning of November 8. Dupuy believed that he had taken forty-five minutes to get to his stop on boulevard de Courcelles, and then (believing he had begun with the latter errand) twenty-seven minutes to reach rue Tronchet, near the church of the Madeleine. He would have spent no more than ten minutes combined at the two addresses. Simply put, it seemed impossible that he could have somehow—between errands—gone back up to his room in Montmartre to pick up a bomb, returned to central Paris, and placed it in front of the door of the Carmaux Mining Company on avenue de l'Opéra. Moreover, upon his return to work, Émile had indeed seemed calm and maintained this demeanor when Dupuy returned with a newspaper describing the horrific explosion in the police station. He had left work at 6 P.M. as usual. Émile Henry was dropped from the list of suspects.

Also on the list was Rullière, the nineteen-year-old son of the mistress of Ravachol, a young man known as "the son of Rava-

chol." The container for the bomb resembled those used by Ravachol, arousing interest in Rullière's whereabouts. Among the other
suspects, seven could be designated only as X because their names
were unknown, although fairly complete descriptions were available for six of them, including a certain "bird merchant on the
avenue de l'Opéra, small, graying, 48 to 50 years of age," and his
female companion, "small, about 40 years old, brown hair, with
a black hat and scarf." A shoemaker, a porcelain decorator, and a
female embroiderer were hauled in; they had attended anarchist
meetings. Foreigners suspected of anarchism appeared on the list,
among them two Italians, a Belgian student, a couple of German
subjects, an Austrian, and a Swiss, as well as various provincial anarchists and a certain Puchel known as "Choucroutemann," presumably an Alsatian who liked to eat—especially *choucroute*, sau-
erkraut—and who had turned up in Paris nine days before the
explosion. Along with an Italian anarchist known as "Macaroni,"
Puchel disappeared immediately after the incident.

Stories came forth, possible explanations. A merchant had observed two young men about nineteen years of age strolling in
front of the building at number 11. They had paused to look at a
combination cane and pistol in the window of the store, so the
merchant continued to watch them until they left. Several passersby had been struck by "the attitude" of a rather slight young
man who walked out of the building.

The police followed up on every possible lead, even the highly
improbable ones. One story had Malato and the brothers Placide
and Remi Schouppe deciding to attack the Carmaux Mining
Company because they assumed that the police would think it the
work of miners (this made little sense, in that anarchists eagerly
accepted responsibility for their violent acts). Gustave Mathieu,
believed to have helped Ravachol construct bombs, would have
made the "engine," with the help of a certain Madame Mollet, who
carried the bomb. When police later interviewed the wife of Ortiz,
the anarchist-burglar, she claimed that her husband had carried

out the attack, and this story had begun to circulate among anarchists. The source was hardly credible—Madame Ortiz was dead drunk at the time.

The massive police search for the bomber reflected the new investigating techniques that emerged in the latter decades of the nineteenth century. Policing had become more scientific, emphasizing attention to tiny but significant clues. The fictional investigator Sherlock Holmes (who first arrived on the British scene in 1887) epitomized this new approach. The interviewing of suspects and witnesses had become more systematic. The press, with close ties to the prefecture of police, was able to follow major cases with often surprising accuracy, thanks to inside information and leaks, some of which were purchased. The success of memoirs published by prefects of police and of both newspaper serials and popular novels focused on crime revealed the intense public interest in this realm. Readers, already woozy from stories of the spectacular scandals involving leaders of the Third Republic, could turn their attention to events even more dramatic and threatening: the anarchist bombings.

Meanwhile, the anarchist press smirked about the "firecracker" that had exploded. In *Père Peinard,* Émile Pouget described 11, avenue de l'Opéra as one of the most elegant corners of a "neighborhood of aristos . . . fancy digs, goddammit! Marble everywhere, gilded things everywhere else, and damned soft rugs on every stairway—a lot softer than the straw mattresses of prol[etarian]s." *Père Peinard* could not help but note that the sergeants who arrived on the scene had refused to carry the package because "it was not done to have a policeman in uniform actually carrying a package." And as for the explosion, "Oh, hell, here was a blow that rocked the whole miserable joint off its hinges. The swine were no longer living!" The government had thought that subjecting Ravachol to the guillotine had put an end to bombings, but "now the really good stuff will begin." Apparently the dynamite missing from Soisy had been found: "It appears so . . . a thousand bombs!"

In the opinion of most people of means, anarchism amounted

to nothing less than a philosophy of murder and theft. They considered all anarchists to be cruel, hateful people who killed the elderly to steal from them, or robbed graves—as Ravachol did—while preparing "diabolical bombs intended to blow the bourgeoisie into another world." Moreover, the theft of dynamite earlier that year from Soisy-sous-Étiolles was common knowledge. It was out there somewhere. Some anarchists had told the *compagnons* that they were combatants in a modern war. They should prepare their dynamite; the moment was not far off when they would be called upon to use it. An anarchist newspaper helpfully provided the formula for mercury fulminate, a great quantity of which could be made for one and a half francs, to which could be added mercury, azotic acid, and alcohol baumé. If one wanted to blow up the theater of Odéon, the Opera, or a café, here was how to do it. The paper illustrated how to make a bomb, with mercury fulminate at the bottom, as if it was as simple and normal a task as making a Provençal beef stew. And if the dynamiter wanted to blow up your house? "Nothing easier!" He could hide a small bomb in his pocket, find a pretext to walk in, and leave behind "this trinket which appears so harmless . . . a quarter of an hour later, you blow up."

The bomb in the police station carried Paris's panic to a new level. Big business and the grand cafés worried about its economic impact, especially with the Christmas holidays little more than a month away. Some wealthy people were afraid to go to theaters, restaurants, shops, or the Bois de Boulogne, where they believed they saw an anarchist behind every tree. According to rumors, bombs were about to explode in churches, poison had been prepared for reservoirs, and the Black Death or cholera was about to descend. (The most recent epidemic of the latter had passed through only eight years earlier.) Police complained that current law limited their ability to repress the anarchists. They feared the possible reconstitution of militant groups such as the Avengers of Ravachol.

In various locations in and around Paris, pranksters planted discarded sardine cans, which were taken to be small explosive devices. From March to November 1892 about three hundred "bombs" were found and transported—very carefully—to the municipal laboratory for analysis. There, a special device had been built in the basement to absorb the shock of an explosion. The "bombs," such as the six that arrived on the morning of November 15, were detonated here. Half of them, like the can found at Les Halles that was filled with mere gravel, were the work of mischief makers. Three turned out to be "infernal machines," though minor ones. But the threat continued. Just after Christmas, a small bomb exploded in the barracks of the prefecture of police.

In mid-December Rose Caubet Henry cleaned out her son's room on rue Véron. She told the concierge that she would return later in the week with a mover from Brévannes. A wagon carried away Émile's few possessions, under the watchful eyes of policemen, who followed it until it passed beyond the fortifications.

Earlier that month, Émile had written a letter from London to the *compagnon* in Orléans to whom he had earlier sent the letter for Dupuy. He apologized for his long silence, caused by many "hassles." Now he was on the eve of a trip, probably a very long one. Émile promised that when they next met, he would relate his "peregrinations" from city to city. His friend certainly had learned from newspapers the details of "the pretty little dance" that had killed five policemen in Paris. Émile had learned from a journalist the day after the explosion that his brother was in prison in Bourges and that the police were looking for Émile himself. Why? He had no idea but was sure that the cops would come to visit him soon. His employer must have told the police where he had been living because no other person knew of his address in Paris (he added, "A serious anarchist knows how to stay hidden in order to be ready to act quickly when the moment comes"). Therefore Émile had left without fanfare and headed for London.

Émile told his friend that he had a little money and would leave London in four or five days. The place bored him. He would go to

Liverpool and await the next boat for New York. After about six months in America, he would return to France. He swore that he would make the bourgeois pay for all of their persecutions and that "until the day that I fall in this battle, I will bite as long as I still have teeth." To his dear friend he said goodbye, and perhaps adieu. He hoped to write from Liverpool, and Émile assured him that no matter where he was, he would have in his heart only love for anarchism and ferocious hatred for "our enemies."

But Émile remained in London. It may have been dull, but it was safe. Police repression in continental European states had turned London into something of a refuge for anarchists. The chief police inspector, the Irishman William Melville, estimated that about a thousand foreign anarchists resided in the city. They had come in waves: the French after the Commune, the Germans in the wake of Bismarck's crackdown on the socialists in 1878, the Italians after the first attempt to kill King Umberto I in 1878, and the Russians after the assassination of Alexander II in 1881. The number had increased after Switzerland became less hospitable in the 1880s, alarmed by the anarchists' incendiary publications and revolutionary activism and pressured by the French government. About four hundred French anarchist exiles lived in London during the early 1890s. Their movements were frequent and unpredictable; therefore the chief inspector's count was simply an estimate (and did not include, in principle, various criminals on the lam, hangers-on, and other refugees passing through).

Italian anarchists, of whom there were several hundred among the five thousand Italians living in London, led the way in activism. Many lived in Soho (a prime location for the down-and-out), Holborn, Whitechapel, or Clerkenwell (northeast of Bloomsbury), or around Fitzroy Square. Extremely poor, they were squeezed together in miserable housing. Many Italian anarchists worked, when they could, in the trades they had learned in Italy, particularly as shoemakers, tailors, or waiters; some taught Italian. One

Italian priest noted that he feared the Italian secret societies and that, of the three thousand Italians living in his parish, only about twelve hundred went to church.

More interested in the philosophy of anarchism, the German anarchists seemed less dangerous because few were tempted by "propaganda by the deed." They were followed in number by the Russians, the Italians, the French, the Belgians, the Dutch, and the Spanish. Although drawn from a variety of countries, the anarchists tended to stay in the same neighborhoods, seeking the solidarity of like-minded souls, something to eat, and perhaps even the possibility of a job.

Great Britain had suffered terrorist attacks from the Fenians, the Irish nationalist organization, but there were few British anarchists, despite the publication of the anarchist newspaper *Commonweal* (which began in 1885) and Kropotkin's *Freedom* (which debuted the following year). They included David Nicoll, who wrote "The Anarchists are 'criminals,' 'vermin,' 'gallows carriers.' Well, shower hard names upon us! Hunt us down like mad dogs! Strangle us like you have done our comrades [in Spain]. Shoot us down as you did the strikers at Fourmies, and then be surprised if your houses are shattered with dynamite." After eighteen months in prison, he continued to write and publish on behalf of anarchism. After one bombing in which innocent people were killed, he wrote that he could not "feel the least pity for those who, living in luxury and splendor, never give a thought to those on whose labors their blissful existence is built."

Immigration played a large role in this "first wave" of modern terrorism, as political refugees moved from one country to another during the closing decades of the nineteenth century—particularly to those places willing to provide sanctuary, notably Great Britain, Switzerland, and the free city of Tangier in North Africa, as well as Egypt. Immigrants provided recruits to the anarchist cause. Italian anarchism was carried to Argentina by immigrants and temporary migrants, including the "swallows"—seasonal workers who returned home each year to Italy. One song sung by Italian anarchists included the line "The entire world is my country." In Europe, only Russia required a passport for entry.

Indeed, the rapid improvement in transportation (of news and goods and people) was largely responsible for the internationalization of anarchism. Shipping lines stretched across oceans, making Barcelona, Marseille, and Buenos Aires important anarchist hubs. Anarchists also found havens in the United States, Argentina, Mexico, Cuba, Brazil, Persia, the Ottoman territories in the Balkans, China, Japan, India, the Philippines, Egypt, and Ethiopia. Russian anarchists operated in France, Belgium, Austria, Japan, and Hong Kong, as well as in Great Britain. Their French counterparts could be found in Spain, Argentina, and even Ethiopia; German anarchists showed up in Britain, the United States, and Australia. The burgeoning popular press of the 1880s carried word of attacks and the ensuing police repression across the world, drawing ever greater numbers to the cause.

In Great Britain, terrorism and the presence—permanent or temporary—of foreign nationals became linked in the popular imagination. During the 1870s, political refugee clubs in London grew in number, and by the time of the Congress of Socialist Revolutionaries and Anarchists in London in 1881, a secret "black international" (the color was derived from the anarchist flag) was rumored to be planning attacks throughout Europe. During the 1880s, immigration to London increased, particularly as Jews fled persecution in the Russian Empire. There were anarchists among them. The steady stream of immigrants generated xenophobia even in this World City, accentuated by a fear that the newly arrived might convert British workers to socialism or anarchism.

The Russian, French, Italian, Belgian, and Spanish governments, among others, viewed the anarchists in London with consternation and alarm, believing that London had become the center of a worldwide anarchist conspiracy. They resented how Britain tolerated the presence of dissidents and gave asylum to political refugees unless they stood accused of a specific crime. After the assassination of Tsar Alexander II in 1881, French and Russian officials pressured the British police to adopt a more aggressive attitude and urged politicians to pass more restrictive laws, but the British government rejected these overtures, viewing them as an attempt to meddle in Britain's domestic affairs. Continental governments complained that British authorities refused to cooperate in the surveillance of anarchists. When in 1891 the Italian ambassador triumphantly showed Lord Salisbury, the British prime minister, an admission ticket for a dance sponsored by the anarchist Autonomy Club to raise money for anarchist propaganda in Italy, the Italian hoped that the Briton would at last grasp the gravity of the threat. But Salisbury dismissed the man, telling him that dancing seemed an unlikely way to start a revolution.

But anarchists in London were in fact being watched. The Special Branch of Scotland Yard, created in 1883 to prevent Fenian bombings, had by the late 1880s turned its attention to foreign anarchists in that city. As it would after World War I, the Special Branch coordinated the policing of anti-colonialists in Britain, the lands that constituted its empire, and other countries. Agents referred to themselves as "Anarchist-hunter[s]" and infiltrated anarchist groups. The officers of Scotland Yard knew well that they had to watch the most prominent anarchists in London themselves and not merely rely on information provided by agents, many of whom were themselves foreigners trying to make ends meet. Knowing that they were the targets of surveillance strengthened the solidarity and determination of refugee anarchists living in London, though the city still remained generally more hospitable than any other in Europe.

As anarchism globalized, so did international cooperation to police its adherents. France, Italy, Spain, Portugal, and Belgium were the first to establish formal agreements to combat terrorism together. As part of this effort, police agents from France, Italy,

Russia, and other countries were dispatched to Britain, where they infiltrated anarchist groups. The Russian police, the Okhrana, opened an office in Paris, with the consent of the French government, in order to monitor the activities and publications of Russian political exiles. Embassies and consulates directly organized such efforts, funneling monthly stipends to spies and informers, some quite well educated, others not at all. Recruits were not in short supply.

Soho, Tottenham Court Road, Fitzroy Square, and other neighborhoods in which anarchist exiles converged were crawling with police and secret agents in the pay of the anarchists' home countries, sometimes to the point of absurdity, as depicted in G. K. Chesterton's *The Man Who Was Thursday.* In this story Gabriel Syme, a detective with poetic pretensions, infiltrates a secret group of anarchists living in London, the European Dynamiters. Each of the seven leaders of the group is known by a day of the week. All turn out to be police spies, although at the beginning none know the real identity of any of the others.

In the London anarchist refugee communities of the early 1890s, suspicion of police spies became a veritable obsession. As in Joseph Conrad's *The Secret Agent,* a novel about the underbelly of anarchism in the back streets of London, it became difficult to tell real anarchists from undercover agents, informers, or even provocateurs. In the novel, Conrad's agent Verloc, whose shop attracts a variety of anarchists, is in the employ of a foreign embassy—obviously Russian. He is summoned to that embassy and told to organize, in the space of a month, a bomb attack that would be blamed on anarchists. So Verloc decides to blow up Greenwich, the point of Greenwich Mean Time: "Go for the first meridian. You don't know the middle classes as well as I do. Their sensibilities are jaded. The first meridian. Nothing better, and nothing easier, I should think." Such an outrageous attack would force the British police to put the squeeze on Russian anarchists in the capital.

Anarchists living in London developed their own counter-strategies. Malatesta eventually created a code, replacing letters with symbols, to communicate safely with colleagues. Because virtually every anarchist exile barely could scrape by, many looked suspiciously upon comrades who seemed to live well, despite having no obvious source of income. When an Italian infiltrater was discovered in 1889, Malatesta used the Italian newspaper in London to warn other anarchists. The Italian anarchist Rubino at one point tried to convince colleagues that he was not a police informer by asserting that he had tried to assassinate King Leopold of Belgium with a pistol bought using funds provided him by an undercover policeman serving as an agent provocateur.

While London police were not allowed to cooperate directly with foreign police, occasionally Scotland Yard or even the London metropolitan police worked informally with embassy-based authorities, who operated a wide network of police informers. However, police in London, as in Paris, Barcelona, Milan, Brussels, and other major European centers of anarchism, sometimes had to depend on reports that were misleading, exaggerated, or simply invented by paid informers—whose most intriguing stories often surfaced when they were pushing for pay raises. Yet the spies collected useful information as well, particularly concerning anarchist publications that were to be smuggled abroad.

In the end, British police did succeed somewhat in monitoring the activities of foreign anarchists living in London. Nicoll, the British anarchist, called Inspector Melville, the chief police inspector, "a really remarkable and astute man." He admitted that Melville was "on terms of perfect intimacy with the police agents of foreign governments . . . he and his gang [had] dogged the steps of the foreign refugees for years." In January 1892, six anarchists were arrested in London and Walsall, a town in the West Midlands near Birmingham, after a small bomb factory was discovered, its products perhaps intended for use in Russia. One of the men was a French Breton, picked up outside the Autonomy Club on Windmill Street in London and found to be carrying a paper bag containing chloroform; another of the apprehended was an Italian shoemaker. Although four of those arrested were convicted and sentenced to long prison terms, two men were acquitted when it became clear that a French agent provocateur named Auguste Coulon had encouraged the operation and then denounced it. The Italian shoemaker also belonged to the Autonomy Club. Another was in possession of a tract called "An Anarchist Feast at the Opera," in which several anarchists bring a bomb to the opera and then leave after the first act, enjoying the anguished screams of their victims. Émile, who was in London during this period, almost certainly read this pamphlet, which was reprinted in 1892.

Many French anarchists, like Louise Michel, lived in Soho (dubbed "La Petite France") or to the north around Fitzroy Square. During this time, Fitzroy Square was far from the exclusive address that it would become (though at the time, George Bernard Shaw lived at number 29, an address subsequently occupied by Virginia Woolf). Still, it was somewhat less shabby than the more proletarian Soho neighborhoods nearby. Small firms of cabinet-makers and upholsterers were located in and around its stucco façades. The London Skin Hospital stood on one corner of the square. People of means had abandoned Fitzroy Square for more chic addresses, leaving behind properties that were divided and then subdivided. Rents were relatively low and the neighborhood attracted political and artistic outsiders. Fitzroy Square and its surroundings thus earned a reputation as a small oasis of left-wing politics and bohemian lifestyles.

Louise Michel, the anarchist known as "the Red Virgin" who had been a leader in the Paris Commune, fell in love with London, "where my banished friends are always welcome." Kropotkin wanted to organize a lecture for her, but she did not speak English. After arriving in the British capital in 1890, she started an anarchist school on Fitzroy Square for the children of political refugees (it lasted until 1892, when police discovered explosives in the building, stored there by a *compagnon*). Michel always wore black in honor of the Communards who had been slaughtered in 1871.

A Parisian journalist described the French anarchists in London as "a collection of poor devils more needy than ferocious." *Compagnons* helped each other, and like immigrants in any city, relied on their fellows as they learned to navigate a foreign place. Zo d'Axa described his time living near Fitzroy Square in London as simply "vegetating," completely cut off from Londoners. For him "isolation compounded the dense sadness of the fog." The lucky ones found work in their trades—tailoring, cabinetmaking, shoemaking. When he was in London, Émile's friend Constant Martin worked for a tailor. Several French anarchists sold flowers to survive, and it was rumored that several were working for a company that manufactured torpedoes for the Royal Navy. A few were burglars. At least two French anarchists worked at swindling people in the wine trade.

The small grocery shop Le Bel Épicier, operated by Victor Richard, a fifty-year-old philanthropic political militant and refugee from the Commune, became a port of entry and gathering place for French anarchist refugees. Richard was something of a local celebrity and well known to the police. He proudly sold only "red" beans, not the "reactionary" white ones, on Charlotte Street, near Fitzroy Square. Some French anarchists and store patrons lived on that street, which parallels Tottenham Court Road and is now so elegant. (Richard almost certainly was the inspiration for Conrad's character Verloc—Conrad also lived near Tottenham Court Road.) On at least one occasion Richard provided funds so that an anarchist sought by the police could get out of England. Nearby, the anarchist bookstore on Goodge Street provided a gathering place for *compagnons* lacking the money to frequent the pubs.

Most of the exiles knew only a smattering of English. Malato, who learned English fairly well, recounted the challenges of heading off into different parts of London armed only with two English words, *street* and *fish*. A raid on Richard's grocery store in 1894 turned up a list of phrases intended, for better or for worse, to help French anarchists get along in London. Along with ferry timetables to and from England and France, Malato's *The Pleasantries of Exile* included the following crib sheet.

French	Written English	Spoken English (how to pronounce)
Ma jolie fille?	My pretty girl?	Maille prêté guile?
Donnez-moi un shilling.	Give me a bob.	G'hive mi é bob.
Je vous tirerai le nez.	I will pull your nose.	Aille ouil poule your nose.
Je vous mettrai mon pied dans le derrière.	I will put my foot on your bottom.	Aill ouille poute maille foute one your botome.
Fermez ça!	Shut up!	Chotte ap!
Je vous ferai des bleus sur le corps.	I'll make rings about your body.	Aill'le mêke rin'gse abaoute your bode.
Ma femme me bat.	My wife strikes me.	Maille waill'fe straïkse mi.

London played an extremely important role in the dissemination of anarchist propaganda and thus anarchism's global reach. Pamphlets, brochures, and newspapers produced there allowed anarchists to communicate across national borders and even oceans, relate inspiring news of anarchist deeds in other countries, and carry on a debate about tactics. Anarchist manifestos arrived in France from London, including "Response to the Gunners," which celebrated the martyrdom of the anarchists in Chicago and saluted the destruction of the restaurant Le Véry. Anarchist papers published in Britain often reprinted articles from similar publications in Italy, Spain, and France, particularly *Père Peinard*. The anarchist press, publishing in London, Paris, Ancona, and other cities, spread the subculture of anarchism through songs about "deeds" and executions of *compagnons*. The French anarchist community in London marshaled enough resources to finance the publication of anarchist newspapers there, including *Le Tocsin (The Alarm Bell)*, edited by Charles Malato, and *La Tribune Libre*. *L'International*, another French-language newspaper, published only eight issues in 1890 but managed to include an excerpt from a brochure titled "The Anarchist Guide: The Manual of the Perfect Dynamiter."

Following the highly publicized bomb on rue des Bons-Enfants, many contradictory and often absurd rumors circulated in the anarchist community in London. According to one account, the person responsible for the attack had already reached America, but the police did not take this seriously. Another anarchist asserted that the author of the attack was now in "a little country" where he would never be found. A certain Wagemans, who had turned down an offer to become a police informant, said confidentially that the person was hiding in a convent run by one of his uncles in a large city in provincial England, perhaps Manchester. This also seemed highly unlikely.

When Émile arrived in London in November 1892, he took a furnished room right off Tottenham Court Road. He spoke some English, although not with ease. He quickly developed a reputation for being a hard-core anarchist, "real, convinced." He spent his time getting to know anarchists in Whitechapel, where many Jewish migrants from eastern Europe had settled. He also was known in pubs around Tottenham Court Road and in Soho. Soon after his arrival, Émile went with Louis Matha, with whom he probably stayed, to the Autonomy Club. A portrait of Ravachol adorned one of its rooms.

The Autonomy Club, founded in 1886 by a German anarchist who had been expelled from a different group, was first located on Charlotte Street off Fitzroy Square. Its facilities included one long and narrow room, a kitchen, and several rooms on the second floor. The club soon moved to a more spacious house on Windmill Street near Tottenham Court Road, operated by an anarchist who lived there with his family. It offered a restaurant, and for a small sum one could have a meal of soup, meat, and vegetables, as well as plenty of conversation. The club, which published the German anarchist newspaper *Die Autonomie*, featured a large room in which *compagnons* presented plays. Ticket sales helped subsidize the families of anarchists in jail or on the run as well as destitute, sickly, or otherwise overburdened supporters of the cause. Proceeds from the bar went to help anarchists unable to find work.

On at least one occasion, Melville, the inspector from Scotland Yard, managed to get into the club.

The Autonomy Club was the unofficial headquarters of the informal network of foreign anarchists in London, what has been called a "shadow circle." In particular, it became the center for French anarchist exiles. The club had enough rooms that *compagnons* could meet by nationality (although Italian, German, and Scandinavian clubs existed elsewhere in that part of the city). This division certainly seems surprising, given the emphasis placed on internationalism in anarchist writings. But as a French policeman who had become an expert on anarchist doings in London noted, it was one thing to theorize about transcending national boundaries and quite another to turn away from those who shared one's own heritage, language, and culture. By the end of 1885, the International French Language Group formed part of the original Autonomy Club, and two years later the Anti-Patriotic Group began to meet there on Mondays. Yet, to be sure, contacts and friendships developed between anarchists from different countries, despite the language barriers. (French worked best as a common language for most of the multinational community of exiles.) For example, Martial Bourdin, a French anarchist and a member of the Autonomy Club who, like his brother Auguste, worked as a ladies' tailor when he could find work, had many anarchist friends who were Italian.

The anarchist clubs did the best they could to welcome the newly arrived to teeming, foggy, cold London and introduce them to its strange food, much of which they could hardly afford. (Malato prided himself on producing wine—a touch of home tradition, though he had to use bananas to make it.) They provided a place to talk politics, discuss events back home, and play chess and cards. The Autonomy Club in particular hosted anarchists expelled from the Continent, including a German advocate of the "right of theft," who had most recently been kicked out of Paris, and Bob Hippolyte, a "man of color"; the London police followed both of them to Windmill Street. On occasion, the rooms of the Autonomy Club were transformed into dormitories. It was difficult to find provisions to feed everybody, and the coffers were more often empty than full.

On one occasion, about thirty Spanish anarchists arrived in London from Buenos Aires without a cent among them. The police shadowed their entire journey from the moment they landed in Liverpool. They marched together from Euston Station to a political club near Tottenham Court Road, where they were provided food and drink and a temporary place to stay. They then were sent off to lodgings in groups of four or five. Within a few months, all but a few had returned to Spain. Not knowing any English, they had found staying in London extraordinarily difficult. Moreover, to the police and to other Londoners who saw them, they seemed "an unwashed, sinister, forbidding crew, and their presence caused a distinct flutter among the other Anarchists, although there were no revolutionary outbreaks."

As important as the clubs were for fostering social cohesion among anarchists in exile, they fueled the myth of a centralized international Dynamite Club, based in London. In Paris, the prefect of the Seine in 1893 described a central anarchist committee that included Kropotkin, Malato, and Matha, who gave orders to the faithful. Kropotkin, to be sure, was of sufficient reputation (he was a friend to William Butler Yeats and Oscar Wilde, among other literary personalities, and also knew George Bernard Shaw) to seem capable of organizing such a motley group. Indeed, he provided the entry on anarchism for the 1910 *Encylopaedia Britannica*. The British press presented anarchist clubs as Conspiracy Central, the very architecture of their meeting places conducive to dastardly plots: complicated entrances that allowed all visitors to be observed without their knowing it, back doors facilitating easy, discreet escape, should the police arrive—as they did, at the Autonomy Club, in 1892 and again two years later. Londoners' obsessive belief in an anarchist plot was an extension of the paranoia that swept Paris in the early 1890s. Malato described how the mainstream press portrayed the modest Autonomy Club as a center of conspiracy for social revolution. According to Malato, journalists "out of ideas and paid by the line were delighted to be able to speculate on bourgeois terror, plots being hatched and ready to go to strike the continent . . . preparing dynamite, potassium chlorate, nitrobenzene, rack-a-rock, and green powder." At a time of rapid technological progress, the public was fascinated by the developing wonders of science but at the same time uneasy about the dangers that might lurk in them. *The Morning Post* in 1892 — the year of Ravachol's bombs — claimed that four hundred French "desparatos [sic], thieves, counterfeiters, and murderers" had swooped down on England. Their goal? To kill all of the wealthy, not only in London but throughout Great Britain, by suffocating them with chloroform. A London magazine described the arrival in 1892 of a well-heeled French anarchist who had come to speak in an anarchist club. Purportedly, he stated that anarchists lived near virtually all major government buildings in Europe and planned to use dreadful new killing machines, invented by one of their own and rigged to explode in such a way that the culprits would have time to escape. The press exaggerated the number of women present in the anarchist clubs, implying that many were prostitutes responsible for the rampant syphilis that supposedly afflicted anarchist men.

The French journalist Henri Rochefort — an arrogant, provocative anti-Semite resplendent in his role as the "prince of the gutter press" — was also living in London. (Rochefort created a parody of what might be stated in an "anarchist constitution." Article 1: There is no longer anything. Article 2: No one is charged with enforcing the previous article.) He had been forced into exile because of the part he played in the Boulanger affair of 1889, when the dashing general Georges Boulanger seemed on the verge of overthrowing the republic and establishing a military dictatorship. Rochefort had served as a correspondent for *L'Intransigeant*, the Boulangist newspaper. Although sometimes unreliable, he offered a perceptive assessment of the London-based anarchists — for whom he had some respect and occasionally even affinity. He understood that Parisians, among other Europeans, believed that London was the center of a worldwide anarchist movement. But Rochefort said, "This is a complete error. The anarchists in London never constituted themselves into secret societies. They retained their complete independence, and only met in very small groups, while all sorts of characters were collected under their banner."

Soon after he arrived in the British capital in November 1892, Émile came to be known as the hero of the explosion at the police station on rue des Bons-Enfants. He seemed to have made it clear that he intended to blow up various public places in Paris. The "associationalists" ("*fraternistes*") considered him "insane," as did some anarchists who revered Ravachol. Émile's presence in London accentuated the hostility between those who rejected "propaganda by the deed" and those who wanted to lash out by using bombs. Thus, the passionate debate unleashed by Ravachol's violent deeds and execution continued around Tottenham Court Road and Fitzroy Square, in French, German, Dutch, Flemish, Spanish, Russian, and Italian. A London detective remembered Émile very well, especially his audacity and arrogance. Those who knew him sensed that he would meet his end at the guillotine. While this surmise might have stopped anyone else, Émile, in the detective's opinion, was not even conscious of his acts. He was as unsettled and volatile as a Parisian street urchin. At other moments, he was shy and insolent, an overgrown boy.

Émile became a darling at the Autonomy Club, which was favored by the "individualists," whose cause Émile had defended in his letter attacking Malatesta in *L'Endehors*. A French group, Free Initiative, met there, and they accused the anarchist grocer Richard and his friends of being soft "associationalists." Members of Free Initiative produced pamphlets in French, fiercely attacking their fellow anarchists who disagreed on the use of violence. Following Ravachol's execution, meetings at the club became so stormy that Charles Malato said, with some irony, that it was not unlike being in the Chamber of Deputies.

To the police, however, most members of this club appeared to fit into one general group, "foreigners of the lowest class" among whom resided anarchists willing to use bombs to further their cause. The police had developed a profile of the typical bomber. He was "a solitary and fanatic individual who has thought about and noted the fault of contemporary society until the moment that his mind becomes demented." He would invariably tell only one or two friends of his plans to launch an explosion. He then would execute his scheme "with unmatched composure and audacity." Even if he knew with certainty that the ultimate sacrifice lay ahead, he would never back down—"he walks to his death with courage and no regrets."

In November 1892, around the time Émile had arrived in London, the French police in that very city were watching the girlfriend of a certain Pomati, who received mail from Fortuné and Émile as well as from Constant Martin in Paris. Now she saw Émile and Martin together in London. The Henry brothers had moved considerably higher on the police's list of suspected potential bombers; they were considered "audacious and determined, and at the point of preparing to strike." These officers also knew that Émile was adept at chemistry, could assemble explosives, and was "cooler and more experienced than his brother."

Almost inevitably, a few *compagnons* in London suspected Émile of being a police informant. Martin noted as much to an anarchist who had recently arrived to interview Louise Michel at Richard's grocery store. The *compagnon* knew Émile and asked Richard to give him his greetings because he had worked with him, and the two were "even somewhat intimate." Richard replied that he did not know Émile Henry, which seemed unlikely.

In fact, Richard, for one, desperately wanted to know whose bomb had blown up the police station on rue des Bons-Enfants. An anarchist brought Émile to the back of the grocery, a place that

Émile had avoided because the police closely watched who came and went. Richard was so pleased with Émile's deed that he gave him three hundred francs "to demonstrate his satisfaction and eagerness that he would continue his work." According to the story, Émile was indignant that the sum was so small.

In the meantime, the French police were getting closer to Émile. An anarchist informer offered to provide information about him in exchange for cash. This man was almost certainly the "friend" who had mailed the letter to Dupuy from Orléans. Now he wanted five hundred francs in exchange for Émile's letter. The police wanted to know if Émile "was involved in the affair" at rue des Bons-Enfants. The informant's answer was an emphatic yes. He had found out on the Saturday before the bombing that it would occur.

The "betrayer" also revealed that Émile tended to lay low and generally avoided the most prominent anarchists in London. Martin had tried to hide the details of Émile's flight from Richard, whose store was constantly under police surveillance. And clearly, Émile was not in England simply to dodge the draft; if so, he would be content to stay in London, rather than move on to America, which he had mentioned to his "friend." The informer reminded the police of the enormous risk he was taking, because if certain *compagnons* learned of his betrayal, he would not be long for this world. To prove that he was well informed, he provided the number of the street where the French anarchist Gustave Mathieu was hiding under the name of Dumont (he could not remember the exact name of the street, only that it was near Oxford Street).

Rochefort had his own view of Émile's involvement in the bombing:

Well! Although he was the son of a former member of the Commune, he was so little in touch with the anarchist party that nobody believed his story, and it was greeted either as a young man's boasting, or else as an imaginative romance invented to get money out of those who might be stupid enough to credit it. I recollect

Malato saying to me one day—"There is a fellow going all over London saying that he is the author of the Rue des Bons-Enfants explosion; he is evidently taking people in."

As the French police investigated Émile, the anarchists turned their attention to Spain, where their movement had grown during the 1870s, particularly in Barcelona (which became known as "the city of bombs") and in Andalusia. Some 4,000 vineyard workers had entered the town of Jerez to free 157 anarchists arrested the previous year. The Spanish Civil Guard responded as if this action constituted a full-fledged insurrection. The guards arrested, beat, and tortured many anarchists, whom they accused of belonging to a secret society known as the Black Hand. Four men who had confessed under torture to planning the insurrection were garroted in Jerez on February 10, 1892. These executions angered and preoccupied Émile.

In retaliation, an anarchist named Paulino Pallás, who had earlier traveled with Malatesta, tossed two bombs at a Spanish general, killing a soldier and five civilians, but not the officer. Pallás too was executed. Vengeance was not long in coming. On November 7, 1893, an anarchist dropped two bombs, made of mercury fulminate, from a balcony onto the main floor of Barcelona's elegant Liceo Theater during a performance of *William Tell,* killing twenty-two people and wounding about fifty others. Police rounded up hundreds of well-known anarchists, charging them with conspiracy, and then executed four of them. The Spanish police arrested the bomber himself, Santiago Salvador, two months later. Claiming conversion to the church—a last-ditch effort to save his life—he was executed in 1894.

Similar attacks had occurred in the United States as well. There Alexander Berkman, who had immigrated five years earlier, tried to assassinate Henry C. Frick, who managed the Carnegie Steel Company, the object of a violent strike in Homestead, Pennsylvania, in 1892. In January of that year, anarchists planned, but could not carry out, simultaneous bombings in London, Paris, and Berlin.

Malato, who had been in London since his 1890 conviction in France, observed that Émile changed dramatically at this time: "The bombs of Barcelona hypnotized him: the only thing he thought of was to strike a blow and die. 'Today is the anniversary of the dancing-lesson,'" he said, alluding to the explosion of the rue des Bons-Enfants. He was proud of having killed five enemies. Malato added, "He grew in his own eyes; he said to himself that his role of avenging angel had only just begun."

On December 21, 1892, two men turned up at an auberge in the Norman village of Fiquefleur-Équainville, along the estuary of the Seine, about five miles from Honfleur. One introduced himself as an English businessman, eager to start up a factory. Both asked about local properties and industries. About a week later, another man joined them, and the three expressed interest in a property owned by a wealthy elderly lady named Postel. They turned up at Mass on January 1, one of the rare occasions in which the woman left her house, where she lived with a domestic servant. Then, on the night of January 7, the same three men, carrying stiletto knives, broke into the lady's house. Wearing long black coats and masks, they subdued the woman by placing a chemical-infused handkerchief over her nose; then they tied her up, along with her servant. Before leaving, they forced the woman to give them keys to a safe and took more than 1,000 francs, some jewelry, and receipts acknowledging the deposit in a local bank of items worth about 800,000 francs. (The slip of paper was, of course, worth nothing.) On January 16, the woman received a threatening letter, telling her to send 30,000 francs to Victor Richard's grocery store on Charlotte Street in London; some of the deposit receipts were tucked into the envelope. A second letter, written five days later, reflected some panic on the part of the thieves, as it suggested that a lesser sum would do.

Later, several people claimed to have seen Émile in Fiquefleur, posing as the English businessman. The second man may have been Léon Ortiz, and the third Gustave Mathieu but more likely Placide Schouppe (the two men looked quite similar). Schouppe was involved in another theft in the town of Abbeville and had been arrested in Brussels at the end of May. Émile may have written the extortion letter; his friend the Egyptian-born anarchist Alexandre Marocco, a London dealer in stolen goods, probably was involved, though not in the heist itself. Matha, who was in London at the time, at least knew about it. The list of suspects was long.

A few months later, in February 1893, Émile seemed to be back in Paris. Police heard that he had met with the anarchist typographer Achille Étiévant in a bar in Clichy. They believed the two were plotting a new dynamite deed, perhaps with explosives that had been hidden nearby when *compagnon* Francis went on trial at the Assize Court in April 1893 for blowing up Le Véry.

The word then went out that Étiévant and another anarchist planned to bomb "The Aquarium," the Chamber of Deputies in the Palais-Bourbon. Reportedly in contact with various groups of anarchist revolutionaries, Émile had told someone that he would be in Paris until May 1 and then return to England. The police knew that his mother lived in Brévannes on avenue de la Planchette and believed that Émile went there from time to time to visit her. But no word of Émile's whereabouts surfaced in any of the anarchist groups the police had infiltrated. He was almost certainly on occasion staying with several of his classmates from the J.-B. Say school.

In March 1893, the police thought Émile to be back in London. They were wrong. Two months later, Gustave Babet, an anarchist shoemaker living in central Paris, a regular propagandist, and an intimate friend of Ravachol, told an undercover policeman that the "affair" of rue des Bons-Enfants had been the work of Émile. Moreover, he claimed to have been aware that the attack was in the works and that a woman he did not know had placed the bomb. Émile was on a list of those who seemed ready to "carry out criminal projects" in April.

Early that month, Émile called on his wealthy conservative aunt, the marquise de Chamborant, in Passy. He seemed at ease, clean shaven and well dressed in a frock coat, vest, black pants, and a nice white shirt with a stand-up collar. He asked for five hundred francs, which he said he would use to start a small business. A man named Duthion, then employed by the marquise, later noted that he appeared unhappy when he left the house empty-handed.

Émile then traveled to Brussels and remained there until May 1. At this time, Belgian workers were staging massive demonstrations to demand the right to vote. When, on April 11, the parliament rejected a bill for general manhood suffrage, the Belgian Workers' Party declared a general strike. The movement spread rapidly. Small bands of men, including anarchists, broke windows in central Brussels, outraging merchants and the public at large. A state of siege was declared, and gendarmes charged at the workers, with swords drawn. Troops killed demonstrators in two Belgian towns. Would the revolution begin in Belgium? On April 18, the Belgian parliament offered a compromise, a cumbersome system of plural suffrage, awarding extra votes to fathers of families, various "qualified" voters, and those men who owned property. Many workers remained dissatisfied.

Living under the name of Martin or Meurin, in a hotel on a main street in the suburb of Saint-Gilles, Émile would later claim that he had taken an active part in the fighting in Brussels, firing a pistol in fact, and was amazed that he was not arrested. Although universal manhood suffrage was not an anarchist cause, Émile supported any action, such as the riots in Belgium, that could ultimately contribute to the revolution. His probable presence there underlines the international character of anarchism. He sent *Père Peinard* an article from a Brussels newspaper denouncing the "treason" of the Belgian socialists for having caved in. In late April, he returned to the hotel to find that a French policeman had been asking about him. He immediately left for Paris, arriving in time to watch the demonstrations on May 1.

From May 20 to July 12, 1893, Émile lived in a tiny room on boulevard Morland, between the Bastille and the Seine, taking the name Louis Dubois. He was apparently learning the locksmith's trade in the Marais, but he earned nothing. When Félix Fénéon brought Émile home to introduce him to his mother, the latter was carrying a tool kit. Fénéon's mother exclaimed, "Ah! You didn't tell me that he was an artisan." Émile was carrying a fine new cane that he had almost certainly stolen from a man of means. Madame Fénéon understood that he was hard up, but nonetheless expressed alarm at the theft. In any case, the fact that Émile desired something as bourgeois as a cane reflects a certain conflicted identity, even as he lived among down-and-out anarchists.

In Paris, Émile slept on occasion in Constant Martin's dairy shop a few steps from the Bourse. There Martin seemed to be the instigator and chief organizer of thefts, as well as the receiver of stolen goods, particularly jewels and precious stones that could be easily unloaded. Yet Émile expressed pride that he was not a thief—if the lifting of a nice cane from a wealthy man could be conveniently forgotten.

A friend of the family, Charles Brajus, a Breton beret maker, with whom Émile, his mother, and younger brother had stayed on occasion, saw Émile in Paris in early July 1893. That month, during student demonstrations in the Latin Quarter, a police inspector recognized him. Émile later expressed contempt for the disturbance caused by the students but admitted that he had been tempted to throw a bomb into a group of policemen who had arrived on the scene. On July 12, he left his room on boulevard Morland without paying his rent. Later that month, Émile was spotted several times in London.

In early August 1893, an unidentified anarchist arrived in London from Paris. He asked for chemical tubes that could be used to make bombs. He wanted four of them, between five and seven inches in diameter, two of which would be divided in the middle by a copper plate, with a hole through which acids could be added. Such material could be used for "reversal bombs," apparently destined for various Parisan financial institutions. In the margin of the police report, detailing the anarchist's inquiries, the officer had written, "Émile Henry?"

By late summer, the Parisian undercover policeman "Thanne"

concluded that Émile had indeed been the source of the bomb that blew up the police station on rue des Bons-Enfants, and that Bonnard, known as Père Duchesne, had been an accomplice and had bragged about it. Thanne believed that the anarchist singer Adrienne Chailley had been the woman seen by the law student on the stairs. She now seemed to have renounced anarchism, hoping to avoid further suspicion. A French police report of August 22, 1893, had Émile leaving London for Paris with Matha. In the fall, Émile was back in London with Matha at the Autonomy Club and could be seen strolling with Marocco on Dean Street almost every day. He was last sighted in the British capital in early December 1893.

In Paris, on November 13, 1893, a young anarchist shoemaker from the Alps named Léon-Jules Léauthier was broke and despondent. He went to a nice Parisian restaurant, the Marguery, spending what money he had left on a hearty meal that included quail, mâconnais wine, and champagne. The nineteen-year-old worker then jumped up and plunged a knife into a well-dressed diner, gravely wounding the man, who turned out to be the Serb ambassador to France. The day before the attack, Léauthier had written Sébastien Faure that rather than die of hunger or kill himself, he would kill a prosperous person: "I would not be striking an innocent person in attacking the first bourgeois who comes along." At his trial, he explained that he had been "at the end of my resources. I did not want to live submissively. I spotted a bourgeois of haughty and ornate appearance, and I planted my dagger in his throat."

The police intensified their campaign against anarchists. They undertook searches, seized newspapers (French and foreign), made arrests for little or no reason, and intimidated employers into firing anarchist workers. Magistrates used existing laws to expel foreigners, including Germans, Austrians, Belgians, Italians, and a Spaniard. The crackdown had greatly reduced the number of known anarchist meetings, and a number of key militants left for London, weakening some organizations. Anarchists no longer met in sizable gatherings, where undercover police agents or informers could report on what was said. Realizing this, the police focused their attention on the *compagnons* espousing "individual initiative," like Émile. These were the ones who disappeared into the shadows. The police continued to watch Martin's dairy store and, in Brévannes, À l'Espérance. Madame Henry had received no letters, and her comings and goings appeared perfectly normal. Where was her second son, Émile Henry?

CHAPTER 6

Two Bombs

ON DECEMBER 9, 1893, Auguste Vaillant, an unemployed worker distraught at being unable to feed his family, tossed a small bomb into the Chamber of Deputies. Born in the Ardennes near the Belgian border in 1861 and abandoned by his father when he was about ten, Vaillant started an apprenticeship with a pastry cook. However, he was let go when he got hungry one day and made a cake for himself. He worked for a time in a sawmill and then briefly as a laborer demolishing a rampart in Charleville. He was arrested for eating a meal in a restaurant for which he was unable to pay. At the age of twelve, an aunt put the young Vaillant on a train for Marseille, although he had no ticket. He was arrested again, and his father, who was a gendarme on the island of Corsica, paid the fine of sixteen francs.

From that day on, Vaillant was on his own. He walked all the way to Marseille. Desperately hungry, he stole food in order to survive as he wandered from place to place. He was jailed four times for theft and for begging.

After working as a quarryman in Algeria, Vaillant left for Argentina in 1890 to try to start a new life. There he tried his hand at farming in Chaco Province for two and a half years. But everything went wrong, and he complained that his situation amounted to a kind of slavery. After returning to France in 1893 and living at first in Montmartre, Vaillant married, and soon his wife gave birth to a baby girl, Sidonie. He got a job as a leatherworker in Saint-Denis. When his employer refused to pay him more than twenty francs a week, Vaillant reminded him that he had a wife and a child to feed. The boss replied, "I don't give a damn about your wife. I hired you." After flirting with socialism, Vaillant became an anarchist, meeting with the groups the Independents and the Equals in Montmartre.

Living in the suburb of Choisy-le-Roi, his family wracked with hunger, Auguste Vaillant decided to strike a blow that would call France's attention to the plight of poor people like him. He purchased materials to make a small bomb, which he filled with green powder, sulfuric acid, tacks, and small nails, enough to hurt but not to kill. He obtained a pass that allowed him to observe a session of the Chamber of Deputies, where he sat in the second row of the balcony. Soon he stood and threw the device, tossing it over the head of an astonished lady in the first row. When the small bomb exploded, the president of the Chamber of Deputies merely announced, with memorable calm, "The session continues."

A few spectators, including a priest, and several deputies suffered only light injuries. Vaillant himself suffered some kind of wound while throwing the bomb and sought assistance at the Hôtel-Dieu (the central hospital). There the staff discovered traces of gunpowder on his hands. He was arrested and readily admitted guilt, saying that he had acted alone. Indeed, he had not told any of his anarchist acquaintances about what he was planning. All the deputies were the same, he insisted, and he had wanted to attack society itself.

In Henry Leyret's bar, Le Déluge, in Belleville, a worker arrived at 7 A.M., laughing and shouting, "Here's some news. 'The Aquarium' blew up!" The news met with little surprise. People had expected it. No one expressed any sympathy for the injured deputies. After all, they were paid twenty-five francs a day for doing nothing. A worker in the bar suggested that President Sadi Carnot decorate the person who threw the bomb, another adding that the anarchists were indeed "tough guys!"

On December 11, the police obtained information about anarchist plans to blow up the entire Palais-Bourbon, and possibly even the Palais de l'Élysée, the residence of the president. The Parisian anarchist groups known as Compagnons of the Fourteenth Arrondissement and No Country favored the first proposal, as did anarchists in London, who believed that the bombing of the Chamber of Deputies would be a particularly effective symbolic attack, since financial scandals had more than tarnished "The Aquarium."

Public opinion turned against the intelligentsia—particularly writers and some journalists—for being sympathetic to anarchism, giving it a measure of respectability. The book *On Intellectual Complicity and Crimes of Opinion: The Provocations and Apologies for Crimes by Anarchist Propaganda,* quickly published in the wake of the most recent anarchist attacks, claimed that intellectuals were in part responsible for the remarkable increase in the number of anarchists in France. The book's author called Dostoyevsky's *Crime and Punishment* "an admirable manual for assassination" and argued that the Spanish anarchist Santiago Salvador, who bombed the Liceo Theater in Barcelona, had been nourished by the work of Malatesta and other anarchist theorists. Cheap newspapers and subversive posters polluted Paris with dangerous ideas, which had a "hypnotic" effect on people already weak from alcoholism. A magistrate equated propaganda "by ideas" with "propaganda by the deed," the former equally as criminal, in his view; the theoreticians of anarchy were every bit as dangerous as the murderers who actually wielded the dagger.

How would France, and the rest of Europe, respond to terrorist deeds? Following acrimonious debate, the Chamber of Deputies and the Senate, on December 12 and 18, passed laws so controversial and deemed so unfair by their critics that socialists dubbed them the "scoundrelly" or "shameful" laws—because these statutes could be used against them too. Under the new laws, anyone who wrote anything sympathetic to anarchism could be prosecuted on the grounds that such writing indirectly provoked crimes. The law of December 12 toughened existing legislation (the law of 1881) related to the media: it was first applied not against an anarchist but against the author of an article in a socialist paper who appeared to express sympathy for the plight of Auguste Vaillant. This signaled to many that the legislation was indeed aimed at all political opposition from the left. The law permitted the seizure of newspapers and preventive arrests. It criminalized any expression of sympathy for anarchist attacks, or for murder, pillage, arson, or any other violence, as well as for antimilitary propaganda.

The second law, which followed six days later, codified the concept of an association of malefactors, or "evildoers," suggesting a massive anarchist plot against people, property, and the public peace. It authorized harsh penalties, including execution, for anyone convicted of building or keeping an explosive device—or any product used to make one.

In the eyes of the law, anarchism took on a new, specific definition; "the anarchist sect" constituted "a veritable association." No matter that it lacked official statutes or constitution—it existed by virtue of a "pre-established agreement" by which it recruited and protected its members. This conception of anarchism resembled the *compagnonnages* (although that reference was not made), which offered lodging and food to skilled artisans who traveled from town to town to hone their skills. In like manner, when anarchists went from Paris to provincial cities or arrived from other countries, they received assistance from local anarchists. To exemplify how the anarchists' network of mutual aid functioned, the police cited the small fund Jean Grave kept in the offices of *La Révolte* on rue Mouffetard, distributed to anarchists in need of a little assistance or to subsidize propaganda. And though a good amount of internal debate characterized the movement, lawmakers argued that all anarchists shared a single goal: to abolish the state through violence. The fact that anarchists often signed their propaganda collectively was cited as proof that all members of the movement acted as one. Thus the government came to a rather sweeping conclusion: that any anarchist who attended a meeting was complicit in this destructive plan. Furthermore, anarchism was to be excised from public debate, in speech and in print. Anarchist newspapers, or any paper that spoke well of anarchism, were "lit matches thrown into the middle of explosive materials."

Thus anarchism itself became a crime. By virtue of the law of December 18, associations of "evildoers" could be indicted not only for committing an offense, but also for appearing to plan, anticipate, or express sympathy for or interest in such an act. Thus, anyone who knew an anarchist or discussed anarchism could be prosecuted, as could members of any anarchist organization, presumed by its very existence to be criminal in nature, a threat to public peace.

According to this aggressive new legal initiative, a person could be considered an accomplice to a serious crime without participating in it at all. One critic provided this possible scenario as a warning: Say an anarchist commits a crime and then is given lodging by a friend. The criminal writes something on a piece of paper given to him by his host, who is not necessarily an anarchist. Thus both the "criminal" and the person he is visiting, who had provided both a bed and a piece of paper, could be prosecuted as members of an anarchist conspiracy and subject to a harsh sentence. Similar examples abounded. A prosecutor could assume that a knife used in any way by the printers of the anarchist newspaper *La Révolte* actually served as a weapon. And in fact, a social reformer who organized meals for the poor was prosecuted because speeches were given as people ate. Police also seized documents about Sicily from the geographer Élisée Reclus, sure that they had found proof of a secret society. Even jokes about anarchism could lead to jail sentences.

The harsh crackdown in France was replicated in Italy and Spain. In Italy, emergency legislation in June 1894 in response to anarchist attacks banned newspapers and parties considered "subversive." The government shipped three thousand anarchists to penal colonies, and hundreds of their colleagues went abroad as exiles. In Spain, the police began to persecute labor organizations, considering them "revolutionary" and therefore dangerous by definition. Any leftist political activity became identified with anarchism. Police harassed socialists and even shut down anarchist cultural publications.

In the meantime, more suspicious objects were being discovered around Paris. Just before Christmas, the city's chief chemist, Girard, examined a dead rat that had been wrapped in paper and sent to a wine merchant. Girard determined that the object was not a bomb.

Waves of police raids and searches targeted all kinds of anarchists. The police drew up a list of more than five hundred of them in Paris, putting together a separate list of foreigners. Fortuné Henry's address was listed as unknown although he was in prison, and Émile could not be located. Beginning at six in the morning on January 1, 1894, French police carried out an especially ambitious 552 searches. During January and February, 248 people were arrested on suspicion of being anarchists, and 80 of them were still in jail after two months had passed, although the police complained that the most recent searches and arrests—the sudden arrival of police wagons with bells clanging, the police waving guns—gave anarchists time to destroy compromising papers or simply disappear. Meanwhile, anarchist bombs in Spain had caused widespread panic. A journalist related that bombs "hang as a menace over the entire bourgeoisie . . . there is no person who does not worry about dynamite, nitroglycerine, and detonators . . . Satan has made himself a dynamiter and tries to be equal with God." In Paris, anarchists were not the only people seething at these systematic roundups. Nothing like this coercive police activity had been seen since the final days of the Commune.

Those arrested in Paris included some familiar faces, including Léveillé, the locksmith arrested and battered in Clichy two and a half years earlier; Achille Étiévant, the anarchist typographer suspected of knowing the whereabouts of the stolen dynamite; and Élisée Bastard, a well-known anarchist orator. Alexander Cohen, a Dutchman who had translated a play for the Odéon theater, was arrested and deported. In Toulouse, a man was charged with "apology for the crime of murder" for shouting "Long live anarchy! Long live Ravachol!" An anarchist received two years in prison for having preached anarchist theory to a man who later stole something from his boss. An anarchist called Rousset was put on trial for having organized evening gatherings that fed up to five thousand people and received contributions from respected writers such as Stéphane Mallarmé, Émile Zola, and Alphonse Daudet. The minister of the interior, David Raynal, requested lists of all people who were not anarchists but had some sort of relationship with one or more members of the movement and who therefore might "come to their aid by personal friendship." Police forbade kiosks from selling *Père Peinard, La Révolte, Revue Libertaire,* and even some socialist papers. Émile Pouget, fearing arrest, left for London in January 1894. (There he may have been involved in a swindle, selling to a collector some teeth supposedly extracted from Ravachol, along with forged autographs of the famed revolutionaries of 1789 — Robespierre, Marat, and Danton.) The police shut down *Père Peinard* on February 21, 1894.

Even then, the press continued to document the overreaching efforts of the police. A news dealer named Desforges, who had a kiosk on place Clichy, was detained with his seventeen-year-old son, who had never been in any kind of trouble. Louis Bouchez, a sculptor, was arrested at his parents' house because he had expressed sympathy for anarchism, though he had done nothing else. Charles Paul, an upholsterer, had joined a gymnastic organization on rue Lepic in Montmartre and was accused of being the friend of a well-known *compagnon* in that center of anarchism. This was enough to get him arrested.

Upon his return to Paris on or shortly before December 18 — he had been seen in London at various points that fall — Émile could already see the results of the draconian measures taken against anarchists — spying, searches, and imprisonment of the innocent. The anarchist had become "a beast tracked everywhere, with the bourgeois press . . . calling for its extermination." Police even stooped to underhanded methods; their spies, for example, entered a suspected anarchist's room and hid packages of tannin there, which were then "discovered" in a police search the next morning. In this way an anarchist whom the police wanted to put away would be sent to prison for three years. (This had happened to Émile's friend Mérigeau.) And then Raynal, the minister of the interior, could triumphantly announce in the Chamber of Deputies that the laws they had passed had "thrown terror into the anarchist camp."

The press promoted a rather fanciful idea about how to capture anarchists: each one could be trailed more or less continuously by a policeman "staying at his side and grabbing his arm at the critical moment." Yet there were many anarchists, and not enough police to follow all of them. Undercover agents could stake out known gathering places and monitor the buildings in which anarchists lived, but there were limits. Not everyone could be watched all the time, and many whom the police sought with special effort, such as Émile, proved difficult to find.

Auguste Vaillant went on trial on January 10. He offered a rambling defense full of heartfelt but vague references to the philosophes of the Enlightenment and the playwright Henrik Ibsen, among others. He condemned imperialism and, above all, "this accursed society where one can see a single man uselessly spend enough to feed thousands of families . . . while one comes upon a hundred thousand unfortunate people without enough to eat." He was condemned to death.

Vaillant's life of deprivation and the plight of his young daughter, Sidonie, attracted great attention in the poor neighborhoods of Paris. How could President Sadi Carnot not pardon her father? "Who knows?" they said at Le Déluge. "Perhaps if he had always had enough to eat for little Sidonie, Vaillant never would have resorted to his little bomb! In any case, he had not killed anyone, and the wounded were healing rapidly. Why cut off his head?" A group of socialist deputies and the moderate politician Georges Clemenceau were among those who asked President Carnot to spare the man's life. A letter from Vaillant's young daughter, Sidonie, to Carnot's wife achieved nothing. The duchesse of Uzès, a monarchist, offered to adopt the girl; the anarchist Sébastien Faure ultimately took charge of her, at Vaillant's request. Paris awaited the execution. The police received an anonymous warning that anarchists renting a room right at place de la Roquette, the site of executions in Paris, planned to throw a bomb in protest. Rumors had anarchists leaping out to stab the chief executioner, Antoine-Louis Deibler, and spirit away his intended victim. The police wondered if anarchists whom they sought might show up at the execution to hear Vaillant's final words.

On the morning of the execution, Vaillant refused to speak with the prison chaplain. When asked if he wanted to drink the traditional glass of eau de vie before being executed, he replied, "I am not a murderer. I do not need to drink alcohol in order to have courage." Dr. Guillotine's blade fell at dawn on February 5, 1894. Auguste Vaillant became the first person in nineteenth-century France to be executed, even though he had not killed anyone.

News of the event spread rapidly through working-class Paris on that gray day, with thick clouds contributing to "a glacial and dark atmosphere of grief." To the working poor, it seemed that society had once again proved itself "implacable." In Henry Leyret's bar, a general sense of bewilderment reigned, "a desolate stupe-

faction, with shouts of anger about the future, and the expecta-
tion of vengeances that were sure to follow." Vaillant's death
was appalling, especially in the darkest, shortest days of winter,
when many people, such as construction workers, could not find
employment and were short on credit. If he had killed people, as
Ravachol had, perhaps Vaillant's execution could be understood.
But Vaillant was an honest man, pushed to the limit by his misery. The hard times were responsible. In January, a Parisian family
of three died in abject poverty, unable to pay their rent or even
eat. In an exceptionally cold winter, such intimate hard dramas
multiplied.

In the factories, workshops, and bars of Belleville, Vaillant's execution recalled the early Christian martyrs, echoing the image of
Ravachol. Leyret overheard someone say, "They wanted to pulver-
ize him in the name of property, and the faubourg does not have
any property . . . anarchism is extending its influence, infiltrating."
Hundreds of arrests "among the humble" gave the impression that
the government and its police force were persecuting the poor on
behalf of the rich. People reasoned that Vaillant had been a victim
of the bourgeoisie, and many more workers became attracted to
the anarchists, while remaining indifferent to much of their political theory. Instead, they shared their bitterness, misery, and
"gloomy despair." Here was something that could threaten the ruling classes even more than "propaganda by the deed": "the anarchism of feeling!" Two of Leyret's clients almost came to blows
when one referred to the anarchists as "bandits," before the latter
adroitly explained that he did not mean Vaillant, but rather men
who used anarchism as an excuse to steal. More than one worker
said that he would not want to be in President Carnot's shoes. It
had also been "in the air" of the faubourgs that "The Aquarium"
would explode. Anything could happen next. Parisians of means,
as well as the police, waited to see how Vaillant's execution would
be avenged.

On about December 15, 1893, Émile went to the watchmaker's
shop where he had apprenticed for a month in the summer of

1892. He asked if there was any work for him, saying that he had been in London but would remain in Paris if he could find employment. He tried to sell the watchmaker a watch that was missing a minute hand, but it was worth nothing.

On December 20, Émile appeared at the Villa Faucheur (named after the owner of the property) on rue des Envierges in Belleville. Saying that he was a mechanic and providing a reference from a previous landlord (which turned out to be a forgery), he took a small room. The rent would be 120 francs a year, and he gave 5 francs to the concierge as a tip. He gave his name as "Émile Dubois" (he had used the name "Louis Dubois" when he lived on boulevard Morland). Despite its rather grand-sounding name, the Villa Faucheur was a modest residence, an immense *cité ouvrière* on a street lined with workers' residences. There were two large entryways at numbers 1 and 3, each with an imposing iron gate. A few bourgeois of modest means lived in the complex, including seven or eight policemen. Poorer residents, like the so-called Dubois, lived farther back in the complex. His room was in the middle of path number 1, about halfway back, on the left, across from a small empty lot. On each side of the small building stood a wall about a yard high, topped by a small iron fence, alongside a tiny garden. On the fourth floor, Émile's room stood across from the stairs, between the lodgings of a copper turner and an older man who was a jeweler.

As Émile walked out of the gate, below him to the right was the Belleville Garden (sometimes called Belleville Park). On a clear day, he could easily see the Eiffel Tower, constructed little more than four years earlier; the Panthéon, where heroes of the state were buried; and Notre Dame de Paris—for Émile, three imposing symbols of the enemy. In Honoré de Balzac's *Père Goriot*, a novel set earlier in the century, a minor noble from the Charentes, Rastignac, looks down from Père Lachaise Cemetery toward the wealthy *beaux quartiers* of Chaussée d'Antin and Opéra. He gestures in that direction and says that henceforth it will be war between him and the world he wants to conquer, until he is accepted in wealthy society. Émile looked toward elegant Paris and pledged another kind of war, one of total destruction.

A neighbor described the new young renter as quite nice and gentle. Sometimes he returned home late, after 9 or even 11 P.M., and on those days, he could be heard singing anarchist songs. During the time he lived there, "Émile Dubois" had but one known visitor, a well-dressed law student who appeared to be about twenty and who stayed with him a day or two, although another neighbor said that occasionally someone would come by and ask for him. He had received two letters during his time there—one from England.

The police grew increasingly interested in this Émile. One agent overheard, in a conversation between Constant Martin and another anarchist in mid-January 1894, that Émile Henry was hiding somewhere in Ménilmontant. He was thought to have transformed his room into an "anarchist laboratory." The police thought that tracking the anarchist militant Jacques Prolo would lead them to Émile, as the two seemed sure to meet. The investigators believed that Émile had returned to Paris with three other anarchists. On February 4 "Léon," an ace among the expanded corps of undercover police agents following militant anarchists, offered his opinion: Émile was somewhere in Belleville or Montmartre. That same day, a police informer reported that Émile was indeed back in Paris.

On February 8, the undercover policeman "Thanne" again expressed certainty that the bomb that exploded on November 8, 1892, had been put together by Émile Henry and Paul Bonnard, an anarchist shoemaker known as "Père Duchesne," who took his name from a radical newspaper published during the French Revolution. Bonnard had been seen in the company of Adrienne Chailley, the anarchist singer, the day before the explosion at the office of the Carmaux Mining Company. If she had carried the bomb into the building, which was by no means certain, Émile would have stood guard at the front door. Thanne was very lucky

The Hôtel Terminus, with the Café Terminus on the right side, and the Gare Saint-Lazare to the left of the hotel.

The village of Brévannes, where Rose Caubet Henry and her family lived.

Rose Caubet Henry, Émile's mother, in her bar, À l'Espérance.
Collection Roger-Viollet

Left: Élisa Gauthey, the object of Émile Henry's unrequited love.
Right: Ravachol, presented as a heroic martyr framed by the guillotine.

The Italian anarchist Errico Malatesta, in exile in London.

Avenue de l'Opéra
in Paris, with the
Grand Opera in the
distance. The offices
of the Carmaux Mining
Company stood at
number 11, three blocks
up on the left.

The Villa Faucheur
in Paris. The woman
is pointing to Émile
Henry's room.
Collection Roger-Viollet

The explosion of
the bomb at the
Café Terminus,
February 12, 1894.
Collection Roger-Viollet

The capture of
Émile Henry.
Collection Roger-Viollet

Émile Henry.
Collection Roger-Viollet

The basilica of Sacré-Coeur, then still under construction.

Police drawings of Émile Henry.

The Palais de Justice, where Émile Henry went on trial, and
the Conciergerie, the prison in which he was held.

Louis Deibler, "Monsieur de Paris," the city's chief executioner.

A guillotine in operation.

to pick up this information, as only two or three anarchists knew about the planned attack beforehand. In order to prove Chailley's participation, Thanne had only to demonstrate that she was the lover of one or the other anarchist, and this he hoped to do by interviewing her landlord, her concierge, or a hotel porter. The growing belief that Émile had been responsible for the bomb made his presence in Paris all the more threatening.

On about February 7, one of the Bourdin brothers — French anarchists who had found refuge in London — was back in Paris and had seen Émile on a street in Belleville. There Émile could easily disappear among the machinery and ironsmith workshops and the bars. He was shrewd and careful. He would probably try to see his friend Martin, who had been spotted several times in the afternoon, apparently hurrying to meet someone near rue Cadet or place Cadet. In London, Émile Pouget had told someone that he had news of his young friend but revealed nothing specific. Yet on February 11, the undercover policeman "Léon" reported that Émile had left Paris three or four days earlier for the provinces. The policeman thought that he might have gone to Brévannes, or even to Normandy, where he was believed to have friends.

The holy grail of those anarchists inclined to violence was the assassination of President Sadi Carnot, who had refused to pardon Vaillant. But the Palais de l'Élysée was too heavily guarded and the iron gate too high, making an attack impossible. So Émile came up with a less ambitious plan: he would target the Opera or a fancy restaurant or café. For a short period, Matha had met with Émile virtually every day, attempting to talk him out of the plan. On February 11, Émile had become irritated, telling Matha "your friendship bothers me." The next day, February 12, Émile did not show up to meet him. That morning, he had told the concierge at the Villa Faucheur that he would be gone "for quite a while."

The bomb thrown on February 12, 1894, by a young man wearing shabby black pants, vest, boots, and a white shirt with a black tie, struck a chandelier in the grand hall of the Café Terminus. It fell to the ground between two tables, not far from the orchestra, exploding with a terrifying boom and producing thick, acrid smoke. Bullets and pieces of lead flew in every direction. Marble tables, metal chairs, and mirrors shattered. The explosion left a sizable hole in the wooden floor and punctured the ceiling. Amid general panic, the screams and shouts of the wounded joined the smoke. Those not seriously wounded ran toward any door they could find, flooding the adjoining streets and the courtyard of the Gare Saint-Lazare.

The waiter who had served Émile his beer and cigar had seen him return to throw the bomb. Madame Leblanc, sitting with her sister and brother-in-law, an employee of the Bank of France, also saw a young man move toward the door and then turn back to throw something. She remembered thinking, at first, that he did not want to pay for his drink. Her sister, Madame Emmanuel, had had exactly the same reaction—"Hey, look, he is running away without paying the waiter." The three of them were hurt. Charles Villevaleix, a former diplomat representing Haiti in Paris, had been sitting near the door; he heard a noise like a loud shout and saw glass falling on the table. Standing up instinctively, he realized that he was bleeding profusely from his left thigh. Charles Beuquet, a bank employee, was sitting near the orchestra when he saw an electric lamp crash to the ground and heard the explosion. He ran outside and then felt a sharp pain in his leg. Eugène Garnier, a self-described man of letters, heard a dull thud as the bomb exploded and immediately shouted that it was a bomb, and then felt a shooting sensation through his left foot, heel, and calf. The widow Pauline Kinsbourg, who was sitting with her daughter between the two doors, saw the bomb explode, flames leaping forward, followed by acrid smoke. Both her legs were bleeding. Ernest Borde, a forty-two-year-old draftsman, was sitting with his good friend Louis-Napoléon Van Herreweghen, his back to the front door. As the small orchestra played the third piece of the first set, he noticed a young man who appeared to be from the provinces;

he was carrying a package wrapped in newspaper and tied with string. It occurred to him that the package might contain a large Camembert. The two men saw him get up and leave, and then the bulbs of the electric chandelier crashed onto the table where they were sitting. An object exploded at their feet. Borde collapsed, gravely wounded. Van Herreweghen pulled a piece of lead out of his right leg. Amid understandable panic, a man yelled, "I am wounded! Let me through!" and then fell into the arms of another victim. Some of the waiters and a few cool-headed souls began to assist the wounded, carrying them to the adjoining restaurants or up into the hotel itself. Others were led to nearby pharmacies for help.

In the meantime, the man who had thrown the bomb had fled before it actually detonated. A waiter who saw him running shouted, "Stop him, stop him!" After almost colliding with another waiter, Émile shouted "There he is!" to distract attention from himself. He ran down rue du Havre, narrowly missing a kiosk before turning back onto the nearly deserted rue de l'Isly. His goal was to reach the Gare Saint-Lazare back around the corner, lose himself among the passengers, and purchase a ticket for the suburbs.

Émile-Joseph Martinguet, who worked in an office near Pigalle and had been walking outside the Café Terminus, gave chase. A waiter, Tissier, also pursued the man, joined by a railway employee who happened to be standing across the street. Émile pulled a pistol from his coat and fired at the waiter. François Poisson, a policeman who had fought with the army in Indochina, was standing nearby on duty—ironically, talking with a Republican Guard about Vaillant's execution—when he heard someone yell, "Stop him!" When Poisson asked what had happened, someone shouted that the man who had run past them had thrown a bomb. Although wearing heavy boots, Poisson ran after Émile, followed by the waiter, who had been grazed by a bullet. An apprentice barber, Léon Maurice, heard someone shout, "Stop, thief, murderer, stop him!" and ran out into the street, still carrying a shaving brush and bowl, before joining the chase. Policeman Poisson gained ground when Émile turned to fire more shots, as policemen Jules Toutet and Émile Gigot took off after the bomber. A bullet hit the barber. Two ticket inspectors of the Tramway Company had heard a shot, first thinking that it was a firecracker tossed by a child. Then they saw policeman Poisson chasing a man, and they too pursued Émile. At the corner of rue de l'Isly and rue de Rome, Poisson grabbed Émile, who fired at him point-blank. The first bullet struck the policeman's black leather wallet in an inside pocket of his overcoat, shredding some papers. The wallet saved his life, though it also helped that Émile's bullets had been flattened in order to do greater damage, which slightly reduced their initial speed. A second bullet grazed the policeman's arm. When Poisson raised his sword over his head, Émile fired again, the third shot barely missing the policeman's face. Then one of the ticket inspectors, Guillemin, hit the suspect with the metal puncher he used to validate tramway tickets. A fishing-tackle merchant, Gustave Petit, had entered the melee when an unknown man apparently hit him over the head with a cane, which led some to suspect, briefly, that Émile had an accomplice. Poisson threw himself on Émile, and the two rolled into the gutter. Holding Émile down, Poisson placed the point of his sword against the bomber's throat, shouting, "If you move, scoundrel, I'll cut you up!" Émile was formally arrested at 9:15 by the agents Toutet and Gigot.

Poisson and the policemen who had joined him now had to protect the suspect from a small but angry crowd. In his attempt to escape, Émile had received several bruises and bled from his nose. His clothes had been torn. The bomber continued to struggle, lashing out with fists and feet, until he was finally subdued. A witness later remembered that because he said very little, Émile seemed more like an ordinary thief than an anarchist. One of the men who helped capture him recounted that the bomber's eyes seemed to be popping out of his head and that he was drenched in sweat. There seemed nothing human about him, especially when he shouted with a husky voice, "Bunch of pigs! I would kill you all." The police contingent now numbered almost twenty. The nearby cafés emptied. A woman fainted.

When asked his name, Émile replied, "Find out for yourself." At first he denied having thrown the bomb, but he was clearly out to get society: "the more bourgeois who get killed, the better . . ." A quick search of the bomber turned up six flattened bullets, a knife with several blades, a stiletto knife, and brass knuckles. He had put poison on a knife blade. When asked why he was carrying such an arsenal, the arrested man replied that he was always armed so as to defend his freedom. He admitted having fired shots at those running after him and regretted that only one policeman had been hit; if he had not fallen after firing his last shot, he would have switched to using his knife.

The captured man carried no identity papers but was wearing around his neck a small locket containing a lock of hair. When one of the policemen, Aragon, asked his name, age, and profession, he replied that his name was Léon Breton. He added that if the policemen did not like that one, then Le Breton would do, or any other they preferred. As for his age, he was as old as he was, and as for his address, the police would not have that, either, nor his profession. He would only say that he was an anarchist and responded to further questions with a political tirade.

"Breton" was taken to the police station on rue de Moscou. Martinguet, one of those who had chased him, was brought along to identify the man in custody as the person who had thrown the bomb. Martinguet reported that he had seen two young men "looking quite suspicious," one wearing a blue smock and wearing a hat, and the other blond and noticeably thin, with a small mustache, standing on the sidewalk outside the café and looking in. Suddenly he saw the second man throw something about the size of a cannonball into the Terminus; then he took off, running. When Martinguet heard the powerful explosion inside the café, he immediately began to run after the man, who turned and fired a pistol, first once, and then three more times, in the direction of those who were following him, before being taken at the corner of rue de l'Isly and rue de Rome. Martinguet's account, however, left the identity of the second man, whom he took to be the bomber's lookout, a mystery. He confirmed that "Breton" was one of the two men he had seen outside the café, and without question the one who had thrown the bomb, for his face had been fully exposed by the streetlights.

A doctor was summoned to treat the suspect's minor injuries, incurred in the scuffle. The bomber seemed to be about twenty years old, if that. The doctor asked his patient why he had committed such a monstrous act and was told that what the doctor considered a "monstrous act" was very natural for anarchists. In order "to arrive at an era of justice and true freedom which will bring happiness to everyone," the bourgeoisie had to disappear from the planet. When the doctor asked if he would kill someone caring for his wounds, he replied that he would certainly do so.

At 9:35 P.M., the policeman in charge at the Gare Saint-Lazare notified the prefect of police and the prosecutor's office that a bomb had been thrown into the Café Terminus and that several people had been gravely wounded. The secretary-general of the prefecture of police happened to be dining in the vicinity, and was alerted. At 11:30, a magistrate arrived to ask "Breton" some questions. And so did Lépine, the prefect of police himself, who had first gone to the Café Terminus to see what had happened. After trying to interrogate the bomb thrower, who refused to say much more than that he had acted alone, Lépine went to see the minister of the interior. "Breton" suddenly stated that he had arrived in Paris from the provinces. From where? No one's business. He had been chased and demanded to know why. He had only been walking by the Café Terminus. Madame Emmanuel, who lived nearby on rue d'Amsterdam, was also brought to the police station to identify "Breton" as the person who threw the bomb. A woman from the neighborhood turned up at the police station hoping to catch a glimpse of the bomber; she had not been in the Café Terminus but had never seen a murderer and was eager to lay her eyes on one. When a magistrate again asked his occupation, "Breton" spat out,

"Write down cabinetmaker or chimney sweep, if you want. Add that I come from Marseille, or Peking, or anywhere else. Go and try to find out . . . it will help pass the time." At 1:15 in the morning, a small crowd of onlookers began to insult him as he climbed into the police wagon. Émile turned and called them cowards.

In the meantime, the Café Terminus had been blocked off by barriers and the metal storefront lowered. Bloodied pieces of clothing, hats, napkins, copies of the evening's program, and a bloodstained newspaper lay among the rubble of wood and metal, broken chairs, chunks of marble, and shattered porcelain and glassware. These were sealed as evidence, along with what was left of an ironworker's lunchbox. The first conclusion was obvious: the bomb was intended not simply to call attention to the plight of the poor—the goal of Vaillant—but to kill. When Lépine arrived at the Café Terminus several hours after the attack, two extremely pale cashiers still sat in their chairs, frozen in fear, obliged to guard the evening's take. A waiter who was exhausted, confused, tired, and hungry asked only to be left alone. In the hotel itself, guests anxiously asked the staff what had happened; some wanted to move out of their rooms immediately. The Café Terminus opened for business the next day at 2:30 P.M., while people stopped by simply to gawk.

Those arrested in Paris and the *département* of the Seine passed through the holding cells at the Palais de Justice on the Île de la Cité. On an average day, about 150 people were brought there. Many arrived in a police wagon pulled by two horses (and now known—without the horses—as "salad shakers" because their small windows make them resemble this kitchen tool). "Breton" was taken into the receiving room, and his assumed name entered on a register, along with the reason for his arrest: attempted murder. He was then led across a small courtyard—really just an open space, with ruins on one side and the wall of the Court of the Girondins on the other—then through a set of doors leading into the holding cells. He was there ordered to take off his shoes, and was searched. He again said that he was Léon Breton and that he had been born in 1874, adding that he would not reveal where he had been born, nor the names of his mother and father. He declared himself to be a cabinetmaker, unmarried, and without a residence in Paris. He refused to sign the copy of the initial interrogation. The process of gathering information and thus preparing the case against "Breton" began immediately, under the authority of the investigating magistrate, Judge Meyer.

The bomber was taken to cell number 8 in the men's block on the right side of the building at 2:45 A.M. The cell could be seen from above by guards patrolling a maze of staircases and iron footbridges. The two-story gallery of jail cells, standing between the halls of the Correctional Courts and Assize Courts, formed a tall, narrow nave, with small cells, each with a small glass window, on both sides. At the far end was a common area, where prisoners often inscribed their signatures and the dates of their visit. Émile climbed onto the bed and quickly fell asleep. Two police inspectors remained with him in the cell until 5:00 A.M., having been told to extract every possible bit of information from him. Two inspectors would occupy the cell with "Breton" at virtually all times, in shifts of twelve hours.

Émile slept until 11:30 A.M. He then asked a procedural question about the judicial investigation and wondered if he would have to remain in the temporary holding cell for long. When told that this would depend on his cooperation, he replied that he would be of no help. Curiously enough, he seemed preoccupied with how investigators would learn his true identity, adding, almost helpfully, that he saw only one way, by publishing his photograph: "as I am somewhat known, someone would recognize me." He readily admitted that he attended anarchist meetings, referring to several notable gatherings, including the one in the Salle du Commerce, after which his brother—and he too—had been arrested for brandishing what appeared to be a cartridge of dynamite. He spoke about a meeting organized by the followers of Boulanger, a gathering in which "the anarchists were very badly

treated." However, he had concluded that such sessions were inef-
fective unless they were immediately followed by "an act of propaganda by the deed."

That same day the prisoner was taken to the "anthropomorphic" department, where Alphonse Bertillon, "high priest" and
creator of the service, took measurements of his head and body,
including his height and the length of his middle finger, left foot,
ear, forearms, and so on. Bertillon also photographed him. At 1:50
P.M. on February 13, the prisoner was taken to see Judge Meyer.
During the twenty-minute encounter, "Breton" briefly changed
his name, saying that he was Léon Martin, admitted that he had
thrown the bomb, and insisted that he had acted alone. He added,
and not for the last time, that he regretted only one thing: that
there had not been more victims.

In his cell, "Breton" asked about the number of victims in the
Café Terminus. (He was told that of the twenty people who were
injured, several had very serious wounds.) He invoked "legitimate
defense" in explaining why he had fired three times at Poisson the
policeman: the man had raised his sword to strike him. He volun-
teered that the *compagnons* were "very strong." He then added that
like other anarchists, he had not been after a particular person, for
example, a certain magistrate, "but rather the entire bourgeoisie,
of which the former was only a representative." He sang the praises
of Vaillant's deed. He warned his guards that he knew all their
tricks. They would never get him to say anything he did not want
to. France would pay because of Vaillant's execution. As the guards
went off their shift, he was praising Ravachol, the "martyr."

Two of the guards, Duchâtel and Duthion, were gradually able
to establish rapport with their charge. "Breton" asked them if Girard, the municipal chemist, had discovered the composition of
his bomb. This question appeared to greatly preoccupy him. He
began proudly to volunteer details. The bomb had comprised
pieces of buckshot weighing about seven hundred grams, and in
all, the bomb weighed more than four pounds. He explained that
he had first gone to the Café de la Paix, and then the Café Améri-

cain, but neither seemed sufficiently full; he had then gone to the Terminus, waiting until it was quite crowded before throwing the bomb.

Some one hundred photos of "Breton" had been distributed to judicial and police offices (but not yet to newspapers) in an attempt to establish his identity. Magistrates in Saint-Étienne quickly noticed that the person in the photo corresponded exactly to a man who had been seen visiting various local anarchists. Reflecting the growing fascination with photos, *L'Éclair* speculated that the young man in the photo seemed about twenty-four to twenty-six years old, appearing "sure of himself, looking straight ahead, his lips seemingly in a mocking pose," and that he seemed intelligent—"his chin somewhat prominent giving his face a rather square, hard aspect," though overall he gave the impression of being a café waiter or an apprentice barber. His clothes were rather ragged—his pants, the journalist guessed, had come from the Belle Jardinière department store, at least in their better days—but they were clean, that is, very bourgeois. Indeed, Émile had dressed in ordinary, even threadbare clothes, in order to give his deed "more of a working-class character." His vest was that of someone who owned a bar and was inscribed, like his underwear, with the letters A.M. An experienced buyer for the department store Bon Marché believed that the clothes had been made in Troyes and that the initials did not signify a brand of clothing but had been marked in special ink by "Breton" or another person. In any case, two letters, at a time when it was perfectly common for ordinary people to wear secondhand clothes, would not help identify the person now under arrest.

Insisting that he would prefer the guillotine to jail, the prisoner told his guards that his first name was Henri-Émile, not Léon, and that his mother lived outside of Paris. On February 14, the police speculated that "Breton" may have come from London, carrying anarchist manifestos that were the work of the Autonomy Club. A particularly violent proclamation printed in London had turned up, asking its readers to slaughter bourgeois and spread the blood of the murderers who were starving the poor to death. *Le Matin* complained that the anarchists finding refuge in the British capital were free to organize plots "under the benevolent eye, indeed even the protection, of Scotland Yard."

Early in the morning of February 14, someone in the prefecture concluded that "Breton" was Émile Henry. "Léon," that very useful undercover policeman, had picked up on the striking similarities between the newspaper descriptions of the bomber and the young anarchist who had fled Paris following the deadly explosion on rue des Bons-Enfants. Anarchist informers had, to be sure, infiltrated many of the anarchist groups. But Émile had remained in the shadows. He had avoided the large meetings that guaranteed surveillance by the police. And no photo of him or his brother had been taken on the occasion of their arrest in 1892.

Émile identified himself to the guards Duchâtel and Duthion on that same Wednesday morning, February 14. He wrote the date and place of his birth in Duchâtel's notebook, saying that his father was dead and his mother still living, although he refused to provide her address. He also mentioned his brother Fortuné, indicating that he was in prison, and offered details of his own arrest, along with his brother, at the end of May 1892. Vanoutryne, his employer on rue du Sentier, confirmed his identity. Léon Breton was without a doubt Émile Henry. He told his guards that they should do their job, and he would do his, which was to destroy the bourgeoisie. He boasted that if he had enough material, he would take it upon himself to blow up all of Paris. If his career as a terrorist was over, others would follow him. He gave the impression that he had more dynamite or other similar explosives in his room. Vaillant, whose execution he wanted to avenge, had put together a "ridiculous" bomb, using mere nails instead of dynamite and buckshot, which had so much more to offer to the cause. Émile's bomb had been very different, as would be those that followed.

Early that same morning, at the Villa Faucheur in Belleville, a neighbor noticed that the door of the room of "Monsieur Dubois" had been left wide open, leaving visible a stark iron bed and straw mattress, a single table, and some papers that had been burned. The door had been forced. The police arrived. Girard, the director of the municipal laboratory turned bomb squad, hurried to Belleville to see the room and found traces of a green powder and pieces of metal. Shown a photo of Émile, the guard identified him as Émile Dubois, the "mechanic" who had said that he would be gone about four days.

As it happened, four hours after they heard about the explosion and their friend's arrest, Matha, Ortiz, Millet, and perhaps Philabert Pauwels, a Belgian anarchist, had gone to the Villa Faucheur. They managed to sneak past the concierge and broke into Émile's room, carrying away enough dynamite, fulminate, picric acid, and chlorate powder to make twelve to fifteen bombs.

By now some working in the prefecture of police believed that Émile was the young blond man seen outside 11, avenue de l'Opéra in November 1892. Émile immediately became a prime suspect in that unsolved case. One of the investigating magistrate's most important tasks was to discover what Émile had done between then and his attack at the Café Terminus. Such information might reveal dangerous accomplices still roaming the streets of Paris or London.

Judge Meyer told the prisoner that the police now knew that he lived at the Villa Faucheur in Belleville. Émile responded that he had never heard of the place. When told that the police had found material for making more bombs there, which was not true, he fell into the trap, saying that he was sure that they were not still there. He thus let slip two things: that those who had cleaned out his room had known about his plan and that they had agreed that if Émile was captured, they would take the explosive materials stored there. Asked if he had accomplices, he replied that he was "a righter of wrongs, not a denouncer." Indeed, he claimed that he had considered biting his tongue in two so that he would be incapable of revealing anything, or mutilating both hands, so that he would be unable to write.

A debate over the attack on the Café Terminus erupted in the

Chamber of Deputies. One deputy blamed the socialists (who in elections the previous August had gained thirty seats) and demanded that their red flag be banned. He also complained about the "scandalous scenes" at the cemetery of Ivry, around Vaillant's tomb, which had become something of a pilgrimage site, asking what measures the government planned to take against the scoundrels who had declared war on society and "who spread death without even looking at their victims."

The press immediately seized upon a crucial element unique to this attack. The bomber had chosen random victims—he simply threw his bomb into a group of people. This time the target was not the government or one of its officials or representatives, or a public monument, or the office or house of a wealthy financier or captain of industry, but rather ordinary people having a beer and listening to music in a café. The risk to the safety of everyday Parisians seemed heightened, and the police were blamed for being unprepared. The press demanded harsh and immediate action: "We must make sure that the instincts of hate and blood that boil over impetuously in certain individuals disappear from our civilized society. The repression must be both dignified and pitiless."

CHAPTER 7

The Trial

THE IDENTITY OF the Café Terminus bomber shocked Paris. He was not a marginal criminal like Ravachol nor a poor devil like Vaillant. The young man now in custody was a bourgeois, an intellectual, a fact that, according to one journalist, reflected "our so troubling and complex contemporary life."

The prosperous city panicked yet again. Where would the next bomb explode? Must Parisians now fear bourgeois bombers as well? Police worried about an identical attack on the Grand Hôtel and guarded major Parisian monuments. Small objects that resembled bombs kept turning up. Police raced to a fort near Saint-Denis, carrying a map found in an anarchist's room that seemed to indicate that dynamite had been buried there. Indeed, a patch of dirt had apparently been turned over. Perhaps the anarchists got there first? Félix Dubois's book *The Anarchist Peril* stirred further alarm by claiming that there were tens of thousands of anarchist believers. The book recounted two decades of anarchist horrors to an eager, if fearful public.

When part of the scenery at the Théâtre de la Gaîté collapsed during a play, some audience members screamed hysterically, and chaos ensued. An electrician told police that a month earlier three men had come to ask him to put together a complicated machine that could be made to explode. He had seen them twice since then, once in Belleville. He remembered that one of them was called Émile. From Marseille, a woman wrote to warn that if the attacks were not stopped, France risked becoming "a new Poland," referring to that country's repeated partitioning by its more powerful neighbors. Montmartre's Concert Lisbonne would soon advertise that it was "the only Concert protected against Bombs," and its posters jokingly offered insurance policies against explosions, this supposedly following a pact made with groups such as The Avengers, Those Without Pity, and The Spiders of Despair.

In the meantime, the police undertook more searches of residences and arrested hundreds of anarchists, acts that ultimately affected some three thousand families. Such moves angered many ordinary people. After all, the government had not taken such aggressive and decisive action against the corrupt officials involved in the financial scandals that had rocked the Third Republic.

From London came news that employees at the Royal Observatory in Greenwich had heard an explosion late in the afternoon of February 15. Martial Bourdin, a young, solitary French anarchist and an acquaintance of Émile, had accidentally blown himself up when explosives he was carrying detonated when he tripped over the roots of a tree. The British too seemed to have something to fear, particularly as the newspapers in London speculated that the material for Bourdin's bomb (intended to destroy the Royal Observatory) had come from Émile's room in Paris and that the Autonomy Club had offered a course in chemistry, with the goal of producing such explosives. In April, two young Italian anarchists who, following the precise instructions of Johann Most for the preparation of bombs, were arrested by Scotland Yard for planning to bomb the London Stock Exchange. Their goal: to kill "moneyed bourgeois."

The police showed up in Brévannes on February 15. Madame Henry tried to appear calm, but she was of course extremely nervous. She did not want to talk about her son, whom she said she had not seen since August 1892. Yet neighbors had seen Émile there on occasion during the previous autumn and believed that his mother had given him some money so that he could get by.

Three journalists made their way to Brévannes the next day by train. They then walked an hour along a path lined with fields and orchards, interspersed by small houses with chickens pecking in the yard. Finally, amid flowering acacias and thorny bushes stood the auberge, recently whitewashed, with the sign À L'ESPÉRANCE, VINS ET RESTAURANT above the door. The auberge had done well enough while the hospice across the road was still under construction. But now, since most of the work had been completed, Madame Henry had less business. Soon hundreds of thousands of readers became familiar with the simple country auberge, with its sparse furnishings and bare walls. They also came to know the small, sad lady of about fifty years with gray hair, her eyes rimmed in red. On the day the journalists visited, she seemed confused but expressed herself clearly in a strong Midi accent. Four workers sat around the wooden table, talking in low voices and sharing a bottle of wine. Her aunt and Jules were there. Madame Henry did not hide the fact that her husband's radical politics had influenced her son, nor that her eldest son was in prison. But she insisted that Émile could not be the dynamiter of the Café Terminus—he was simply incapable of hurting anyone. She had no reason to be ashamed of Émile, who adored her and had given her nothing but satisfaction. Over the next few days, several of Émile's classmates went to Brévannes to express their incredulity. And Émile's mother began to receive upsetting, anonymous letters, some merely vulgar insults written in the margins of articles clipped from the Parisian press about her son.

On February 16, Judge Meyer ordered Émile's transfer from a holding cell to the Conciergerie. In 1826 the original entrance had been walled up, ultimately replaced by a new gate constructed on the quay. The old cells of the Conciergerie, which had held Louis XVI, Marie-Antoinette, and the revolutionaries Danton, Saint-Just, and Robespierre, were no longer in use, replaced by seventy-three modern cells that were now part of the complex of the Palais de Justice. Learning that Ravachol had occupied the same cell, Émile enthused that he seemed to be breathing in an ethereal atmosphere: "I am transfigured! Oh, Ravachol, give me counsel, help me, I beg you!"

Cells numbers 1 and 2 had been transformed into a larger single cell to accommodate the two guards who would be with Émile around the clock. They were ordered to obtain as much information as they could. The prisoner tried to convert his guards to anarchism, as Ravachol had tried to do. Émile got along particularly well with the guard Duthion. The two had coincidentally seen each other in April 1893, when Émile went to pay a call on his aunt, the marquise de Chamborant, in the hope, unrealized, of obtaining five hundred francs; Duthion had worked for her then. All of Paris soon knew of the conversations between Émile and his two guards, as journalists confidently placed quotation marks around the comments and revelations they reported; some of the information obviously came directly from the guards, in exchange for cash. Two newspapers quickly mentioned that Émile was well known in anarchist circles and meetings for "his easy gusto and his mocking irony" and that he had earned the admiration of his fellow anarchists and the attention of the police.

On February 17, a magistrate, three gendarmes, two clerks, and a policeman arrived at the auberge in Brévannes and tore through everything, including Madame Henry's bed and the rooms rented out to workers. In the kitchen they tasted the salt to make sure it was not some sort of deadly explosive. Émile's mother explained that a pot contained potassium, used for cleaning. They took several small tubes that the elder Fortuné had used to store minerals collected in the mines of Catalonia, and bullets from an old rifle that had belonged to a childhood friend. They seized letters that Fortuné had sent his mother from the Clairvaux prison, as well as the letter purportedly sent by Émile from Germany just as he was supposed to enter the army. They also took a photo of Fortuné, taken in Dijon in April 1892 with a group of anarchists, on which could be seen a black flag with the words DEATH TO THE BOURGEOISIE! At the back of the garden, in the middle of a group of poplar trees, was a hole several yards in circumference. Six steps led down to a sparsely furnished cave, with a table and two chairs. There the police found a wooden box, full of anarchist brochures, such as Fortuné's "Ravachol, an Anarchist? Absolutely!"

A second investigating magistrate, Judge Espinas, was charged with solving the mystery of the explosion at 11, avenue de l'Opéra fifteen months earlier. Émile at first denied having had anything to do with the bomb that ultimately exploded in the police station. But on February 23, he asked to be taken to see Judge Espinas. He told him that he had left the bomb in front of the Carmaux Mining Company, describing its composition with pride.

A week after the explosion at the Terminus, Émile gave the investigating judge Meyer a letter for his mother, listing the return address as the Conciergerie.

My dear little Mother,

You must have suffered when newspapers reported what I did last Monday. Believe me that before I committed that act, I thought very much about you and all those who are so dear to me. But what can one do? Motives that you cannot understand won out, and I threw my bomb into the Terminus. Since my arrest, I have often thought of you, and I have suffered because I realize the sadness into which you must be plunged. Nevertheless, dear Mother, you must overcome your pain. You must not let your tears be paraded before the spiteful and the indifferent. You must not believe those who will say that your son is a criminal. You know me and can say to them that the real criminals are those who make life impossible for anyone with a heart, those men who uphold a society in which everyone suffers. You can tell them that those who in our society refuse to accept a role that their very dignity rejects will take vengeance. On the side of the people, they devote themselves totally to their emancipation. Understand that very well, my

Mother. Far from being embarrassed by me, whom you have nursed and given heart, be proud of what I have done. You will carry with you the esteem, the sympathy, and the affection of the only people who should really matter. I will have the pleasure of seeing and kissing you, my dear Mother. Ask my judge M. Meyer for authorization to see me, but promise me that you will be strong. Give a hug to my little Jules. If you can bring him with you, please do. He must have grown quite a bit since I last saw him, and he probably has begun to understand. Do not forget my Aunt Michalet, who must also be suffering. As for Fortuné, I will write him myself. Remember me to all our friends. See you soon, my little Mother. A thousand kisses from your son.

On reading Émile's letter admitting responsibility for the bomb at the Café Terminus, Rose Caubet Henry exclaimed, thinking of the suffering of her family after her husband had been condemned to death in absentia by the French state and moved to exile in Spain, "He has avenged his father!" When his mother was the next day brought into the office of Judge Meyer, the bomber was at first visibly moved by seeing her, turning pale, with tears welling up in his eyes. He then returned to his steely demeanor, exhorting her to have courage. When she started to ask about what he had done, the son rebuffed her. "Don't speak to me about it. What I did, I wanted to do. Your tears serve no purpose." He told his mother that before the bombing he had selected a lawyer, knowing that he would likely be captured. He had thought of everything. To which his mother replied, "Everything, my poor child, except your mother."

However, the lawyer Émile had chosen refused to take his case. His mother then chose a young lawyer called Hornbostel, a nationalist and a political reactionary. Hornbostel was one reason Parisian newspapers were so well informed about Émile. The lawyer furnished *Le Temps* with his account of his first meeting with the accused. Leaks to the press originated with judicial sources as well as prison guards: one published report referred specifically to piece number 462 of the dossier.

Hornbostel initially insisted that he could save Émile's life, despite the latter's admission that he had been responsible for the earlier bomb, which complicated things considerably. When news came that Borde, one of those wounded at the Terminus, had died from his wounds on March 12, Émile's only reaction was that this would add one more victim to his total. Borde's death put an end to any hope Hornbostel had entertained of avoiding the death penalty.

At the paper store on rue La Fayette, where Émile claimed to have purchased the metal pen case that he had transformed into a detonator, the merchant produced a bill of sale that matched the date—November 4, 1892—that Émile had provided. During a reconstruction of the morning of November 8, he demonstrated without the slightest hesitation that he knew the building well at 11, avenue de l'Opéra, although he had not seen a mirror at the end of the vestibule, thinking it a passage instead. He recalled that there had been a sign for the company, indicating that the offices were up one floor. The sign was no longer there, but when the investigating magistrate asked an employee of the Carmaux Mining Company to find the old sign, it turned out to be exactly as Émile had described it. Judge Espinas viewed Émile's summary of events on the morning of November 8, 1892 as conclusive.

Understandably frantic, Rose Caubet Henry made contact with Dr. Goupil, the friend of the family who had cared for Fortuné upon his return to Paris. Could Émile's actions be explained by madness? The doctor, a gray-haired, robust presence, believed that a neurasthenia "always threatens exhausted brains"—he had in 1876 written about such a theory. He believed that a person could not work more than eight hours a day without risking serious mental disorders. Émile had had a great amount of work imposed on him in school. Could the stress have caused lasting damage?

In the meantime, Émile could hardly complain about his conditions in the Conciergerie. The relative comfort of his cell was making him "lazy and passive," as he put it. He often stayed in bed "like a *rentier*" after ten hours of sleep. If the guards woke him up too early, they risked his bad humor. He had the right to one hot bath per week and could wash his feet each day. His mother dropped off clean linen, and every few days, Madame Denaples, who ran a small restaurant on rue Saint-Martin in central Paris, where Émile's widowed seventy-year-old aunt had long worked as the cashier, brought clean clothes and homemade food. Local restaurants provided the guards' food, which they sometimes shared with their charge. After lunch, Émile lay on his bed or on a mattress on the floor, reading what books were available in the prison library—some with pages missing because prisoners needed them to serve an alternative, hygienic use. The director of the Conciergerie and Hornbostel brought him other titles to augment the prison's paltry selection. He read Alexandre Dumas, Herbert Spencer's *First Principles of Biology,* and three novels by Zola, including *La Débâcle,* about the terrible year of 1870–71, which Émile's father had seen firsthand, and *Germinal,* as well as Dostoyevsky's *Crime and Punishment,* which was his favorite.

Following what he called "a rather amicable discussion" in his cell with the director of the Conciergerie on February 27, Émile penned a long account of anarchist ideas. The director had asked him to do so, perhaps out of curiosity or in the hope of uncovering evidence that could be used against his prisoner. Describing authority, property, and religion as enemies of humanity in the quest for "absolute equality," Émile predicted that two or three generations were all it would take "to save mankind from the influence of the artificial civilization to which it is subjected today. We must throw down this antiquated, rotten edifice. And that is what we are doing."

Sometimes Émile walked in the prison garden, which was really just a large exercise yard decorated with three miserable little shrubs—two dwarf lilacs and a collapsing spindle tree—which nonetheless brightened the gray pavement and red brick wall with a splash of green. In the evening, he smoked his pipe and sometimes played cards, for tiny sums of money, with his guards, for whom he occasionally wrote verse. Upon waking in the morning, he often sang anarchist songs. "Dame Dynamite" was one of his favorite tunes. On one occasion, he shocked his guards by announcing that he was about to say his morning prayers, at which point he paused and began singing "The Martyrs of Anarchism."

Visiting days at the Conciergerie were Sunday and Thursday. For one hour, prisoners could sit across from their visitors, separated by wire screens. On one occasion he told his mother that the long-awaited social revolution might well come before his trial, and thus she should not worry. Overall, Émile seemed surprisingly uninterested by what was happening outside the prison, rarely looking out at the quays.

In the meantime, newspapers debated the significance of the man in prison and his bomb. Maurice Barrès, the right-wing nationalist, considered Émile's attack a turning point in modern French history. He did not have much good to say about young people in France in the early 1890s. Barrès wondered if the disenchanted and dangerous Émile Henry might be part of a new wave. Henri Ribeyre of *La Revue Blanche,* a journal of literature and art, countered by arguing that it was difficult to blame the educational system. Uneducated workers had shown themselves capable of making bombs that were just as effective as the one tossed into the Café Terminus. Could it be a generational thing, involving those born at about the time of the Commune? The victory of the bourgeoisie over the Communards in 1871 had been total and devastating. (One journalist insisted that Émile had been conceived during the Commune, which explained it all.) The amnesty of 1880 had never really been accepted by the French upper classes, who had refused to pardon the insurgents. The flame of vengeance for the Commune still burned, and now it had killed. Émile had chosen as his target ordinary bourgeois, the base upon which the republic had been built. Émile's father had suffered at their hands. They would now pay the price.

The largely upper-class readership of Le Figaro was given yet another indictment of French youth. Émile Henry was a young citizen of the fin-de-siècle, bringing to the disinherited "a new formula." Rather than accept their suffering or be consoled by religious faith, such young people engaged in open rebellion against the laws of society. Émile seemed to be "a bacillus" of modern education, lacking any instruction in the principles of morality. The right-wing La Patrie recalled a prediction made by one of Proudhon's early enemies, who wrote in 1840 that educated young people who could not find a proper place in society could become the enemies of society.

Amid daily police searches and arrests of anarchists, a small bomb exploded in Lyon, and another one was discovered in Saint-Étienne. In Paris, railroad workers discovered a bomb placed against a pillar near a train about to leave for Mulhouse. To the Conciergerie, Hornbostel brought news that a small bomb had exploded on the evening of April 4 in the small, elegant restaurant of the Hôtel Foyot, across from the Luxembourg Palace, where the Senate met. The prince of Wales liked to eat there when he was in Paris. Only two full tables were occupied at the time in the restaurant. By incredible coincidence, at one of the tables sat Laurent Tailhade, a critic and poet with anarchist sympathies. His dinner companion was Lia Mialhe (also known as "Madame Roux," as well as "Violette"), a milliner, with whom he lived. The bomb, which had been placed outside on a windowsill near the table, exploded as the waiter was describing a dish to the couple.

Laurent Tailhade was perhaps best known for his rather flippant commentary after Vaillant threw his small bomb into "The Aquarium": "What do the waves of humanity matter so long as the gesture is beautiful!" The explosion at the Foyot took out one of Tailhade's eyes. The bomb was probably placed by the anarchist literary critic Félix Fénéon, perhaps inspired by his friend Émile.

That evening Fénéon coolly took an omnibus home to rue Lepic in Montmartre. When someone on the bus exclaimed that he had heard that another bomb had gone off, Fénéon indicated that it had been at the Foyot, a fact not yet known. He later admitted that he was responsible. In his cell, Émile appeared "delighted" by the news. "Once more, the idea [of anarchist bombs] has shown its value," he commented.

Émile had not been allowed to see any of the letters that had arrived at the Conciergerie for him; they were apparently being kept by one of the prosecuting attorneys in an attempt to gather other leads. On March 6, Girard, the chemist, came to the Conciergerie. He was carrying a pot half full of sand. When he asked Émile to show him how he had closed the bomb after assembling it, he refused to do so. This convinced the judge that someone (probably Paul Bonnard, "Père Duchesne") must have helped him assemble it.

Then there was the woman seen by the law student on the stairs at 11, avenue de l'Opéra. Who was she? The anarchist Mérigeau, recently imprisoned, had told an undercover agent that the woman seen on the stairs was "Rosalie," Mariette Soubère, a twenty-four-year-old ribbon worker and anarchist from Saint-Étienne who lived with *compagnon* Joseph Béala in Saint-Denis. Both had been accused of helping Ravachol kill two women in July 1891 in Saint-Étienne. However, a meeting in the judge's office made it clear that Mariette Soubère and Émile had never before met. The police then arrested the singer Adrienne Chailley, known as "Marie Puget." She knew the Henry brothers and closely resembled the woman seen on the staircase. The undercover agent "Thanne" believed that she had carried the bomb into the building and up to the mezzanine. Following the explosion at the police station, she had stopped singing, drank even more, and now thought she saw police agents behind every plant. When confronted in the judge's office with Adrienne Chailley and Bonnard, Émile turned pale but shook Bonnard's hand and winked at the woman. Back in his cell he told the guards that he only knew Bonnard, although he later asked if Adrienne Chailley had been released, indicating that they did indeed know each other.

On February 23, police raised the possibility that the woman seen on the stairs might have been Émile himself, in drag. His youthful appearance and short stature might have helped him momentarily pass for a young woman; his short hair could easily have been covered by a woman's wig.

Judge Espinas, hoping to discover the identity of the woman, became obsessed with discovering Émile's mistress, someone willing to serve as an accomplice. In one session, Émile was confronted with Madame Élise Schouppe (most recently the mistress of the anarchist burglar Ortiz), who had lived near him on rue Véron. Émile had been seen on rue Lepic several times with her husband. Espinas believed Madame Schouppe had also been Émile's lover. Émile had once taken her and her children on a country outing to Brévannes but insisted that he "had never had relations with that person." He had certainly had lovers but said that for such an operation as making and planting a bomb, he would never have trusted a woman.

Ten francs arrived for Émile at Meyer's office, sent by someone called Élisa. At first agents thought the money was from Madame Élise Schouppe. In fact, Élisa Gauthey had sent it—the strands of hair Émile had carried with him in his locket were of course hers. Meyer had Madame Gauthey arrested as a potential material witness on March 13.

On March 15, the Belgian anarchist Philibert Pauwels, a friend of Émile, entered the church of the Madeleine, carrying a bomb. Pauwels was much more like Ravachol than Émile. If anyone most fit Bakunin's ideal of an anarchist—"the devil in the flesh"—it was Pauwels. Born in Flanders in Belgium in 1864, he had been an awful pupil in school, of limited intelligence, compounded by eye and ear problems. Pauwels was the black sheep of a respectable working-class family—his father was a master cabinetmaker known as "Rouge-Barette" who worked and drank hard; his mother was a caring parent. Two well-respected uncles worked in nearby mines. Pauwels was a disreputable character who even cheated in games with other children. Leaving home at the age of fourteen, he went to Paris in the early 1880s and found some work in the glove-making industry before returning to Belgium, where he skipped out on military service.

Pauwels had first came to the attention of the police as a militant anarchist in January 1885 in Saint-Denis, where he founded the group Anarchist Youth of Saint-Denis and participated in other groups in Montmartre, Montreuil, and Paris. At a meeting of the Equals of Montmartre, he met the young Auguste Vaillant, as well as Sébastien Faure. However, after a violent argument, Pauwels never returned to that particular group. Whenever he found employment, he was considered a good worker. He sold copies of the anarchist newspaper *Land and Liberty* and provided other reading material to workers who came to his house, where he displayed the black flag of anarchism. He married Albertine Lardon, an embroiderer working in Saint-Denis, in 1886, and four years later they and their young daughter moved to Argenteuil. Pauwels's wife, who suffered from tuberculosis, also became a militant anarchist. She once told her husband that the day she felt that the end was near, he should get a bomb for her, and her final effort would be to use it against the bourgeoisie.

The Belgian made contact with Dutch, Russian, German, and Spanish anarchists, as well as French and Belgian *compagnons,* cranking out antimilitary propaganda and traveling frequently to Brussels. In 1891, he found a job in a factory in the Parisian suburbs. He turned up at an anarchist gathering at place de l'Opéra, the heart of enemy territory, and later in Saint-Denis, where he gave a fiery speech asking the *compagnons* to stay away from work on May 1 and burn down their factories and the town hall for good measure. He was ordered to leave France in April 1891, in part because of his role in another strike. But he had disappeared.

In early July, police undertook a clumsy search of the residence of Pauwels's wife, in Argenteuil. They failed to discover letters that were poorly hidden—and which his wife burned after the men departed. On July 21, 1891, police swooped down on an apartment in Paris where Pauwels was staying and discovered explosives. Expelled from France, he penned a request asking to be taken to the Luxembourg border (he could not be returned to Belgium because no agreement existed for the extradition of those fleeing military conscription). Gendarmes took Pauwels there in a police wagon.

During the next year, Pauwels bounced between Luxembourg, from which he was also eventually expelled, Geneva, and Paris, where he was suspected of being involved in a plot to blow up the police station in Levallois-Perret. He abandoned his wife and daughter, who moved to Saint-Denis, where they lived with her parents and two brothers in abject misery on the ground floor of a brick hovel that was blackened by the smoke of nearby chimneys.

In 1892, Pauwels assumed the identity of a worker from the provinces, "Claude Defosse," one of many aliases that he used over the years. A heavy drinker of absinthe, that dangerous and potentially addictive drink made from wormwood, Pauwels developed a reputation for brutality, which alienated many *compagnons,* who considered him unbalanced. Also known as "Pointy Nose," the somber, sad Pauwels always spoke of the bourgeoisie with hatred, promising to wipe them out. He now survived by working as a tanner, borrowing money from militants in Saint-Denis and elsewhere, stealing (or living off the thefts committed by others), and receiving small sums from anarchist groups. Élisée Reclus may have given him a little money. Throughout his travels, he remained a frenetic propagandist, heaping abuse on Sébastien Faure, whom he called a "Jesuit." Pauwels carried a pistol and distributed propaganda encouraging soldiers to desert. Late in 1892, he was in Switzerland, and in January 1893, in Marseille and then Barcelona. While working for a time in a factory in Saint-Ouen, Pauwels found or stole the papers of a coworker named Rabardy from Rouen, and assumed the man's identity.

While *compagnon* Émile awaited trial in the Conciergerie, Pauwels decided to strike. On February 12, he entered the extremely modest Hôtel des Carmes on rue des Carmes, and, refusing to give his name, he deposited four francs for a stay of eight days in a fifth-floor room. The next morning, he said he was Henry Sabauth, thirty-eight, a traveling salesman from Bordeaux. He told a young employee of the hotel, to whom he spoke Spanish, that he had arrived from Barcelona. Wearing a black felt hat and dark clothes, Pauwels carried a small suitcase made of gray cloth. A package about the size of a hat was attached to the suitcase with a wire.

On February 20, Pauwels left the Hôtel des Carmes for two even shabbier hotels, taking a room in each. In both he placed a small bomb, which he rigged to explode the next time the door was opened. His goal was to kill policemen. He then left a note near two police stations, saying that he, Étienne Rabardy, was going to kill himself in his hotel room. A policeman went to the hotel on rue Saint-Jacques and went up to the room with the elderly concierge. They opened the door and the bomb exploded, mortally wounding the old woman and inflicting only light injuries on the policeman. At the miserable rooming house on rue du faubourg Saint-Martin, another policeman pushed open the door. The bomb, made from a can and suspended from the door, did not explode. The policeman called for experts, who detonated the device. Five days earlier, police had found bombs of exactly the same composition—dynamite, picric acid, and chorate powder—in a bank.

At 2:40 in the afternoon of March 15, Pauwels entered the church of the Madeleine, the site of some of Paris's most elegant baptisms and marriages. In the small foyer, the bomb he was carrying exploded with such force that it could be heard across the Seine in the Chamber of Deputies. Pauwels fell to the ground, his right hand hanging by a thread, with serious wounds to his stomach and spinal column. A bullet, which had struck him in the head, was later deemed the cause of death. The anarchist may have had the strength—and the presence of mind—to shoot himself. Pauwels carried with him a picture of Ravachol, along with details of the martyr's execution. No one else was injured, and damage to the church was slight.

Paris continued on high alert. Policemen went from rooming house to rooming house, carrying photos of Pauwels and searching for information on men of ages twenty-five to thirty-five who had not returned to their lodgings on the night of March 15. They came up with five names, including two described as "miserably dressed," hardly a distinguishing characteristic. Employees of the Hôtel de Carmes formally identified Pauwels as the person staying in the hotel. His father-in-law came to identify him at the morgue but refused to claim the body.

In his cell, Émile speculated at first that the bomber of the church of the Madeleine was Meunier, an anarchist recently condemned to death in absentia. But when Émile asked for part of a newspaper to serve as toilet paper, a guard inadvertently gave him half of *Le Petit Journal* of March 17, which identified the dead man as his friend Pauwels. It certainly seemed that this bomb had been made from the stash of dynamite taken from Émile's room. Where was the rest?

On April 27, Émile Henry went on trial for his life in the Assize Court. The court was within the Palais de Justice, that monumental stage for Paris's major and often theatrical trials. Standing between two enormous corridors that joined the east and west entrances, the rectangular hall stood above the renovated Conciergerie prison. The space devoted to Émile's trial, and the other anarchist trials that had preceded it, reflected the Third Republic's desire to showcase its progressive system. Journalists and other spectators, entering by the door opposite the judge's bench, crammed into every available space. The upper classes, often including a disproportionate number of women, sat in front. Some clutched opera glasses so as not to miss a single detail of the spectacle. The people whom Émile hated the most would be sitting closest to him.

Magistrates and lawyers made majestic entrances through one of the two doors. The judges wore red robes trimmed in white fur, the lawyers black robes and elaborate traditional hats. Below them sat the lawyers who would represent the prosecution and the defense.

The prosecutor was Bulot, of the Clichy trial, whose apartment Ravachol had attempted to blow up. Two long galleries of seats lined each side of the courtroom. The jury sat on the same side of the room as the prosecutor. Across from them stood a small enclosed dock for the accused, guards posted on either side. Another dock seated more than fifty journalists from twenty Parisian newspapers, ready to cater to the public's intense fascination with the trial. Windows across from the prisoner's dock flooded the courtroom with light, leaving the jury in the shadows. In the middle of the hall stood a table, on which was placed material evidence: the battered remnants of tables; a dozen chairs piled one upon the other, some peppered with holes; bloodstained clothes; broken pitchers and pieces of tableware; shattered boards and other wreckage brought from the Café Terminus. In front of this dramatic evidence and before a painting of Christ, witnesses would swear to tell the truth. At the back of the court the public waited eagerly—some occupying reserved seats, others boldly pushing their way forward in the back section. As the bourgeois press described it, the crowd was bathed in the plebeian aromas of sausage and garlic.

Guards led Émile from the prison below, up the spiral staircase between the two courtrooms, and through the little door into the courtroom. His entrance hushed all conversation. Every eye focused on him. He had the bearing of a young student at an elite school, awaiting an exam. Dressed properly, even elegantly, this dandy of anarchism wore a nice white shirt with a stiff, starched white collar, a black jacket, and a black satin tie. In the back of the courtroom sat his mother, wearing an old dress, an equally worn cape, and a hat, decorated with a small branch of wisteria. She seemed beaten down, resigned to the suffering that had overwhelmed her. Near her sat Dr. Goupil.

The prisoner's ironic smile seemed to broaden when he saw the packed courtroom. Before sitting down, he paused to gaze at the public. Five or six court artists took up their pens and brushes in order to immortalize him. Now doors swung open, and the lawyers entered.

The presiding magistrate opened the trial, asking the prisoner to state his age, occupation, and residence: "Émile Henry, age twenty-one and a half," he replied in his husky, adolescent voice. His domicile? "The Conciergerie." Émile listened impassively to the charges—one murder and twenty attempted murders at the Café Terminus and five murders at the police station in November 1892—and occasionally, he reached up nervously to rearrange his hair. But on the whole he seemed very sure of himself and his ability to handle any question. He reacted to the charges with smiles, shrugs, or gestures of denial. Several times, with his eyes half shut, he seemed to be reliving the acts of which he stood accused.

On the side of the defense stood the bearded defense lawyer Hornbostel. Virtually unknown in Paris, the son of a prominent lawyer in Marseille, Hornbostel knew that playing on the big stage of the Assize Court of the Seine could make his career. To prepare, he had taken ten elocution lessons from Silvain, a well-known actor at the Comédie-Française, who himself was in the courtroom, eager to see his pupil perform. But Hornbostel was outmatched. He had not yet mastered the dramatic, theatrical gestures so necessary to arguing a case, and did not use his shoulders to impress judge, jury, and audience. He mumbled. And he defended a man determined to be convicted and executed, one who sought revolutionary immortality.

The role of the presiding magistrate, Judge Potier, would ordinarily have been to "unmask" the accused, poking holes in his defense with leading questions. This trial would be different. Émile admitted, with unrestrained pride, to virtually all the charges against him. He contradicted or corrected minor points in an arrogant, mocking tone. He had not entered the Café Terminus at 8:30 P.M., but at 8. He had not hidden a bomb under the belt of his pants, but rather in the pocket of his overcoat—"I wasn't going to unbutton my pants in the middle of a café!" When asked why he had chosen the particular location for his attack, he replied, "Because it was a *grand café,* frequented by the bourgeoisie." Why had he not stopped in the other big cafés he had passed along the way? "There weren't enough people. The apéritif hour of these folks was over." This sent a collective shudder through the courtroom. When asked if he had told the investigating magistrate Espinas that he wanted to kill as many people as possible to avenge Vaillant, he replied, "Absolutely," mimicking Simon *dit* Biscuit, Ravachol's boyish accomplice.

Potier interjected, "You have contempt for the lives of others?"

"No." Émile corrected him. "Only those of the bourgeosie."

He confirmed that he had fired point-blank at Gustave Étienne, the railway employee referred to by Potier as "a courageous citizen," who ran after the bomber and grabbed him. And that he had fired at the barber Léon Maurice—Émile interrupted sarcastically: "A second courageous citizen." He regretted having shot only one policeman. When the presiding judge reminded him that several of those whom he had tried to kill were workers, Émile's response was that they should have minded their own business. If he had had a better revolver, he would have killed them too. When the judge noted that the accused had constructed the bomb with the care of "a veritable artist," Émile thanked him for the compliment.

The presiding magistrate then began to try to show that Émile was anything but a victim of bourgeois society, but rather someone who "had found along his road only hands reaching out to him, protectors, and benevolent, generous people." He was, after all, a bourgeois. When Émile recounted his trip to avenue de l'Opéra that fateful afternoon, he noted wryly that he had taken public transportation. "As a good bourgeois, I did not go on foot," he said, drawing smiles. Potier pointed out that he might have been admitted to the prestigious École polytechnique. Why had he not wanted to be an officer in the army? "Nice career, in which one kills the unfortunate, as at Fourmies. I would rather be here than there!"

Potier evoked Rose Caubet Henry's "great despair" that her son had avoided military service and had been classified a deserter, then mentioned, provocatively, "another person, whose name it is useless to mention, and who, since that time, has stopped loving you," a clear reference to Élisa Gauthey. The presiding judge wanted the accused to disclose his activities during the eighteen months before the Café Terminus attack, thereby identifying accomplices. Émile would admit only to having worked for six weeks as a mechanic. He said that he had received income "from my work" and thus had been able to pay for the bomb materials himself. Émile rejected, with some indignation, the judge's suggestion that he had lived off the thefts of Ortiz. But the president insisted that "even in depriving oneself, one still needs resources in Paris." His white hands were not those of a worker, and they were "now covered with blood from murder." Émile rose to his feet and replied, "Covered with red like your robe, *monsieur le président.*" He denied being the man who had posed as a British businessman and, along with Ortiz, robbed the wealthy lady in the Norman village of Fiquefleur.

The police were still looking for Placide Schouppe and Paul Reclus, the nephew of Élisée Reclus and an advocate of the "right to theft," whom they suspected of helping Émile prepare the bomb, perhaps with Schouppe's help. Émile concluded, "'Justice' will not be satisfied with only one head—it must have two. Once again, I prepared, closed, and carried the bomb myself."

When Émile was under investigation immediately following the first bombing, the police had concluded that he would not have had time to return to rue Véron to get the bomb and take it to avenue de l'Opéra. Now an employee of the district attorney's office had duplicated the trek Émile claimed to have taken and had demonstrated that it was indeed possible to do so.* Potier finally appeared to accept Émile's version of events.

Victims of the Café Terminus bombing, ordinary people, simply told their stories, without cross-examination. Some walked with difficulty, with the help of canes or supported on the arm of someone who had been a bit luckier. Tapping his fingers incessantly on the wooden gate of the prisoner's dock, Émile looked on indifferently, remarking that he had seen many worse injuries in mining or factory accidents. Would he have used the other bombs in his room? "Naturally." When Potier interjected that he was cynical, Émile corrected him. "It is not cynicism, it is conviction!"

Potier reserved a hero's welcome for the policeman Poisson, who was wearing his new cross of the Legion of Honor, and, under his uniform, scars from two bullet wounds. Madame la Baronne d'Eckstedt, a wealthy woman who owned at least one building, and her sister both trembled when they related their evening at the Café Terminus. They had not wanted to give their names to the police, for fear of anarchist vengeance. The minister of the interior had awarded an indemnity of fifteen hundred francs to Madame Kinsbourg, another *rentière*, who had suffered three leg wounds.

A small parade of "experts" followed. The role of such witnesses became increasingly important in French legal proceedings during the last decades of the nineteenth century. Girard, the omnipresent director of the municipal laboratory, flattered Émile by saying that the bomb had been well put together, shattering marble tables and cast iron supports like flimsy wood. He described Émile's two bombs, the "reversal" device that had killed on rue des

---

* Was it remarkable for Émile to cover so much ground so quickly? A detective later made the same trek and found it took about the same time. I tried it myself in September 2005, replacing, of course, tramways and omnibuses with a bus and the métro, and the carriage with a taxi. Subtracting the thirteen minutes when my taxi could not turn left onto avenue de l'Opéra because of construction, I finished the same trip in about two hours and fifteen minutes. Parisian traffic congestion keeps today's vehicles moving at the pace of nineteenth-century tramways and omnibuses.

Bons-Enfants, and the fuse-detonated bomb that had exploded in the Terminus. When Hornbostel asked which was the more dangerous, Girard replied, "Both!" The second bomb could have been even more powerful but for a small fault in its mounting. Girard acknowledged that he and Émile had discussed this (scientist to scientist) and had agreed on the nature of the error. In Girard's opinion Émile would have needed someone to help him close the bomb, but the accused continued to insist that he had acted alone.

On the second day, the court summoned character witnesses for the defense, including one of Émile's former teachers. When Dupuy, his employer at the time of the explosion on rue des Bons-Enfants, completed his testimony, Émile cocked his head in a way that seemed to say, What is the use of defending me? His former boss replied with a shrug that suggested he had simply told the truth about the quality of his work. The comte Ogier d'Ivry, son-in-law of the marquise de Chamborant, an army officer, and a self-styled man of letters, spoke as "a bourgeois condemned to death like all the others." He testified that he considered Émile a maniac and showed his disgust for his distant relative's crimes. He explained that all the Henry family had been "rebels"—republicans under the monarchy, Communards under the Republic, and now more anarchist than anarchy itself. Throughout the parade of witnesses, Émile demonstrated emotion only when his uncle Jean Bordenave, who had returned to Paris from Italy, left the dock. The accused man's eyes became moist with tears, and he said, "Thank you, and adieu! I will never see you again!"

Dr. Goupil, after asserting that he could not swear before a God in whom he did not believe, contended that Émile was mentally disturbed, perhaps a result of the typhoid fever he had suffered when he was twelve. In Goupil's opinion, he should be examined by specialists. Émile interrupted defiantly. "Pardon, but I don't want any of that. I am not in any way mentally disturbed." The accused took full responsibility for his acts: "My head does not need to be saved. I am not mad. I am perfectly aware of what I am doing." He stated that his notable academic success demonstrated full recovery from typhoid fever. Fortuné Henry, whom the presiding judge of the court had refused to let testify as a character witness, had written Hornbostel from Clairvaux prison to support the view that his brother was insane, a result of his father's being condemned to death in France in absentia and then "reduced to wandering in a foreign land." Dr. Goupil contended that Émile suffered from oversensitivity—it was "disgust, anger, and passion" that had led to his act.

Two days before the trial, Émile had written to the judge, saying that his mother had wanted to attend but that he had tried to dissuade her from doing so, even though Hornbostel wanted her to testify on her son's behalf. She spent all of the trial (except its first moments) waiting in a small room with several friends; each day of the trial, the press depicted her plight. Fearing how the ordeal might affect her, Émile at one point stood and asked Potier to disallow her attendance at the remainder of the proceedings. Spectators murmured their support, and the presiding judge momentarily suspended the trial.

Bulot summarized the prosecution's case and demanded the death penalty. Émile seemed to be an example of "a perfect little petty bourgeois." He was a property owner in Brévannes who had received the assistance he needed from his family and teachers. He had become "profoundly proud, envious, and marked by an implacable cruelty." His poor mother inspired only great pity, but her suffering should not influence the verdict. Her son's bombs had left five widows and ten orphans. Did the accused intend to solve the gnawing problem of poverty by killing people? Only capital punishment could "provide satisfaction." Émile would try to save himself to kill again. Even if he were sent to the hellhole of a prison in Cayenne in French Guiana, Émile would escape. When Bulot said that the accused had forgotten his duties to his mother, Émile exploded, standing up and shouting, "Do not insult my mother! You will not reproach my attitude toward my mother! You never cared if she was dying of hunger!"

Émile was then asked to present his own defense, the "Declaration" that he had written in the Conciergerie. He did so, speaking slowly and clearly, at first from memory, until finally asking for his notes. He defended anarchy and "propaganda by the deed." His presentation was compelling, even riveting—impressive even to those prepared to hate him for what he had done. He began by insisting that as an anarchist, he was responsible to but one tribunal, himself.

Émile went on: The state had guillotined a man who had killed no one—Auguste Vaillant. But the bourgeoisie and its police had not counted on unknown men, waiting in the shadows, appalled by police action, eager to lash out, "in turn, to hunt the hunters." Émile really did not need a specific provocation to kill, but the timing of the bomb at the Café Terminus was in his eyes a response to the repressive campaign against the anarchists and to the judicial murders of Ravachol and Vaillant.

Vaillant had been unknown to almost all *compagnons* before his arrest, Émile explained. Yet the police campaign against anarchists had made them collectively responsible for his act. Now it was the turn of the bourgeoisie to be collectively responsible for his execution. Should anarchists carry out deeds only against deputies who pass laws against us, magistrates who apply them, or policemen who enforce them? No. The police were acting on behalf of the bourgeoisie, who profit from the labor of workers. The petty bourgeois was no better than the others, applauding the acts of the government. Living on three hundred to five hundred francs a month, they were "stupid and pretentious, always lining up on the side of the strongest." They were the ordinary clientele of the Café Terminus and the other *grands cafés*. That is why he had struck so randomly. It was time for the bourgeoisie to understand that "those who suffer have finally had enough: they are showing their teeth and will strike even more brutally than they have been abused." The anarchists had no respect for human life because the bourgeoisie itself had shown none. Those who had murdered ordinary people in Fourmies should not call others murderers:

[We will] spare neither women nor children because the women and children we love have not been spared. Are they not innocent victims, these children, who in the faubourgs slowly die of anemia, because bread is rare at home; these women who in your workshops suffer exhaustion and are worn out in order to earn forty cents a day, happy that misery has not yet forced them into prostitution; these old men whom you have turned into machines so that they can produce their entire lives and whom you throw out into the street when they have been completely depleted?

Émile remarked that he had no illusions. His act would not be understood by many ordinary people. Many workers would consider the anarchists their enemy. It did not matter. Even some anarchists would reject "propaganda by the deed," as they spent their time drawing a subtle distinction between theoreticians and terrorists. They were too cowardly to risk their lives: now was the time for "action without weakness" or retreat. In the war without pity, anarchists would ask for none. They dispensed death and knew how to submit to it. He would await the verdict of the jury with indifference. His would not be the last head that would be cut off, because those who were dying of hunger were beginning to know how to find "your cafés and great restaurants."

And then, in a remarkably brazen flourish, he concluded:

You will add other names to the bloody lists of our dead. You have hanged us in Chicago, decapitated us in Germany, garroted us in Xerez, shot us in Barcelona, guillotined us in Montbrison and in Paris, but what you can never destroy is anarchy. Its roots are too deep, born in a poisonous society which is falling apart; [anarchism] is a violent reaction against the established order. It represents the egalitarian and libertarian aspirations which are opening a breach in contemporary authority. It is everywhere, which makes anarchy elusive. It will finish by killing you.

Émile's defense caused a marked, prolonged stir in the court-room. Henri Varennes of *Le Figaro* was amazed by his composure: "He is perhaps a monster, but he is not a coward."

Maître Hornbostel, immeasurably less eloquent than Émile, de-scribed his client as "an intellectual pushed to the extreme. Noth-ing exists except what he thinks." Hornbostel asked pity for Émile, "a dreamer, a fanatic," who believed that his acts would serve hu-manity. His crimes thus should be considered crimes of passion. The lawyer earned laughter the hard way when he reminded the jury that the first bomb placed by his client was "his first infrac-tion against the rules of society!"

Hornbostel's defense was disastrous. (The actor Silvain assessed his pupil's performance, after about a dozen lessons, in this way: "He knew very well what his role should have been, his speech for the defense. I taught him certain intonations. But in the court-room, it was nothing but shit, shit, and more shit.") The journalist Varennes mocked Hornbostel's Marseille accent and "historical and literary references thrown out in no particular order, making a sort of bouillabaisse out of which emerged the names of Descartes, Mohammad, Jean-Jacques Rousseau, Voltaire, Napoleon, etc."

The jury entered the deliberating room at 6:30 P.M. and re-turned in less than an hour. Émile bounded up the stairs like the schoolboy he had recently been, smiling as he awaited the verdict. He stood with his hands in his pockets, telling a court artist sitting not far from him, "You will cut off my head." The jury found Émile guilty on all counts, with no extenuating circumstances. Asked if he had anything to say about the verdict, Émile replied that he ac-cepted it. Judge Potier pronounced the sentence of death at 7:45, to which Émile uttered, "Good." Led from the courtyard, he said to no one in particular, "Courage, comrades! And long live anarchy!"

The court clerk came to Émile's cell to ask if he wanted to ap-peal the court's verdict. He did not, adding that he would not re-quest a presidential pardon. At 9:15 he was transferred to the prison of La Roquette, in a *quartier populaire* he knew very well, near the cemetery of Père Lachaise, below the Villa Faucheur.

Rose Caubet Henry and Dr. Goupil were still convinced that it was possible to save Émile in spite of himself. The doctor wanted the court to order a psychological examination. His fixed gaze at the trial and "his loss of the instinct of self-preservation" could reflect an unstable mind. Goupil contended that "monomaniacs" spoke sensibly as long as their specific aberration had not taken over. In his view, Émile was not responsible for his acts and should not be executed. Goupil believed that at least four of the jurors had been inclined to consider "extenuating circumstances." Émile's defiance had prevented Goupil from carrying this argument further at the trial. Madame Henry hoped to plead her case to President Sadi Carnot in person, as only the president could commute the death sentence. The socialist Paul Brousse, who had left anarchism behind after originally helping create the concept of "propaganda by the deed," agreed with Hornbostel on at least one point: Émile Henry's execution would only create another martyr. Such a death "is the life of anarchism: to kill the doctrine, we must spare the indoctrinater."

On May 1, Émile wrote to his mother. He hoped that her strong will would sustain her during "this final test." She would still have two sons left. This, to be sure, was hardly what she had hoped for her middle son, "on whom she had pinned so many great hopes." This "beautiful dream" could not be realized "because life today has only suffering for us." She would hear that he was a murderer, but if he had killed, it was for "a great idea." Friends would console her and ultimately they would see in her a victim of society, which took away her son. He hoped that his younger brother, Jules, whom he believed would certainly later become "a very fierce and energetic *compagnon*," would be strong, signing "a thousand kisses from your Émile."

Émile's mother had indeed emerged as a tragic figure, a subject of public fascination and pity. When Madame Henry came to Paris, she nervously scurried here and there, always dressed in the same black dress, scarf, and simple hat adorned with a little blue flower. Her eyes reddened by tears, she sadly noted that the days were going by too quickly. She carried with her two little black bags. One contained letters regarding her son's trial; the other was full of articles clipped from newspapers, a letter from Émile, the certificate for good work in school awarded Émile by the king of Spain and by one of his French schools, and various other letters, including several from priests. A nun had sent her a "miraculous image" of the Virgin Mary, with instructions that she should pray before it round the clock, because Mary would never refuse her. She was to instruct her son to swallow the postage-stamp-sized Virgin Mary—"you give it to him by rolling it up like a little meatball, or in a little wine," so that he would not actually see the figure of Mary. "Believe me, Madame, this will really change his heart." The name of her auberge, À l'Espérance, seemed more ironic than ever. There was not much hope left.

Madame Henry implored her son to sign the appeal for clemency on May 2, the last possible day. But her son awaited execution as a deliverance—not unlike the radical revolutionary Maximilien Robespierre during the French Revolution. Émile too sought revolutionary immortality. Several days later, when told that his mother was coming to see him again, Émile told his guards, "It's useless. I don't want to see her! I don't want to see anyone!" When she arrived, he told her that her visits now hurt him. She should abandon efforts to see President Carnot. Madame Henry had already written to the president's wife, who had replied that only a defense lawyer could appeal for clemency. Émile then asked the guards to return him to his cell, and turning toward his mother, he held her two hands and said goodbye.

In the meantime, Élisa Gauthey had become a star in the Parisian press. Now all of Paris had read Émile's 1891 letters to her. As his mother put it, he was "so gentle, in those times." Two journalists went to see her in the attic apartment she shared with her husband on the sixth floor on boulevard Voltaire. Élisa was wearing her bathrobe, sometimes struggling to keep it properly closed. She would (for a price?) break her silence. She quickly insisted that she had never been the mistress of Émile. Had his passion for her brought about "the strange evolution in his mind?" She related the awkward moments during her visit to Brévannes with her husband in 1891. Since then, Émile had not ceased to proclaim his love for her, although she had time and time again reminded him that she was married to a man he knew. But he had continued to pursue her. She had never consented, never. Did she regret it? "Yes, and I will not hide it. If it is true that this passion was disastrous for him, I will always reproach myself that it was cruel for him." She could not sleep. She had stopped living. Yes, she wished that she had been his mistress.

Meanwhile, Hornbostel awaited the call to go to the Palais de l'Élysée, where he would plead his case. By tradition, no one condemned to death could be executed before at least a lawyer had spoken about the situation with the president of the republic.

In the middle of place de l'Opéra, policeman Poisson was directing traffic, surrounded by carriages and buses. The policeman had no interest in going to see the blade fall: "If they cut off his head, there will be one less of those bandits."

For days rumor had the execution set for May 12. Yet in the wee hours of each day earlier that month, a small crowd showed up at place de la Roquette just in case. The police too were there, to maintain order. Bars in the vicinity stayed open late to accommodate revelers, before closing at 3 or 3:30 A.M., when it became clear that the guillotine would not be operated that night. A bomb exploded on the elegant avenue Kléber on May 11.

Invented during the French Revolution by a doctor of the same name, the guillotine, popularly known as "the Widow," became a symbol of the French nation. Reflecting the empire of "reason," it eliminated both class distinction and hideous torture from state-sanctioned executions, and it delivered instantaneous death. Public executions became something of a spectacle, and the scaffold first stood at place de la Révolution, where revolutionary justice would be dispensed by the "national razor." Enormous crowds watched the execution of Louis XVI, Marie-Antoinette, Danton, Robespierre, and many others, carefully studying the comportment of the executioner and, above all, those about to die. Viewers leaned forward to catch the final words of the condemned and watched as the executioner triumphantly held up each severed head.

In 1851, the scaffold was moved outside the gates of the prison of La Roquette in Paris. It was also reduced in size from its previous more theatrical dimensions. During the Commune, a crowd seized the guillotine from its place near the prison and burned it at the foot of a statue of Voltaire. The guillotine returned with the smashing of the Commune, but in 1872 its scaffold disappeared altogether. Henceforth, the guillotine stood on the ground, bringing to an end that dramatic final walk up the stairs. As the priest blessed the victim, the executioner's assistants grabbed him and instantly threw him down onto the plank, so that he would not have time to realize what was happening. During the period 1800–1825, about 120 people were guillotined per year. That number declined in the following decades, to about 28 a year in the 1860s and then about 10 to 12 a year into the mid-1880s.

The role of the head executioner, "Monsieur de Paris," remained paramount, extending in a well-known lineage from the famous Sanson, who worked during the French Revolution, to Anatole Deibler, who would carry out the last public execution shortly before World War II. Executioners, like butchers, were considered a blood trade. They existed as a caste apart, and their families intermarried.

In 1894, Monsieur de Paris was Antoine-Louis Deibler, the son and grandson of executioners. Like past masters of the guillotine, his was a household name, his renown reinforced by his handiwork with Ravachol and Vaillant. He had received death threats, and one rumor had hinted at a plot to kidnap him. Someone had even tried to steal the guillotine itself. Old and ill, Deibler walked with an unsteady gait, and his hands trembled. Now in the twilight of his distinguished career, he would retire four years later, having executed 360 people, 154 as chief executioner, and he would be succeeded by his son.

On Saturday, May 20, Maître Hornbostel finally received a summons to see President Carnot at the Palais de l'Élysée in the afternoon. In what was only a very brief encounter, the president promised to examine with care both Émile Henry's dossier and the request for clemency put forward by Madame Henry and Dr. Goupil. Hornbostel naively left the palace with a sense of hope, believing that, at a minimum, the execution would be put off. Yet the lawyer was barely out the door when Carnot sent the dossier to the minister of justice, denying a pardon. The order for Émile's execution went out at 4:30 P.M. At 8 P.M. on Sunday, May 20, two gendarmes carried the orders to Deibler, popularly known as "Doctor Deibler" even though all his "patients" expired on the table. Deibler was ordered to report for work at the Roquette prison at 4:00 A.M. on Monday, May 21. The news of the impending execution was kept secret until about 10 P.M. Sunday night, in order to make possible anarchist attacks hard to plan so swiftly, as well as to limit the crowds that would inevitably flock to place de la Roquette. In Barcelona, six men accused of a bloody attack against the Liceo opera house were executed the same day.

Maurice Barrès walked, at about 2 A.M., through place Voltaire (now place Léon Blum), where the "personalities"—journalists, politicians, writers, and others having prefectorial authorization—were allowed to pass on the way to place de la Roquette. There, they could stand in the equivalent of theater boxes at the site of execution. Walking up rue de la Roquette, he passed the Petite-Roquette on the left, where young convicts and children were incarcerated. To the right stood the prison de la Roquette, which had been constructed in 1836 to accommodate convicts condemned to death—their stays would be short—and to hold some others with life sentences. It consisted of two buildings of three floors each. Beginning in 1851, the guillotine was placed there on five stone slabs. Thus the prison was also known as the "Abbey of Five Stones."

The site seemed intentionally provocative. To decapitate criminals just off a street that leads from place de la Bastille to Ménilmontant was "to put on a play for the 'dangerous classes' right at the frontier of their territory, [showing them] the pitiless rigor of justice."

Barrès and his friend Charles Formentin, armed with cards that identified them as journalists, passed through the police barriers. Place de la Roquette could accommodate only about 150 people. The politician Georges Clemenceau was there, as well, with his felt hat pulled over his ears, discussing in animated fashion the upcoming event with journalists. Some people of "dubious" appearance had managed to pass through the barriers without proper credentials. Formentin was a novice observer. He had heard dramatic tales of the assembly of the guillotine—the arrival of the cavalry, the sound of sabers being drawn, all amid the flickering of lights piercing the predawn fog. He awaited "a solemnity of horror and majesty" but found only "the absolutely coldest and most disgusting performance."

Peering into the night, Barrès could see the lights of the prison shining through a single door, the one that would lead Émile to his death. Gradually he could see small groups of policemen assembling. Above the square, windows of apartment houses were lit up, providing a perch for well-placed residents. Could Émile's anarchist friends be planning an attack? At the corner of rue de la Roquette and rue de la Folie-Regnault, "Monsieur de Paris" was playing cards with his assistant, the same game that Émile had enjoyed with his guards.

The door of a nearby café had been shut to protect Deibler from gawkers, and policemen were posted outside. Yet at 2:30, relatively few people had gathered. Émile was not well known to the petty criminals who sometimes showed up at executions to express sympathy and solidarity. He was a mere "aristocrat of crime," whose death would be witnessed by a carefully chosen public. In a neighborhood bar, hardly fifty people had assembled. The owner of the bar complained. Vaillant's execution had not brought him much business either. Some executions brought in more than eight hundred francs. Tonight, the take would be about forty. "Don't talk to me about anarchists," he snarled.

Five hundred policemen, four companies of municipal guards, and two squadrons of cavalrymen arrived to take up their positions. A platoon of twelve gendarmes and their commander marched in at precisely 3 A.M., accompanied by a cold wind from the north. Plainclothes policemen placed themselves here and there, ready to record in writing any interesting conversations they might overhear. Shadows began to appear in the windows of nearby apartments. One Englishman tried to force his way into the reserved viewing space, finally settling for a dangerous spot on a nearby roof, for which he paid three francs. The chaplain of the prison, l'Abbé Valadier, arrived in a carriage, soon joined by an investigating magistrate sent by a judge to take down any last-minute revelations offered by Émile Henry.

Only high-ranking functionaries from government ministries and journalists who had managed to get official passes were allowed into the reserved area on place de la Roquette. The latter included Madame Yver, a female reporter, who was believed to be the first woman authorized to witness an execution in France—at least up close—since the Revolution.

As they waited, people spoke little, and their words were soft, almost inaudible. Then, at 3:15 A.M., lights appeared in the distance, and the sound of wheels on pavement indicated that two wagons, escorted by guards, were approaching from the direction of Père Lachaise Cemetery farther up the hill. The first carried Deibler's principal assistant, the second, the "the wood of justice." At first sight, they could easily be taken for the wagons of traveling entertainers arriving for a provincial fair. They stopped to the left of the short avenue that led to the square, in front of the prison itself, where the scaffold would be placed on the five famous stones. The executioner and several of his assistants left the café to go to work, dressed in frock coats and tall hats. Drivers and ordinary workmen in blue overalls joined them. A sense of horrific anticipation settled over the small square. A horse began to whinny, and continued to do so about every five minutes. The assistants stepped forward, cigarettes between their pursed lips.

The workmen laid the pieces of the guillotine near the sidewalk. Under the executioner's watchful eye, the structure was assembled like a giant toy. Not a single nail was needed. The red leather sheath containing the huge triangular blade leaned against a post. A new light suddenly appeared, a lantern held by Deibler, who was overseeing all. He wanted the barriers moved back. "I need space and air and I don't have any," he said. In good form, although grumpy as always, "Monsieur de Paris" barked out expert orders left and right. The soles of his shoes scraped against the cobblestones as he hobbled along, occasionally leaning on his cane.

A lantern marked the place the guillotine was to be set. Pulleys would raise the blade above the cradle, on which the condemned man's neck would be positioned, awaiting the blade. The way Deibler checked each piece of the apparatus reminded viewers of the scrupulousness of a watchmaker or a surgeon, although Deibler was in more of a hurry. There was nothing remotely "judicial" about him. He greeted any attempt to draw him into the conversation with a dismissive grunt. Asked if his clients usually died well, he replied, "They generally are thugs—you have to drag them!" When someone bumped into a pail, he snarled, "Why are you fucking around with my accessories?" An assistant removed the blade from the sheath. The executioner tried out the guillotine blade twice, expressing satisfaction with the dry, metallic thud it made after plunging down along the grooves of the frame. The equipment needed for the aftermath was also in order: the body would be rolled down a plank into a large box, alongside the basket that would accommodate the head. "Everything is ready," Deibler announced to no one in particular, while his young, chubby, red-cheeked assistant looked on. To Clemenceau, "Monsieur de Paris" was "as miserable as his machine."

Some of the workmen, their tasks completed, went back to the wagons to change into their regular clothes. They would now become part of the audience. Many in the crowd had witnessed several executions: they followed the preparation of the guillotine, silently checking off each step.

Dawn arrived slowly, another gray Parisian day. The trees growing here and there on place de la Roquette seemed sickly, with only scrawny tufts of leaves. The gas lamps, which had put an end to night executions by torchlight, were extinguished. Deibler's lamp alone still shone, moving slowly about. Some of the assistants stacked sponges and cloths, placing nearby a basket with small pieces of absorbent wood. An "awful brute, sort of a stable hand," arrived with a broom. Deibler checked that several buckets had been filled with water and that a broom had been left nearby. The ground would be covered with blood. In the distance, a dog barked incessantly.

Émile could see nothing of these preparations. He had gone to bed at 9 P.M. He too would be getting up very early and needed some sleep. He had written several letters, which he left in the drawer of the table in his cell. When various magistrates, the prison clerk, Abbé Valadier, and the chief policeman for the neighborhood entered his cell, Émile was sound asleep, his head resting against the wall next to his bed. The guard Brun tapped him lightly on the shoulder and offered him the traditional stiffening word: "Courage!" Telling the condemned man that his appeal had been turned down by the president of the Republic seemed pointless. Émile dressed while sitting, pulling on the pants he had worn on the day of his arrest and a large red belt. He said only that he did not need courage because he had always had that; he would not be a coward in the face of death. He did not want to speak with the prison chaplain and refused the traditional offer of a glass of brandy. Louis Deibler, with one or two of his assistants, had entered the prison door, over which was inscribed LIBERTY, EQUALITY, FRATERNITY. Led to the office of the prison clerk, Émile greeted the executioner: "It's you, Monsieur Deibler." Outside, all eyes rested on the door, including those of five little girls who sat close together on a nearby roof to watch. Gendarmes mounted their horses.

The executioner pushed down the collar of Émile's shirt, while his assistants bound his hands tightly, so tightly that Émile asked several times if they could loosen the bonds a bit. They shackled his legs, so that he could walk only in tiny steps, and with great difficulty. The object of their attention pointed out that he had no intention of trying to escape. But there was almost certainly another reason for ensuring so much discomfort: to make it difficult for Émile to appear too brave. A magistrate asked if he would care to make any revelations about accomplices "at the supreme hour." Émile noted that this was at least the thousandth time he had been asked the same question. For the last time he affirmed that he had acted alone. The small procession walked toward the prison door.

At precisely 4 A.M., the silence on the square was broken by the sound of the interior gate opening beyond the prison door, followed by the roll of drums and the rifles of soldiers snapping into position. Deibler led Émile, his chest largely uncovered, toward the guillotine. With his hands folded in front of his stomach, he was being pulled more rapidly than his shackled legs could move. In the first light of the new dawn he could see spectators perched on roofs and a photographer pointing a camera in the direction of the apparatus, which Émile could not yet see. He saw the mounted cavalry of the Republican Guard, and the gendarmes, with sabers drawn, in a semicircle. Someone said, "The poor lad! You wouldn't think him more than fifteen years old." Another witness remembered how incredibly calm his face looked. Conversations stopped and hats came off, as if a religious service were about to begin. The chaplain was two steps behind Émile, with nothing to do. Émile looked quickly right and left, as if looking for someone he knew in the crowd. He had been contemplating his final moments for three weeks and wanted to project a noble image. Twenty steps from the guillotine, his face became paler. After a few more steps, he stopped and shouted what everyone expected to hear: "Courage, comrades! Long live anarchy!" As he reached the scaffold, he repeated, "Long live anarchy!" Deibler's aides then grabbed him, pushed him down brutally against the plank so that he lay flat, and shoved his head through the little window, which resembled the porthole of a ship.

Twenty seconds later, the dull sound of the guillotine reaching the end of its rapid descent could be heard. Émile's head fell to the ground and was quickly tossed into the awaiting basket just as casually as one would throw a large wad of paper into a small bin. An almost inaudible gasp of horror rippled through the crowd; some people turned on their heels and moved rapidly away. Several of Deibler's assistants had not even bothered to watch the blade fall. They had seen it many times before and had already begun to organize their departure. Two assistants pushed the body into the waiting box and then carried it quickly to the executioner's wagon.

The death certificate read that Émile had died at 4:10 in the morning on May 21, 1894, at 168, rue de la Roquette, that special address. A band of young drunks staggered by, singing obscene songs. The wagon left with the body, escorted by mounted gendarmes. The crowd departed quietly. The police arrested three men. One had shouted "Long live the Commune!" when the wagon with Émile's body went by, adding that it was not Émile who should have been guillotined but rather President Carnot and his ministers. By 7 A.M., newspapers were already being hawked on the boulevards of Paris relating the details of Émile's execution only three hours earlier.

The politician and journalist Georges Clemenceau left place de la Roquette horrified by the "crude vengeance" of French society that he had just witnessed. Émile's terribly pale face disturbed him: he saw the young man as a tormented Christ, "trying to impose his intellectual pride upon his child's body." Émile's ideas could not be cut off as easily as his head. In an article, Clemenceau expressed hope for "a humanization of customs . . . Let those for the death penalty go, if they dare, to smell the blood of La Roquette. We'll talk about it afterward."

The wagon carrying the remains of Émile headed toward the cemetery of Ivry-sur-Seine, a corner of which, popularly known as "the turnip field," was reserved for those who had been guillotined. Police stood guard. A grave had been dug, near the tomb of Vaillant. Émile's body, with his arms still tightly bound behind his back and his fists blue from the tautly cinched rope, lay in a casket of white wood. He was pale, his eyes closed, his lips slightly parted. Bloodstains here and there besmirched his white shirt. The body and head were placed in a simple wooden coffin, the head situated between the legs. Abbé Valadier prayed briefly. Following a simulated burial in front of the policemen and gendarmes on duty, Émile's remains were taken to the medical school near Odéon to be examined, despite his mother's wish that he be buried immediately in the family plot in Brévannes-Limeil.

At 11 p.m. a journalist had informed Madame Henry's aunt of the impending execution. Three hours later, she had seen troops moving toward place de la Roquette, so she immediately departed for Brévannes to tell Madame Henry. Hornbostel had already left for a vacation in the country.

Newspapermen raced to see who could first reach Brévannes following the execution. One managed to get there by 7:30 a.m. He knocked on the door. He asked the elderly cook if Madame Henry was available. The cook replied that she was ill. The dishwasher asked if the news was true. Yes, the journalist replied, he had been there. In another room, Jules Henry looked away because he had been crying. Workers employed across the way at the hospice began to arrive, to talk and drink. No one mentioned what had happened a few hours earlier. Did Madame Henry know? The cook thought so, but she was in bed. Several workers chatted away, trying without success to converse and joke with the boy. The mailman arrived in good humor. He had a letter for a workman renting a room at the auberge.

Élisa Gauthey had entered the house through the garden. Since Émile's arrest, she had enjoyed the public attention, particularly spending time in the offices of the big papers to tell the story of the bomber's passion for her. She did not know how to keep quiet, even on this dreadful morning, babbling about Émile's love for her and relating intimate details of their "relationship." Élisa had treated him like a child, but in the end "he had shown himself to be an extraordinary man." Again, she expressed regret that she had not given herself to him. It would have made an even bigger story.

The journalist Madame Yver immediately went to Brévannes. She told Madame Henry, who was with Dr. Goupil, that she wanted to offer her consolation. She informed the grieving mother that her son had died bravely, walking to the guillotine with a sure step, his head held high. Madame Henry asked whether Émile had spoken of his mother before his execution. Madame Yver did not reply. Said Madame Henry, "What madness! Him, dying for the workers! But he was bourgeois to his soul. You understand, it was bad advice that lost him, as in the case of my other son." She then asked the journalist if she had actually watched the decapitation. No, said Madame Yver. She had turned away.

On May 24, Émile was buried in the cemetery of Limeil. Jules Henry and several *compagnons* later returned to plant a shrub at the tomb. In Belleville, as news of the execution spread, people looked at each other and asked, "Who is next?"

CHAPTER 8

Reaction

"To those who say: hate does not give birth to love, I reply
that it is love, human love, that often gives birth to hate."

— ÉMILE HENRY

A WEEK AFTER Émile Henry's bomb exploded in the
Café Terminus, the anarchist art and literary critic Octave Mirbeau wrote, "A mortal enemy of anarchy could
not have done more than Émile Henry against his cause when he
threw his inexplicable bomb into the middle of quiet, anonymous
people who had gone to a café to drink a beer before going home
to go to bed." Charles Malato shared this view. Émile was an anarchist of great intelligence and courage, but his bomb "had above
all struck anarchism." Malato approved any and all violence aimed
at the enemy—the state and its props—but "not that which lashes
out blindly," as had the bomb of his former friend. Émile Pouget,
whose violent language in *Père Peinard* had helped set the tone for
"propaganda by the deed," viewed the recent attacks as an embarrassment to the anarchist cause.

At Leyret's Le Déluge in Belleville, the reaction to Émile's Café
Terminus bombing was mixed. Unlike Vaillant's bombing of the
National Assembly, there was no great joy about Émile's "deed."

Why strike ordinary people sipping drinks in a café after work? That Émile was not a worker, like Vaillant, or "vulgar" like Ravachol, but rather an "intellectual born into the bourgeoisie" became a topic of conversation and reflection. There was something disconcerting about Émile's throwing away his diplomas and going on the attack. Yet there was also perhaps grudging admiration. Those frequenting Le Déluge had paid close attention to what Émile said during his trial, hanging on every word, repeating what he said, and taking pleasure in the way that he seemed to dominate his inquisitors. Leyret knew few workers, even socialists who remained inflexible adversaries of anarchists, who had not read and reread Émile's "Declaration." Émile, this self-proclaimed "resolute avenger, deliciously full of hate, supremely contemptuous," impressed even his critics in "People's Paris," with his learning and "by the precision of his tough reasoning." Still, Émile's execution brought considerably less sadness and anger than that of Vaillant. It had seemed inevitable.

Ordinary workers now pondered their fate. Would the state and bourgeois society triumph? The future would tell. Some workers who had suffered greatly over the past years seemed to be licking their wounds, perhaps preparing for vengeance. The faubourgs had once placed their hopes in the Third Republic, but they had been let down. The Panama Canal scandal had enriched some well-placed politicians and further fueled contempt for the upper clases and the state that defended their interests. Despotism and corruption had dashed workers' hopes for true fraternity and equality.

The conservative press generally approved of the execution of Émile. To *L'Écho de Paris*, Émile entered History, carrying, like Saint-Denis, his young head in his hands. It was shameful and even grotesque that this mere boy had already become a historical personage, complete with his legend and his apologists. The anarchists had succeeded in making society tremble. Most people living in cities and towns would have wanted to spare his life, not out of sympathy, but out of terror. This particular writer found the state of the contemporary French soul "nauseating." Too many people had already forgotten Émile's victims. Foreign visitors had packed up and fled the epidemic of dynamite in Paris. Industry and commerce had slowed, and winter, usually bustling, had been a dead season. And despite all of this, Émile had his adherents. The anarchists had become "our emperors: Hail, Caesar! The bourgeois about to die salute you!" A new era seemed to have dawned: Émile had not chosen prominent figures of state and capitalism as his targets, but rather peaceful citizens selected randomly by his "monstrous hatred."

Yet something of a minor cult of Émile began, and not only among anarchists. A Belgian newspaper published a special edition devoted to his life. Its correspondent in Paris was sent searching for copies of his poems and correspondence. Items related to or belonging to Émile Henry were briefly traded much like baseball cards are today. Anonymous articles that had appeared in anarchist newspapers were now attributed to him. Old copies of *Père Peinard* sold for a high price. Émile's portrait circulated in the French provinces, especially in the Loire, the birthplace of Ravachol. People lined up to buy a photo of Émile distributed by a publicity agency in Paris. In London, anarchists penned poems in his honor, and the "individualist" faction of the Italian anarchists in London smuggled into Italy a pamphlet saluting his deed and calling for vengeance.

The "propaganda by the deed" anarchists hailed Émile. In November, someone put red and yellow flowers on his tomb, and on that of his father, in the cemetery of Limeil-Brévannes. On the second anniversary of his execution, an article in an anarchist newspaper in Paris asked why Mirbeau, such a conscientious writer, had condemned the courageous young anarchist's deed. Émile had reacted reasonably to the increasingly evident inequalities in a poisoned society. If he had lashed out, it was because "his sensitivities so full of love" had been tortured by the sad scenes he saw in Paris. He had begun with love and ended with an "impla-

cable hatred for those directly responsible for our miseries." Ravachol, often depicted as a savage beast, had gone hungry while giving what he had to the miserable vagabonds he encountered. Émile
was a model of charity, as had been Vaillant. Only death could
have extinguished Émile's hatred. In contrast, anarchist theoreticians were too cowardly to risk their lives. Acts of revolt under-
taken by "those who love," like Émile, would be the motor of
progress.

His wife expecting a child, the anarchist Augustin Léger playfully suggested naming their new baby Émilienne-Henriette, in
honor of the executed anarchist, or even Ravacholine. In the end,
he and his wife named their baby boy Henry. The child, born into
misery, died as an infant. Léger could not contain his bitterness.
He had lost one child, and his two other children shivered virtually unclothed on the sidewalk. He hated the "dirty bourgeois"
with all his soul. Shortly after the death of his son, his spouse, Cé-
lestine, also died of pneumonia.

Vengeance for Auguste Vaillant had not been long in coming. For
Émile, it also came quickly. On June 24, President Sadi Carnot visited Lyon. As his carriage drove down rue de la République on the
way to an elegant evening at the Grand Theater, a man jumped
past guards into the carriage and plunged a knife into the president. Twenty years old, Santo Caserio, a former apprentice baker
from Lombardy and an anarchist, had read in a newspaper about
the execution of Émile and noticed, by chance, that the president
of France would be traveling to Lyon. He rode a train from the
small French Mediterranean port town of Sète for as far as he
could afford the fare; Caserio then walked the rest of the way to
Lyon. His knife avenged Émile Henry. Carnot died of his wounds
several hours after the attack. Another head of state had fallen. Caserio, who evoked "the great human family" in his defense, was
condemned to death and guillotined on August 15, 1894. (At his
trial, when the prosecution claimed that he wanted to kill both the

king of Italy and the pope, Caserio joked, "Not both at once . . .
they never go out together.")

The "dynamite psychosis," which the Parisian press succeeded in
deepening, led the Chamber of Deputies to pass a third "scoundrelly law" on July 28, 1894. While the previous laws had cracked
down on anarchist publications, the new law sought to abolish
the movement altogether by expanding further the definition of
anarchist propaganda and what constituted complicity with anarchist deeds.

A professor of criminal law named Garraud was among those
defending the new laws. In his view, anarchist intellectuals had
formed a "school of crime" wherein masters worked to recruit students. Peddlers of anarchism had successfully infiltrated proletarian neighborhoods, where they helped form anarchist groups. No
longer content to "intoxicate" workers with anarchist doctrine, the
movement's intellectuals had directly provoked violent acts, even
publishing formulas for putting together bombs. Then, in various
publications, they celebrated those who undertook such deeds,
depicting them as martyrs. Anarchist newspapers were one of the
chief instruments of the cause's success. Therefore the law of December 18, 1893, took aim at them: it made it possible to repress
"associations of evil-doers," whose ranks were now expanded to
include newspapers or other publishers of "clandestine propaganda." Correctional tribunals were endowed with the right to
suspend publication of any of them. The sweep of this new law
raised concerns even outside anarchist circles; socialists feared
that it would allow judges to conflate any form of political opposition with anarchism, despite the minister of justice's contention
that it was aimed only at proponents of "propaganda by the deed."

Trials for provoking or excusing "acts of violence" were taken
away from juries, who tended to be lenient. This gave the judge
more power. Misdemeanors committed by anarchists had not
been previously considered political in character. Now anyone ac-

cused of spreading anarchist propaganda could be prosecuted to the full extent of the law, a measure added at the request of (the aptly named) Léon Bourgeois, a former minister of justice. The third law also designated as "propaganda" what anarchists said in their own defense in trials—as in the case of Émile's widely read "Declaration." Judges could prevent newspapers from reporting what had been said in court, defining such statements as "propaganda enacted through the judiciary." The law effectively banned the publication of trial proceedings.

The December law aimed at "associations of evil-doers" led to the arrest and trial of thirty anarchists the following year. The "Trial of the Thirty," which began on August 6, 1894, lasted eight days and put in the docket intellectuals such as Sébastien Faure, Félix Fénéon, and Jean Grave, along with three anarchist thieves, including Léon Ortiz. All stood accused of belonging to an association formed with the goal of destroying society through theft, pillage, arson, and murder. The most prominent among the accused were Émile's friends. Partly because of the lack of evidence and partly because the prosecution was overwhelmed by the intellectual firepower of the defendants, the Trial of the Thirty proved an embarrassing failure for the prosecutor, Bulot, and the government.

At one point, Bulot interrupted the proceedings because "a package arrived for me by mail containing fecal matter!" He asked to go and wash his hands. Fénéon quipped that no one had washed his hands "with so much solemnity" since Pontius Pilate. Fénéon helped destroy the prosecution's case with his biting humor. When the judge accused him of being "the intimate friend of the German anarchist Kampffmayer," Fénéon replied, "The intimacy could not have been very great. I do not know a word of German, and he does not speak French." When the beleaguered judge held up a flask of mercury that had been found in Fénéon's office in the ministry of war (a most unlikely place for an anarchist to find employment), Fénéon indicated that it had belonged to Émile. When the judge reminded him that mercury could be used to make mercury fulminate, Fénéon reminded the court that it could also be used to make thermometers and barometers. Ortiz and the two other thieves were convicted, the former sentenced to fifteen years of hard labor. The intellectuals were all acquitted.

The acquittals helped bring an end to the dangerous days of "propaganda of the deed" in Paris. A historian warned not long after that "exceptional legislation should be avoided. It is in no way justified . . . Punishment appears to fanatics who long for the martyr's crown as no longer a deterrent but atonement." After all, the executions of Ravachol, Vaillant, and Émile Henry did not prevent the assassination of Carnot. Did this mean "that society is helpless in the face of anarchism"? His answer was yes, if the state relied on repression "and not the power to convince." Many people had turned to anarchism because the state treated them as common criminals simply for harboring anarchist sympathies. Only justice and freedom could defeat anarchism, not sheer force and continued injustice. Maurice Barrès had already come to the same conclusion. In his view, Émile's execution was a disservice to society. The battle against anarchist ideas required intellectual weapons, not Deibler's "accessories." Marie-François Goron, a former head of security, also believed that intimidation had proved a poor deterrent. Fear of imprisonment or even execution had not stopped Ravachol or Émile. Ultimately it was self-defeating to arrest hundreds of people who had been denounced by police informers, separate them from their families, and increase their hatred for the state and society. The most recent roundup of anarchists had brought extremely meager results. The jury in the Trial of the Thirty had shown more sense than had the police. The acquittals helped end anarchist attacks because there was nothing to provoke retaliation. Previously, the state's overreaction to the words and deeds of anarchism had incited further violence. This cycle was broken now.

For several years, a small group of *compagnons* commemorated Émile's execution by making a pilgrimage to the auberge in Brévannes. But over the years, their numbers dwindled. In 1896, someone managed to get into the cemetery to leave flowers, with the inscription MEMORY AND VENGEANCE. A rock was also placed on Émile's tomb, on which was written MURDERED, A VICTIM OF SOCIETY. In 1901, Madame Henry had apparently made it known that she would welcome "comrades" as she would any other clients but that she would not tolerate speeches and singing. Élisa Gauthey, although still living in Paris, had reappeared in Brévannes on at least one anniversary of Émile's execution, chatting with the few *compagnons* present.

After his release from prison, Fortuné Henry took a job working for the Central Pharmacy in Paris, where he had earlier been employed. In 1896, Fortuné and Jules told anarchists who came to the auberge to pay homage to Émile that the two of them would become "men of action" only after their mother's death. But in 1904, Fortuné founded an anarchist community in Aiglemont in the Ardennes, renting a small piece of land. He constructed a hut made of clay and branches. He later purchased the place for eight hundred francs, but because he never did believe in property, a friend became the nominal owner. Fortuné began raising vegetables and managed to attract eleven people there. This seemed to be the kind of ideal, natural community that Proudhon had predicted would bring happiness and transform society. However, the participants began to quarrel, perhaps because of Fortuné's rather authoritarian personality. The community struggled until 1909. After five years of "ridiculous deprivations and hurt feelings, the attempt just collapsed miserably." Fortuné's practical experience in anarchism had failed. As for Jules, he took over his mother's auberge when he came of age, several years after the execution. Instead of becoming a militant anarchist, he started a small business selling eggs and butter, and he prospered.

Once "propaganda by the deed" no longer attracted adherents, anarchists turned their efforts to unionization, hoping that such organizations would provide a base for the future revolution. Unions had been illegal in France until 1884 (although in fact they had existed in many trades through aid or friendly societies, and some had served as "resistance societies" when necessary to support strikes). The National Federation of Unions was created two years later. In 1892, anarchists in London, among them Kropotkin and Malato, had already called for more involvement with unions. Pouget, in particular, had become impressed with the success of British trade unions and led his followers toward syndicalism. Like Errico Malatesta—whom Émile had attacked for his "association-alist" views—Pouget came to believe that the strength of the state could be countered only with organized labor. Moreover, unions pressed for reforms like the eight-hour day and, in doing so, helped integrate workers, unions, and socialism into the politics of the Third Republic.

In 1895, *Les Temps Nouveaux,* begun in May of that year with the support of Reclus and Kropotkin, published an article by the militant labor organizer Fernand Pelloutier, "Anarchism and the Trade Unions." Fatally ill with tuberculosis, Pelloutier described what he hoped would be the "dying society" of capitalism and explained his shift to syndicalism. What was sometimes called "anarcho-syndicalism" insisted that the shop floor offered not only the best means of planning revolution but also a glimpse of future human solidarity and organization. To Pelloutier, such a view did not require dynamite to be heard. Direct action through unions, not individual action or bombs, or involvement in politics, would be the means to revolution.

More militant workers, including many anarchists, also turned to unions, which made good use of the Labor Exchanges (Bourses du Travail) that had begun to spring up in French industrial cities in the late 1880s. Workers could go there to learn about job opportunities and to discuss their grievances and hopes for the future. Moreover, the Bourses provided solidarity and a social life for working-class families. The "heroic days of syndicalism" that began in 1895 and lasted in France until 1907 brought more strikes, as workers pursued the dream of a grand future General Strike, which would bring the capitalist state to its knees. In 1902, the Bourses joined the General Confederation of Labor (C.G.T.), which had been created in 1895 as an umbrella structure for trade unions. Achieving some palpable successes in reform, such as establishing an employer's legal liability for industrial accidents and reducing the workday to ten hours for women and children, the unions gradually improved the lives of many workers.

In 1898, a character much like Émile appeared in French literature, in Zola's *Paris* (1898) as little Victor Mathis, "slight and almost beardless, with a straight, stubborn brow, gray eyes glittering with intelligence, a pointed nose and thin lips expressive of stern will and unforgiving hatred." Like Émile, Mathis was an educated bourgeois, and he could have entered the École normale. In the story, Mathis avenges the guillotining of the character Salvat, as Émile had that of Vaillant. Mathis is, like Émile, "the destroyer pure and simple, the theoretician of destruction, the cold energetic man of intellect . . . in his desire to make murder an instrument of the social evolution . . . a poet, a visionary, but the most frightful of all visionaries . . . who craved for the most awful immortality." But by the time *Paris* was published, the era of "propaganda by the deed" in France had drawn to a close.

Despite the fact that the "scoundrelly laws" had made the printing of anarchist propaganda extremely difficult, anarchists still published twelve newspapers in France in 1914. But they remained a small minority, on the fringe. In London, the anarchists had dispersed. Even Victor Richard's grocery store on Charlotte Street was considerably less welcoming to them. The funeral of Martial Bourdin, the French anarchist who had been blown up by a bomb as he walked through Greenwich Park on his way to destroy the Meridian, had been marked by counter-demonstrations, and the windows of the Autonomy Club had been smashed by a mob. The club closed in February 1894, and anarchists moved discreetly into more distant neighborhoods. They faced increasing hostility in London. On May Day of that year, crowds harassed anarchists gathering in Hyde Park.

Across Europe, the number of militant anarchists was beginning to decline. In early March 1894, the prefecture of police concluded that no more than five hundred of them resided in Paris, a dramatic decline. In 1897, a police expert gave the figure of four thousand, out of a French population of 39 million people. Those considered truly dangerous were few and were loners, like Émile and Caserio, men who virtually never spoke or acted but readied themselves in the shadows. No one, not even the militant anarchists, could predict their intentions. The solitary actor, of which Émile was the prime example, was above all discreet, and his transformation into a murderer, an avenger of social wrongs, was often sudden. It was almost impossible to monitor such people.

Isolated anarchist acts still occurred, to be sure. From December 1911 to May 1912, a band of self-styled violent anarchists terrorized France and Belgium. Led by a petty criminal and auto mechanic turned anarchist, Jules Bonnot, these men used automobiles (and thus were very modern) and rifles in a series of audacious and on occasion murderous hold-ups, notably of banks. They were killed or captured by the police, and three members were guillotined. Bonnot's band terrorized on a small scale but did not set off a revival of "propaganda by the deed." The members of the band were "illegalists," on the fringes of what remained of the movement. In 1914, on the eve of World War I, only about a thousand militant anarchists lived in France. Terrorism was no longer seen as an effective means to an end; even hard-core anarchists shared this conclusion.

Elsewhere anarchism continued a checkered course. In Italy, government restraint after the assassination of King Umberto I in 1900 by the anarchist Gaetano Bresci undercut the movement, reducing anarchist attacks. As in France, workers increasingly turned to unions and politics. In contrast, in Spain anarchism remained extremely potent, especially in the port and industrial suburbs of Barcelona and among the miserably poor, exploited laborers in rural Andalusia. In close alliance with nobles and churchmen, the government undertook a program of brutal repression following the enactment of legislation in 1896—which allowed, among other things, the torture of suspected anarchists— and this swelled the anger of the poor. As one Spanish anarchist put it, "The problem was not only one of bread but one of hatred." Executions brought reprisals, continuing a chain of violence.

In May 1906, as King Alfonso XIII and his new bride, a granddaughter of Queen Victoria of Great Britain, traveled by carriage from their wedding ceremony to the royal palace, an anarchist threw a bomb at them. They were unscathed, but the attack killed twenty-three people and injured more than a hundred. Three years later, Spanish soldiers and police killed more than two hundred people during "the Tragic Week," five days of combat in the streets of Barcelona during a general strike in which anarchists played a major part. The torture of a well-known anarchist, Francisco Ferrer, attracted worldwide attention, garnering sympathy for anarchists as well as disdain for government policies. That the Spanish labor movement remained relatively disorganized relative to its French and Italian counterparts meant that many workers looked to anarchism for hope. Thus, while the press in many other countries helped affirm the stereotype of the anarchist as a dangerous bomber, in Spain his image remained that of a martyr, victimized by the state. Anarchist attacks in Spain continued following World War I. Despite the duplicity of their Stalinist rivals, anarchists would play a major role in the defense of the republic against Franco's nationalist forces during the Spanish Civil War (1936–39). But in the end the shaky alliance defending the republic lost, and the 150,000 people executed by the new government included thousands of anarchists.

In the United States, anarchist attacks killed more than fifty people from 1914 to 1920. In 1919, about thirty bombs were sent through the mail to U.S. officials, ranging from the attorney general to mayors. Two months later, explosions rocked the residences of officials in seven cities. On September 16, 1920, an attack on Wall Street, possibly the work of an Italian anarchist, killed thirty-three people and wounded more than two hundred. In Russia, the revolution of 1917 quickly turned into a nightmare for anarchists. By 1920, the Bolsheviks had crushed their anarchist allies, with whom they had united in the Civil War against the White forces in Ukraine. A largely popular revolution was transformed into a dictatorship. "They have shown how the revolution is *not* to be made," Kropotkin insisted. The anarchist told Lenin, "Vladimir Ilyich, your concrete actions are completely unworthy of the ideas you pretend to hold . . . What future lies in store for communism when one of its most important defenders tramples in this way on every honest feeling?"

The "dynamite club" in France was more imagined than real. It was the creation of fearful Parisians, with the help of the popular press. A well-placed police specialist at the time wrote that those who believed that anarchist deeds were the result of an organized plot were flat wrong. The real threat came from individual anarchist bombers, like Émile. This did not make the upper clases any less anxious, but it did suggest that going after organized plots was folly. In the words of this particular agent, "there weren't any."

So what did link the anarchists who went to the guillotine? Ravachol was a marginal character, "a great bandit, a savage rebel who had put himself in the service of the anarchist cause." Vaillant was a family man crushed by hunger and misery, unable to feed his family, who lashed out in a desperate attempt to call attention to the plight of poor people. Pauwels was an occasional laborer, a thug, and a born killer. Caserio, alone in his misery at age twenty-one, learned to hate the rich.

Émile was different. He was a young middle-class intellectual who might have enjoyed a productive life, were it not for his father's treatment at the hands of the state, exacerbated by the appalling poverty that Émile witnessed in Paris. Émile remained a complex person, a self-detesting bourgeois who proclaimed over and over his hatred for "the bourgeoisie." He was confident, proud, even arrogant, distant, indeed cold, dismissive of the "crowd" that he considered "cowardly" and ignorant of their true interests. "In contrast to Vaillant, who loved the people," Charles Malato remembered, "Émile Henry only loved the idea. He felt a marked estrangement from the ignorant and servile plebs, a feeling shared by a number of literary and artistic anarchists," by whom Malato meant, among others, Camille Pissarro, Laurent Tailhade, and Émile's own friend Félix Fénéon. During his final days in his cell in La Roquette, Émile wrote, "I love all people in their humanity for what they should become, but I have contempt for what they are."

In his own way, Émile could be described as a nineteenth-century Hamlet. He took arms against the sea of troubles devastating much of humanity, seeking to bring an end to them with his bombs.

In 1900, Paris proudly presented itself to tourists as "a pacified capital, far from the tragic and bloody days of revolution." The omnipresent police, with garrisons of soldiers always ready to assist if necessary, ensured public order. The City of Light was a different place, even wealthier than before. The traditional revolutionary neighborhoods of the center Right Bank had gradually become less densely populated, the very texture of some neighborhoods destroyed or at least altered by Haussmann's boulevards. Moreover, ordinary people increasingly lived on the urban periphery. Paris had been subdued.

The French state, against which the anarchists struggled, helped lead Europe into a murderous war in 1914. The Great War killed about 9 million men, including 1.5 million French soldiers, and unleashed the demons of the twentieth century.

ACKNOWLEDGMENTS

NOTES

BIBLIOGRAPHY

INDEX

Acknowledgments

In following Émile Henry around Paris, I benefited from the kindness of the staff of the Archives de la préfecture de police, in the Commissariat of the fifth arrondissement of Paris. I am still struck by the contrast between researchers coming down from the archives, carrying their laptop computers and passing by people (including many tourists) who turned up in the same establishment because their wallets were stolen or their cars or bicycles impounded. The coffee machine is still in the martial arts gym where the police train.

In the course of working on this book, I have asked many friends and colleagues questions on detail and more. They have always graciously responded. Thanks to Richard Sonn, Steven Vincent, Paul Jankowski, Mark Micale, Stephen Jacobson, Vanessa Schwartz, Dominique Kalifa, John Monroe, Brian Skib, Leon Plantagna, Victoria Johnson, Carl Strikwerda, Judith Walkowitz, Richard Bach Jensen, Constance Bantman, Robert Fishman, Ray Jonas, Steven Englund, Mathieu Fruleux, Chris Brouwer, Valerie Hansen, Timothy Messer-Kruse, Beverly Gage, Pascal Dupuy, Darrin McMahon, Martin A. Miller, Eugenia Herbert, George Eisenwein, Yves Lequin, Bruno Cabanes, Carl Levy, and Pietro DiPaolo.

It was a pleasure to give talks and receive comments on Émile Henry and anarchism at Montana State University, Florida State University, the University of Connecticut, the University of Southern California, the University of Minnesota, Washington University in St. Louis, the University of Edinburgh, the University of Newcastle, Stanford University (where the French historians of northern California met), Carleton College, Yale University (Department of French), and Brooklyn College. For my research in Paris, I received funding from the Whitney Griswold research fund at Yale.

I benefited from participating in a conference in Arlington, Virginia, in June 2007, organized by David Rapoport: "What Can and Cannot Be Learned from History About Terrorism: A Dialogue Between Historians and Social Scientists."

Three dear friends read the original draft of this book and, as usual, offered shrewd, helpful comments. So many thanks to Jay Winter, David Bell, and Don Lamm, who, with Emma Parry and Christy Fletcher, have encouraged and represented this project from the beginning.

I have been very fortunate, for decades, to enjoy the inspiration and friendship of Peter Gay and of my late friend Charles Tilly. They taught me how to do history. I will always owe them so much.

At Houghton Mifflin, the tough-minded, outstanding editor Amanda Cook helped shape this book. I am much indebted to her. I also greatly appreciate Susanna Brougham's wonderful manuscript editing.

Carol, Laura, and Christopher Merriman have heard versions of this story in a variety of places. Thanks and much love to my family, as ever. Chris too has had the rather strange experience of dining in the café-restaurant that the principal character of this book blew up on a February evening more than a century ago.

Balazuc, June 25, 2008

Notes

Prologue

2 a black wagon carrying . . . the guillotine: Gérard A. Jaeger, *Anatole Deibler (1863–1939): L'homme qui trancha 400 têtes* (Paris, 2001), p. 117.

3 Account from *Le Soleil,* Feb. 13, 1894; *Le Gaulois,* Feb. 17, 1894; *Le Figaro,* Apr. 15 and 28, 1894; Archives of the Prefecture of Police, Ba 1115, prefect of police, Feb. 14, 1894.

4 "the history of remainders": words of Charles Tilly.
   assassinations and bomb attacks: Richard Bach Jensen, "The International Campaign Against Anarchist Terrorism, 1880–1914/30s" (unpublished paper), p. 2; by Jensen's calculations 160 people were killed and at least 500 wounded by anarchist attacks during the period.

1. Light and Shadows in the Capital of Europe

7 "the rebellious century": Charles Tilly, Louise Tilly, and Richard Tilly, *The Rebellious Century: 1830–1930* (Cambridge, Mass., 1975).

8 "cold and lined up": Robert L. Herbert, *Impressionism: Art, Leisure, and Parisian Society* (New Haven, 1988), p. 15.
   "its irregular curve": T. J. Clark, *The Painting of Modern Life: Paris in the Art of Manet and His Followers* (New York, 1984), p. 35.

10 "colossal monster": Émile Zola, *Paris* (Paris, 1898), p. 394.
   "The straight line": Charles Yriarte, "Les types parisiens—les clubs," *Paris-Guide* (Paris, 1867), pp. 929–30, from Jean-Pierre A. Bernard, *Les*

deux Paris: Les réprésentations de Paris dans la seconde moitié du XIXe siè-cle (Seyssel, 2001), p. 199.

somewhat unreal spectacle: See Rosalind H. Williams, *Dream Worlds: Mass Consumption in Late-Nineteenth-Century France* (Berkeley, 1982), pp. 84–85; Bernard, *Les deux Paris*, p. 193; Vanessa R. Schwartz, *Spectacular Realities: Early Mass Culture in Fin-de-Siècle Paris* (Berkeley, 1998).

11 aisles appeared to be an extension: Philip Nord, *Parisian Shopkeepers and the Politics of Resentment* (Princeton, 1986), p. 133.
British and American influence: Bernard, *Les deux Paris*, pp. 218–19.
spectacle of the boulevards: A point made by, among others, Vanessa R. Schwartz.

12 The Opera, which opened: Karl Baedeker, *Paris and Environs, with Route from London to Paris* (Paris, 1896).

13 "heart of the great city": Zola, *Paris*, p. 91.
"I live at your expense"; Roger Shattuck, *The Banquet Years: The Origins of the Avant-Garde in France, 1885 to World War I* (New York, 1968), pp. 5–6.
"at the proper moment"; Ibid., p. 10.
"On the boulevard each day"; Bernard, *Les deux Paris*, pp. 208–9.

14 "steam-powered journalism": Schwartz, *Spectacular Realities*, p. 28.

15 the expanding French colonial empire: Pascal Ory, *L'Expo Universelle* (Paris, 1989), p. 95.
some bourgeois came to feel disconnected: See Clark, *The Painting of Modern Life*, chapters 3 and 4.

16 "the world has changed less": Shattuck, *The Banquet Years*, p. xv.
"What I saw": Augustin Léger, *Journal d'un anarchiste* (Paris, 1895), pp. 308–9.
"away in the distance": Norma Evenson, *Paris: A Century of Change, 1878–1978* (New Haven, 1979), p. 13, quoting Edmondo de Amicis, *Studies of Paris* (1882).

17 hastened by Haussmann's construction: Lenard R. Berlanstein, *The Work-ing People of Paris, 1871–1914* (Baltimore, 1984), pp. 11–12.

19 wells stood near cesspools: Ibid., pp. 58–59.

20 about twenty-five thousand: Henry Leyret, *En plein faubourg* (Paris, 2000, originally published 1895), p. 8.

21 "barely furnished with basic": Ibid., pp. 20–21.
"everyone for himself": Ibid., pp. 142–46.
"Life is not just a bowl of cherries": Ibid., p. 67.

22 "Goddammit, there are real men in Paris": Ibid., p. 114.
"spread from the Latin Quarter": Ibid., pp. 115–16.
From his hospital bed: *Le Libertaire*, Feb. 4, 1895.

23 "the masters of society . . . take heed": Eugenia Herbert, *The Artist and*

Social Reform: France and Belgium, 1885–1898 (New Haven, 1980), p. 153, from Zola, *Oeuvres,* 50, 650 (Dec. 1885).

2. The Exile's Second Son

26 On Fortuné Henry and Émile Henry's early life: Archives Nationales, BB24 853; Archives of the Prefecture of Police, Ba 1115, telegram of Feb. 16 and report of Mar. 13, 1894; *Le 19e Siècle,* Feb. 20, 1894; *La Paix,* Feb. 18, 1894; *L'Intransigeant,* Feb. 17, 1894; and Charles Malato, "Some Anarchist Portraits," *Fortnightly Review,* 333, new series, Sept. 1, 1894, pp. 327–28.

28 a collection of songs: Fortuné Henry, *Les chants de l'enfance* (Paris, 1881); *L'Écho de Paris,* Feb. 16, 1894.

29 in Brévannes: Marie F. de la Mulatière, *Regards sur Limeil-Brévannes* (Saint-Georges-de-Luzençon, 1988), p. 41. The 1896 census: 1,234 (total population, 1,527, counting those at the hospice, with Limeil 259 and Brévannes 975).
   À l'Espérance: Ba 1115, police report, Aug. 23, 1893; *L'Intransigeant,* Feb. 17, 1894.

30 Émile received a small scholarship: *L'Écho de Paris,* Feb. 18, 1894; *Le Journal,* Feb. 17, 1894; *Le Petit Temps,* Feb. 16, 1894; Jean Maitron, *Le mouvement anarchiste en France,* I (Paris, 1975), pp. 239–40, and Malato, "Some Anarchist Portraits," p. 328.

32 "I hope to build a good future": *Le 19e Siècle,* Apr. 27, 1894.
   outside Venice: Henri Varennes, *De Ravachol à Caserio* (Paris, 1895), pp. 229–31; *Le 19e Siècle,* Feb. 20 and Apr. 27, 1894.
   happy to have received letters: *Le 19e Siècle,* Feb. 20, 1894.

33 hoped to return to France: Ba 1115, "Notices sur Émile Henry," Feb. 13, 1894; *Le Petit Temps,* Feb. 16, 1894; *Le Figaro,* Feb. 16, 1894; *Le 19e Siècle,* Feb. 20, 1894; *La Paix,* Feb. 18, 1894; *L'Éclair,* Feb. 17, 1894.

34 Émile was short: Malato, "Some Anarchist Portraits," p. 330.
   "the most perplexing philosophic speculations": Ibid., p. 329.

35 "Me, a Spiritist?" *L'Intransigeant,* Feb. 16, 1894; *Le Temps,* Feb. 20, 1894; *Le 19e Siècle,* Feb. 20, 1894; Malato, "Some Anarchist Portraits," p. 329. Thanks to John Monroe.

36 "a reposing creature of love": *Le Journal,* May 17, 1894.
   "reign of attraction": *L'Intransigeant,* Feb. 19, 1894.

37 "how many afternoons": Malato, "Some Anarchist Portraits," p. 330.

38 "I would like simply to disappear": *Le Journal,* May 17, 1894; *Le Gil Blas,* May 9, 1894.
   "that madness would take me over": *Le Gil Blas* and *L'Intransigeant,* May 9, 1894; *Le Journal,* May 17, 1894.

39 on one occasion, a cow: Joan U. Halperin, *Félix Fénéon: Aesthete and Anarchist in Fin-de-Siècle Paris* (New Haven, 1988), pp. 269–71.
"the present morality": Daniel Guérin, ed., *No Gods, No Masters* (Oakland, 2005), pp. 398–401.

41 possible military conscription: Ba 1115, Feb. 14, 1892, and Feb. 17, 1894; *L'Intransigeant*, Feb. 17, 1894. Émile later also claimed that he went to Berlin, but a report filed by "Léon" on Feb. 23, 1894, dismissed this: "The time that Émile Henry claims to have spent in Berlin is purely imaginary."

42 "no rights over a woman": Ba 1115, Émile Henry, Feb. 27, 1894, double cell nos. 1 & 2, Conciergerie.
"Long live the Commune!": Ba 1115, reports of Mar. 12 and 14, 1894.
"royal rule of gold": K. Steven Vincent, *Pierre-Joseph Proudhon and the Rise of French Republican Socialism* (New York, 1984), p. 17.

43 "Anarchy is order": George Woodcock, *Anarchism: A History of Libertarian Ideas and Movements* (New York, 1962), p. 276.
"organized, living society": Daniel Guérin, *Anarchism: From Theory to Practice* (New York, 1970), p. 42.

44 quality to anarchism: See Émile's "Déclaration"; Varennes, *De Ravachol*, pp. 235–41.
"robbed you of your victory": Woodcock, *Anarchism*, p. 276.

45 "a man under vow": Alexandre Varias, *Paris and the Anarchists: Aesthetes and Subversives During the Fin-de-Siècle* (Paris, 1996), pp. 41–42.

46 "the freedom of others": Guérin, *Anarchism*, p. 33.
"Let us not become": Ibid., p. 3.

47 the only two perfect lives: James Joll, *The Anarchists* (New York, 1979), p. 142.
"a doomed man": Marie Fleming, "Propaganda by the Deed: Terrorism and Anarchist Theory in Late-Nineteenth-Century Europe," in *Terrorism in Europe*, eds., Yonah Alexander and Kenneth A. Myers (New York, 1982), p. 13.

49 "with one to reach a hundred": Woodcock, *Anarchism*, pp. 301–3.
"in the name of liberty": Joll, *The Anarchists*, p. 114.
Anarchist attacks: Woodcock, *Anarchism*, pp. 300–3, 366–67; Jean Préposiet, *Histoire de l'anarchisme* (Paris, 2000), pp. 391–92; David Stafford, *From Anarchism to Reformism: A Study of the Political Activities of Paul Brousse* (Toronto, 1971), p. 84; Joll, *The Anarchists*, pp. 112–14.

3. "Love Engenders Hate"

51 thirteen anarchist groups: Archives Nationales, F7 12506, Dec. 1893.
slang (*argot*): Richard D. Sonn, "Marginality and Transgression: Anarchy's Subversive Allure," in Gabriel P. Weisberg, ed., *Montmartre and the Making of Mass Culture* (New Brunswick, 2001), p. 132.

52 "dangerous classes": Gérard Jacquemet, "Belleville ouvrier à la belle époque," *Le Mouvement Social,* 118 (Jan. 1982), pp. 61–77.

53 Vengeance of Anarchist Youth: Ba 1508, poster.

54 "Death to the pigs": Ba 77, Dec. 13, 1892.

"hysterical madwoman": Ba 1115, report of Mar. 14, 1894; *Le Matin,* Feb. 23, 1893.

Henry Leyret, the Belleville: Henry Leyret, *En plein faubourg* (Paris, 2000, originally published 1895), pp. 130–31, 151–52.

55 "midnight movers": Léger, *Le Journal,* p. 291.

Jean Grave published: F7 13053, Moreau, 1897; *Le Figaro,* Jan. 18, 1894; *La Révolte,* Apr. 7, June 11, and Dec. 17, 1892.

56 *Père Peinard:* Edward Peter Fitzgerald, "Emile Pouget, the Anarchist Movement, and the Origins of Revolutionary Trade-Unionism in France, 1880–1901" (unpublished doctoral dissertation, Yale University, 1973), esp. p. 189.

57 *"kif-kif":* Sonn, "Marginality and Transgression," p. 131; *Père Peinard,* Mar. 20–27, 1892; Fitzgerald, "Émile Pouget," pp. 194–96.

58 a miners' strike in Decazeville: Roger Langlais, ed., *Père Peinard* (Poitiers, 1976), p. 31, from Dec. 15, 1889.

seven judicial condemnations: Fitzgerald, "Émile Pouget," pp. 242ff.

Zo d'Axa then became: *Endehors,* a presentation by J.-P. Courty, Paris, 1974; Halperin, *Félix Fénéon,* p. 245.

59 an editorial, "First Shout": Jean-Jacques Lefrère and Philippe Oriol, *Zo d'Axa: Un patricien de l'anarchie* (Paris, 2002), pp. 14–17, 21.

anarchist Félix Fénéon: Halperin, *Félix Fénéon,* pp. 252–53, 268–270; Ba 1115, "Léon," May 15, 1894.

Charles Malato, another anarchist: "Charles Malato," in *Dictionnaire biographique de mouvement ouvrier français: 1871–1914,* Jean Maitron, ed. (Paris, 1973).

"the noisy, vapid, and often dubious individuals": Malato, "Some Anarchist Portraits," p. 330.

60 a transformation in Émile: *L'Écho de Paris,* Feb. 20, 1894.

Émile's "indominable will": Malato, "Some Anarchist Portraits," p. 328.

"To those who say": Walter Laqueur, *A History of Terrorism* (New Brunswick, 2006), p. 127: "High strung like a violin string, the anarchists weep and moan for life, so relentless, so cruel, so terribly inhuman. In a desperate moment, the string breaks."

"thanks to his coolness": Ba 1115, Mar. 13, 1894.

61 Émile found a position: Ba 1115, police reports, May 31 and Aug. 4, 1892.

different anarchist groups: Richard D. Sonn, *Anarchism and Cultural Politics in Fin-de-Siècle France* (Lincoln, Neb., 1989), pp. 84–86.

"it is a beautiful dream": Roderick Kedward, *The Men Who Shocked an Era* (London, 1971), p. 112.

returned to "compete barbarism": Joll, *The Anarchists*, p. 149.

62 *Enemy of the People:* Sonn, *Anarchism and Cultural Politics*, p. 76.
"Oh, the songs of Bruant": Uri Eisenzweig, *Fictions de l'anarchisme* (Paris, 2001), p. 177.
"lively as dynamite": Sonn, *Anarchism and Cultural Politics*, p. 168.
"anarchists without throwing bombs": Laqueur, *A History of Terrorism*, p. 111.

63 "idle word-spillers": David C. Rapoport, "The Four Waves of Modern Terrorism," in *Attacking Terrorism: Elements of a Grand Strategy*, Audrey Cronin and James Ludes, eds. (Washington, 2004), p. 50.
"Permanent revolt": André Nataf, *La vie quotidienne des anarchistes en France, 1880–1910* (Paris: Hachette, 1986), p. 76; see also Ze'ev Iviansky, "Individual Terror," *Journal of Contemporary History*, 12 (1977), pp. 43–63; Guérin, *Anarchism*, pp. 44–45; Fleming, "Propaganda by the Deed," pp. 12–13.
"Yes, we are guilty": Ibid., p. 18.
"We who . . . seclude ourselves": Joll, *The Anarchists*, p. 134; Fleming, "Propaganda by the Deed," pp. 22–23.

64 "professional risk": Joll, *The Anarchists*, p. 111; Carl Levy, "The Anarchist Assassin and Italian History: 1870s to 1930s" (unpublished paper).
"men of courage": Fleming, "Propaganda by the Deed," pp. 13–15.
"lonely sentinels": Ibid., pp. 13–14.

65 "two vicious germs": Ba 1115, Feb. 27, 1894; Émile Henry, Feb. 27, 1894, double cells nos. 1 & 2, Conciergerie.
"no anarchist forgot": Kedward, *The Men Who Shocked an Era*, p. 59.
Émile read Kropotkin's: Ba 1115, "notices sur Émile Henry," Feb. 13, 1894; Ba 1115, Émile Henry, Feb. 27, 1894.
"all belongs to all": Peter Kropotkin, *The Conquest of Bread* (New York, 1927), p. 3.

66 "highest expression of order": Nataf, *La vie quotidienne*, pp. 32–33.
published in *La Révolte: La Révolte*, Feb. 5–11, 1892.

4. Dynamite Deeds

70 On Ravachol's early life: Jean Maitron, ed., *Ravachol et les anarchistes* (Paris, 1964), pp. 46–73, dictated as he awaited execution. See Ba 1132, dossier Ravachol.

71 For several months in 1898, in Fourmies: Raymond Manevy, *Sous les plis du drapeau noir* (Paris, 1949), pp. 134–36.

72 "At the top": Kedward, *The Anarchists*, pp. 54–56; Varennes, *De Ravachol*, pp. 2–5.
described the "martyrdom": *L'Endehors*, Sept. 1, 1891.

73 "the life of a policeman": Ba 77, Aug. 3, 1891.
"all seemed to point": *L'Endehors*, Dec. 27, 1891.
the theory and practice of dynamite use: F7 12830–31.

74 In 1875 a law: F7 12830–31.
deadly new "infernal machines": F7 12, 830–31, minister of foreign affairs, June 18, 1883, drawing from the *Sunday Herald*, May 27, 1883.

75 "The Science of Revolutionary Warfare": Louis Adamic, *Dynamite: The Story of Class Violence in America* (New York, 1931), p. 45.

76 "in the pocket without danger" and Most: Ibid., pp. 46–47.
"the good stuff!": Ibid., pp. 45–48; Joll, *The Anarchists*, p. 123.
"At last a toast to science": Laqueur, *A History of Terrorism*, p. 56.
"Do you want some dynamite?": Fleming, "Propaganda by the Deed," p. 16.
such as the "Dynamitards": Ba 75, July 9 and Oct. 17, 1886.

77 dance to the "Dynamite Polka": Varias, *Paris and the Anarchists*, p. 39.
the Haymarket affair: James Green, *Death in the Haymarket: A Story of Chicago, the First Labor Movement, and the Bombing That Divided Gilded-Age America*, pp. 141, 169–72, 203–8; Laqueur, *A History of Terrorism*: "It was a violent age, when public opinion freely held that workers who went on strike for higher wages and shorter working hours should be shot" (p. 59).

78 The image of the bodies: Félix Dubois, *Le péril anarchiste* (Paris, 1894), pp. 55–59.

79 Ravachol's bombs: Ba 1132; F7 12504; Woodcock, *Anarchism*, pp. 310–11.

80 "hoped for and counted on": Ba 77, Mar. 13 and 31, 1892.

81 the journalist Zo d'Axa: Jean-Jacques Lefrère and Philippe Oriol, *Zo d'Axa: Un patricien d'anarchie* (Paris, 2002), pp. 46–47, 55–61, 66.
Meunier and Jean-Pierre François: Ba 140, extract of report: Dec. 17, 1892; Ba 1115, "Thanne," Aug. 16 and Sept. 2, and Nov. 2, 1893; police report, Oct. 26 (or Dec.) 1893; Ba 1085, report of Oct. 14, 1892 and *La Révolte*, Dec. 3, 1892, Sept. 25 and Dec. 8, 1893; Feb. 24 and Mar. 13, 1894; Ba 1509, Sept. 16, 1894.
Ravachol's trial took place: Varennes, *De Ravachol*, pp. 8–27.

82 "If I killed": Woodcock, *Anarchism*, p. 309.
"To be happy": Varennes, *De Ravachol*, p. 47.

83 "the murder of Ravachol will open": Sonn, *Anarchism and Cultural Politics*, pp. 17, 165.
"the peal of thunder": Ibid., p. 17.

83 Ravachol as "a redeemer": Varias, *Paris and the Anarchists*, pp. 84–85.
Ravachol, a "violent Christ": Sonn, *Anarchism and Cultural Politics*, p. 260; *L'Endehors*, July 24, 1892.
"noble bearing " before death: Daniel Gerould, *Guillotine: Its Legend and Lore* (New York, 1992), pp. 94, 195–97.

84 Ravachol's "dandy adaptation": Fitzgerald, "Émile Pouget," p. 242, from *Père Peinard,* Jan. 1–8, 1893.

"Ravachol, an Anarchist?": Ba 77, July 20, 1892; Lefrère and Oriol, *Zo d'Axa,* p. 70.

elusive anarchist lurking: Eisenzweig, *Fictions,* pp. 155, 279.

"the conspiracy of silence": *L'Endehors,* Nov. 27–Dec. 4, 1892.

"La Ravachole": Jean Maitron, ed., *Ravachol et les anarchistes,* pp. 75–76; *Almanach du Père Peinard 1894.*

85 "Dame Dynamite": Natat, *La vie quotidienne,* p. 141.

86 a rapidly increasing threat: Ba 508–10.

"profession of judge": Jean Grave, *Quarante ans de propagande anarchiste* (Paris, 1973), pp. 280–82.

hundreds of scrawled messages: Ba 508–510.

87 "to wipe out the work": Jean-Pierre Machelon, *La République contre les libertés? Les restrictions aux libertés publiques de 1879 à 1914* (Paris, 1976), p. 405.

"Such acts," he said: Maitron, *Le mouvement anarchiste,* I, p. 240; Pierre Miquel, *Les anarchistes* (Paris, 2003), p. 206.

Montbrison or Saint-Étienne: A. D. Loire, 1M 533, telegram, June 23, 1892; Ba 1115, June 22 or 23, 1892, and police report, Feb. 15, 1894.

88 101, rue Marcadet: Ba 1115, prefect of police, Aug. 4 and police report, Oct. 26, 1892.

"Since a temple has burdened it": Sonn, "Marginality and Transgression," p. 125.

destroying Sacré-Coeur: Ba 77, July 18, 1892; Sonn, *Anarchism and Cultural Politics,* p. 82.

89 Guillaume Froment could savor: Zola, *Paris,* p. 451.

These men shared a hatred: Ba 1115, Apr. 13, 1893, police report, Mar. 24, 1894.

Salle du Commerce: Ba 78, prefecture of police, Apr. 20, 1893; Lefrère and Oriol, *Zo d'Axa,* p. 51; Ba 1115, "Notices sur Émile Henry," Feb. 13, 1894.

90 One speaker set the tone: Ba 77, May 30, 1892; Ba 1115, May 30–31 and June 4, 1892 and "Notices sur Émile Henry," Feb. 13, 1894.

92 "dictated by fear": Ba 77, July 3, 1892; Ba 1115, "Notices sur Émile Henry," Feb. 13, 1894.

93 "as are those who are no longer": Émile Henry, *Coup pour coup* (Paris, 1977), p. 23.

the offices of *L'Endehors:* Lefrère and Oriol, *Zo d'Axa,* pp. 60–61.

Fortuné continued to be a regular: Ba 1502, posters and police report, July 11; Ba 77, July 3, 5, 11, 20, and 27, and Aug. 17, 1892.

94 enough nitroglycerin: Ba 1132, "Zob," July 6, 1892; Ba 77, July 16, 1892; police report, Feb. 15, 1894.
Émile spent much of July: Ba 77, June 8, 1892, and Ba 1115, police reports, Nov. 22, 1892, and Feb. 16, 1894.
concept of "propaganda by the deed": Maitron, *Histoire du mouvement*, pp. 220–21; Halperin, *Félix Fénéon*, p. 268.
95 Errico Malatesta expressed: *L'Endehors*, Aug. 21 and 28, 1892; Pietro DiPaola, "Italian Anarchists," pp. 57–60; *La Révolte*, Feb. 16, 1892; Ba 1509, "Léon," Apr. 13, 1894: "Malato, Malatesta, and Kropotkin have clearly announced that they are against propaganda by the deed."
97 "a model employee": Ba 1115; "Notices sur Émile Henry," Feb. 13, 1894, and police report, Feb. 15, 1894; *L'Écho de Paris*, Feb. 16, 1894; *La Libre Parole*, Feb. 16, 1894.

5. Carnage at a Police Station

100 The Carmaux strike: Rolande Trempé, *Les mineurs de Carmaux, 1848–1914*, I (Paris, 1971), pp. 323–24, 401–7, and II, pp. 551–71; Joan W. Scott, *The Glassworkers of Carmaux: French Craftsmen and Political Action in a Nineteenth-Century City* (Cambridge, Mass., 1974), pp. 91, 112–16, 130–35, 139–42.
101 the Russian anarchist Souvarine: Émile Zola, *Germinal* (New York, 2004), p. 144.
"insolent triumphs": Joll, *The Anarchists*, p. 118.
102 "great popes of socialism": Anne-Léa Zévaès, "Sous le signe de la dynamite: Émile Henry," *Vendémiaire*, Dec. 30, 1936 and Jan. 6, 1937.
at 11, avenue de l'Opéra: *L'Écho de Paris*, Feb. 26, 1894; Ba 1115, Dec. 1, 1892, and Feb. 13, 1894.; Ba 140, police reports, Nov. 9 and 12, 1892; F7 12516, Nov. 8, 1892; *Le Figaro*, Mar. 15, 1894; Varennes, *De Ravachol*, pp. 221–23.
105 "the cowardly assassins": *Bulletin Municipal Officiel*, Nov. 12, 1892; Ba 1115, police report, Nov. 11, 1892.
106 a boat to London: Zévaès, "Sous le signe"; Ba 1115, Nov. 22 and 26, 1892, the latter a copy of Henry's letter to Dupuy.
107 180 possible suspects: Ba 140, police reports, Nov. 9, 10, and 12, 1892; Ba 1115, Apr. 12, 1894; *Le Journal*, Feb. 17, 1894; Ba 1115, Nov. 22, 1892. He left his room on quai de Valmy on Oct. 31.
108 Émile's precipitous departure: Ba 1115, Nov. 22–23, 1892.
police interviewed Émile's boss: Ba 1115, Nov. 22 and Dec. 1, 1892.
109 Also on the list: Ba 140, "Individus signalés comme ayant pu participer à

l'explosion de la rue des Bons-Enfants"; telegram, Nov. 8, 1892, 11:55 A.M.; police reports, Nov. 10, 11, 23, 1894; 4M 582, commissaire spécial, Mar. 20, 1895.

attended anarchist meetings: Ba 77.

The police followed up: F7 12504, F7 12516, Nov. 9. 1892, Apr. 11, 1893, and Apr. 27, 1894.

110 the "firecracker": Langlais, *Père Peinard,* pp. 111–14.

111 leave behind "this trinket": Flor O'Squarr, *Les coulisses de l'anarchie* (Paris, 1892), pp. 34–35.

112 Avengers of Ravachol: F7 12512, Nov. 8–11, 1892.

on the eve of a trip: Ba 1115, police reports, Dec. 14–16, 18, 1892.

"the pretty little dance" and view from London: Ba 1115, "Zob," Dec. 21, 1892, copy of Émile's letter of Dec. 7; "Léon," Feb. 17, 1894.

113 "I will bite": Ba 1115, report of "Zob," Dec. 21, 1892.

About four hundred French: Constance Bantman, "French Anarchist Exiles in London Before 1914" (unpublished dissertation, Université de Paris XIII, 2007), pp. 251–52, basing this figure on the estimate of Charles Malato.

Italians living in London: DiPaolo, "Italian Anarchists," pp. 34–47, 89–91; *L'Éclair,* Mar. 3, 1894, interview with Inspector Melville, putting the number of French anarchists at about a thousand; John Sweeney, *At Scotland Yard: Being the Experiences During Twenty-Seven Years of Service of John Sweeney* (London, 1904), p. 243.

114 "The Anarchists are 'criminals'": Ibid., pp. 219–24; *Commonweal,* Nov. 25, 1893.

"first wave" of modern terrorism: Rapoport, "The Four Waves," pp. 46–73.

115 "The entire world is my country": Thanks to Carl Levy for providing this quotation.

important anarchist hubs: Rapoport, "The Four Waves," pp. 2–3.

could be found in Spain: Sweeney, *At Scotland Yard,* pp. 278–79.

immigration to London increased: Richard Bach Jensen, "The International Campaign Against Anarchist Terrorism, 1880–1914/1930s" (unpublished paper), p. 10.

immigrants generated xenophobia: See Michael Collyer, "Secret Agents: Anarchists, Islamists, and Responses to Politically Active Refugees in London," *Ethnic and Racial Studies,* 28, 2 (March 2005), pp. 278–303, noting the association of anarchism in London with Jewish immigration (p. 280); Bantman, "French Anarchist Exiles," p. 414.

116 ticket for a dance: DiPaolo, "Italian Anarchists," p. 15.

"Anarchist-hunter[s]": Sweeney, *At Scotland Yard,* p. 204.

117 a veritable obsession: Bantman, "French Anarchist Exiles," pp. 298–300.

118 looked suspiciously upon comrades: Ba 140, police reports, Nov. 9, 1892, Mar. 26, 1893, and Feb. 21 and Mar. 26, 1894; *Le Gil Blas,* Feb. 16, 1894.

The Italian anarchist Rubino: Pietro DiPaola, "The Spies Who Came in from the Heat: The International Surveillance of the Anarchists in London," *European History Quarterly,* 37 (2), pp. 192–93.

reports that were misleading: See Richard Cobb, *The Police and the People: French Popular Protest, 1789–1820* (New York, 1972).

collected useful information: DiPaola, "Italian Anarchists," p. 257. David Nicol on Melville: Sweeney, *At Scotland Yard,* p. 226.

concerning anarchist publications: H. Oliver, *The International Anarchist Movement in Late Victorian London* (London, 1983), p. 79; F7 12518, "Les Dynamitards aux Panamitards," printed in London, ordered seized on Dec. 19, 1893; Bantman, "French Anarchist Exiles," pp. 15–17.

police did succeed somewhat: Dominique Kalifa, *Crimes et culture au XIXe siècle* (Paris, 2005), p. 12.

six anarchists were arrested: Sweeney, *At Scotland Yard,* pp. 209–20.

119 "La Petite France": Bantman, "French Anarchist Exiles," p. 260.

around Fitzroy Square: Hugh David, *The Fitzrovians* (London, 1988), pp. 81–82, 85, 88–89; Mike Pentelow and Marsha Row, *Characters of Fitzrovia* (London, 2001), p. 8; Walter Besant, *London North of the Thames* (London, 1911), p. 406.

"where my banished friends": Pentelow and Row, *Characters of Fitzrovia,* p. 50; Oliver, *The International Anarchist Movement,* pp. 64–65; Bantman, "French Anarchist Exiles," p. 334.

120 "a collection of poor devils": J. C. Longoni, *Four Patients of Dr. Deibler: A Study in Anarchy* (London, 1970), p. 146, from *Le Figaro,* Feb. 17, 1894.

simply "vegetating," completely: Bantman, "French Anarchist Exiles," p. 301.

street and *fish*: Charles Malato, *Les joyeusetés de l'exile* (Ossas-Suhare, 1985), p. 31.

Richard's grocery store: Ibid., p. 47; Fitzgerald, "Émile Pouget," pp. 254–60; Ba 1504: Oct. 17, 1894 (Z.1.); Bantman, "French Anarchist Exiles," p. 260. See also Jean Maitron, *De la Commune à l'anarchie* (Paris, 1894), p. 276.

a list of phrases: Malato, *Les joyeusetés,* pp. 174–75.

121 edited by Charles Malato: Malato, "Some Anarchist Portraits," p. 331.

122 "a little country": Ba 1115, "Z no. 2," Dec. 25, 1892.

When Émile arrived in London: Ba 1115, "Zob," Dec. 21, 1892; Ba 1509, Sept. 16, 1894; Bantman, "French Anarchist Exiles," p. 258.

to the Autonomy Club: The term "shadow circle" is that of George Woodcock; Bantman, "French Anarchist Exiles," pp. 18–22, 210–11; Sweeney, *At Scotland Yard,* p. 216; Ba 1509, Jan. 25, 1894.

123 The anarchist clubs did the best: Malato, *Les joyeusetés*, pp. 45–46, 96, adding that "so bitter was life in this little anarchist republic that those who composed it had only one desire: to leave"; DiPaola, "Italian Anarchists," pp. 220–31; National Archives of Britain, HO 144/587/B2840C, chief constable, Sept. 15, 1892.

discuss events back home: Murray Bookchin, *The Spanish Anarchists: The Heroic Years, 1868–1936* (San Francisco, 1998), pp. 107–8; Oliver, *The International Anarchist Movement*, pp. 84–85. The bomb in the Liceo Theater can of course also be considered as an originating or at least defining moment in the origins of modern terrorism.

124 paranoia that swept Paris: Jean-Pierre Machelon, *La République*, p. 405, quoting P. Boilley, "L'idée anarchiste," *Revue Bleue*, Dec. 23, 1893, p. 406; O'Squarr, *Les coulisses*, pp. 34–35, 97, 104–5, 116–18, 294; Georges Blond, *La grande armée du drapeau noir: Les anarchistes à travers le monde* (Paris, 1972), pp. 217–18; Ba 1115, Dec. 30, 1892; Varennes, *De Ravachol*, p. 7.

125 The French journalist: Henri Rochefort, *The Adventures of My Life*, vol. 2 (London, 1896), pp. 400–401.

126 The "associationalists": Bantman, "French Anarchist Exiles," pp. 213, 285, 294–95. Thanks also to Carl Levy.

127 "audacious and determined": Ba 1115, Z.2 from London, Dec. 21 and 25, 1892.

"even somewhat intimate": Ba 1115, "Zob," Dec. 6, 1892.

128 "to demonstrate his satisfaction": Ba 1504, Z.1, Oct. 17, 1894. "a solitary and fanatic": Ba 77, Aug. 11, 1892; Ba 1509, Sept. 16, 1894, "Diabolical Plots: Their Organization and Execution," written by a London inspector of police.

The "betrayer" also revealed: Ba 1115, letter from Orleans, Dec. 8 and of [smudged] Lacalee [?] or could be Zévaco, Dec. 10, 1892.

"Well! Although he": Rochefort, *The Adventures*.

130 "The bombs of Barcelona": Malato, "Some Anarchist Portraits," pp. 331–32.

Fiquefleur-Équainville: Ba 1115, Mar. 27 and 28 and May 2, 1894; Ba 1503, Jan. 26, Feb. 2, 17, 27, Mar. 13, Apr. 8, 15, May 27, and June 1, 9, 27, 1893, *Radical*, May 4, 1894; Ba 1503, "Léon," Apr. 15, 1894.

131 to be back in Paris: F7 12516, report of Apr. 11, 1893; Ba 1115, minister of the interior, Feb. and Mar. 21, 1893, police report, Apr. 14, "Thanne," Aug. 16 and Sept. 2; police report, Oct. 26 (or Dec.), 1893; Ba 1085, reports of Oct. 14, 1892 and Sept. 25 and Dec. 8, 1893, Feb. 24 and Mar. 13, 1894, and *La Révolte*, Dec. 3, 1892; Ba 1115. Int. Feb. 20, Mar. 14, 21, 25, Apr. 12 and 21, 1893; F7 12516, Apr. 11 and Ba 1115, Apr. 14, 1893; Ba 1115, police report, May 23, 1893; "Thanne," Mar. 24, 1893; Ba 1115, Duthion, Feb. 17.

132 the Belgian Workers' Party: Ba 1115, report of Pratz and Thiéry, Feb. 21,

1894; *Le Journal,* Feb. 27, 1894; Longoni, *Four Patients,* p. 152; Franz van Kalken, *Commotions populaires en Belgique, 1834–1902* (Brussels, 1936), pp. 133–40; Janet Polasky, *The Democratic Socialism of Emile Vandervelde: Between Reform and Revolution* (Oxford, 1995), pp. 27–29; E. H. Kossmann, *The Low Countries, 1780–1940* (Oxford, 1988), p. 344; Jules Destrée and Émile Vandervelde, *Le socialisme en Belgique* (Paris, 1903), pp. 146–51; Louis Bertrand, *Histoire de la démocratie et du socialisme en Belgique depuis 1830,* vol. 2 (Brussels, 1907), pp. 491–94.

133 "Ah! You didn't tell me": Halperin, *Félix Fénéon,* p. 394.

he was not a thief: Ba 1503, June 16, 1893.

in early July 1893: Ba 1115, police report, Feb. 15 and Mar. 4, 1894; Ba 78, July 6, 1893.

arrived in London from Paris: Ba 1115, Aug. 3 and 6, "Thanne," Sept. 2, 1893; Z.6, Aug. 18 and 19, Ba 1509, Jan. 12, 1894, "Populo."

"Émile Henry?": Ba 1115, Aug. 7, 1893 and Feb. 8, 9, and 10, 1894.

134 Léon-Jules Léauthier: Ba 1115, "Z.6," London, Aug. 16, 18, and 22 or 23, and Sept. 2, 1893; "Z.6," Aug. 6, 1893; Oct. 26 (or Dec.), 1893; Ba 1085, report of Oct. 14, 1892, Sept. 25 and Dec. 8, 1893; Feb. 24 and Mar. 13, 1894; and *La Révolte,* Dec. 3, 1892; Ba 1509, "Z.6," Feb. 19, 1894. Francis told the police that Henry was still in London at the beginning of September. Ba 1503, Nov. 23, 1893.

The day before the attack: Varennes, *De Ravachol,* pp. 165–75; Maurice Garçon, *Histoire de la justice sous la IIIe République,* I (Paris, 1957), p. 233; Sonn, *Anarchism and Cultural Politics,* pp. 121–22, quoting *L'Éclair,* Dec. 18, 1893, and 256.

The police intensified: Ba 77, list of anarchists, Apr. 1, 1892, etc., Mar. 23 and Aug. 11, 1892; Ba 1115, police report, Aug. 3, 16, 18, 21, and 23, 1893; "Z.6," Aug. 19, 1893; Ba 1509, "Z.6," Feb. 19, 1894. One report had Matha returning to London only on Aug. 19 from Paris, "where he left the brother of Fortuné."

6. Two Bombs

137 August Vaillant, an unemployed: Ba 141, Auguste Vaillant; André Salmon, *La terreur noire* (Paris, 1959), pp. 294–98; Maitron, *Histoire de mouvement,* pp. 212–17; Varennes, *De Ravachol,* pp. 98–133.

138 "Here's some news. 'The Aquarium'": Leyret, *En plein faubourg,* p. 155.

139 police obtained information: F7 12516, Dec. 11, 1893.

On Intellectual Complicity: M. P. Fabreguettes, *De la complicité intellectuelle et des délits d'opinion: De la provocation et de l'apologie criminelle de la propaganda anarchiste* (Paris, 1894–95), pp. 6, 19–22, 34–35, especially chapter 8.

propaganda "by ideas": Guillaume Loubat, *Code de la législation contre les anarchistes* (Paris, 1895), p. 188.

140 "scoundrelly" or "shameful" laws: Ba 1500, Jan. 5, 1894; Loubat, *Code de la législation,* passim; Machelon, *La République,* pp. 413–14, 436–40; *Journal Official,* Dec. 19, 1893; Manevy, *Sous les plis,* p. 140. See Eisenzweig, *Fictions,* pp. 300–302; searches, F7 12508.

142 replicated in Italy and Spain: Levy, "The Anarchist Assassin," p. 10, noting that in Italy the anarchist attacks "opened the way for a reconciliation of the 'Extreme Left' (the socialists and the radicals) with the liberals, a turning point in Italian history"; George Eisenwein, "Sources of Anarchist Terrorism in Late-Nineteenth-Century Spain" (unpublished paper), pp. 9, 15.

examined a dead rat: Ba 66, Girard, Dec. 23, 1893.

suspicion of being anarchists: F7 12504, Apr. 27, 1894, prefecture of police.

"hang as a menace": Jensen, "Daggers, Rifles, and Dynamite," p. 138.

143 Those arrested in Paris: Ba 1500; Machelon, *La République,* pp. 418–19, 432; Sonn, *Anarchism and Cultural Politics,* p. 20; F7 12508; Halperin, *Félix Fénéon,* p. 51; 432; Varennes, *De Ravachol,* pp. 140–45.

"personal friendship": Ibid., p. 101.

involved in a swindle: Fitzgerald, "Émile Pouget," p. 262; F7 13053, Moreau, commissaire special, "Anarchisme en France," 1897.

the overreaching efforts: *La Libre Parole,* Jan. 28, 1894.

144 "staying at his side": F7 12504, Apr. 27, 1894, prefecture of police.

Vaillant went on trial: Ba 79, Jan. 29 and 30, 1894; Varennes, *De Ravachol,* pp. 108–33; Leyret, *En plein faubourg,* pp. 156–60.

146 "a desolate stupefaction": Ibid., pp. 159–60.

147 a Parisian family: Manevy, *Sous le plis,* p. 60.

"in the air" of the faubourgs; Leyret, *En plein faubourg,* pp. 153–54; Ba 79, Feb. 1, 1894.

Anything could happen next: Ba 79, Jan. 29, 1894.

the watchmaker's shop: Ba 1115, "Notices sur Émile Henry," Feb. 13, 1894.

147 the Villa Faucheur: *Le Figaro,* Feb. 16, 1894; *L'Éclair,* Feb. 17, 1894; *L'Écho de Paris,* Feb. 18, 1894; *Le Matin,* Feb. 16, 1894.

"Émile Dubois": *L'Intransigeant,* Feb. 17, 1894.

148 The police grew increasingly: Ba 1115, "Populo," Jan. 15, 18, 23, and 24, 1894; "Léon," Feb. 4 and 6, 1894.

"Léon," an ace: Ba 1115, Feb. 11–12, 1894.

Adrienne Chailley: Ba 1115, "Léon," Feb. 8, and "Thanne," Feb. 8 and 9, 1894.

149 "your friendship bothers me": Maitron, *Le mouvement anarchiste,* p. 239, citing a conversation with Madame Matha, July 28, 1946.

"for quite a while": Ba 1115, "Léon," Feb. 10 and 11, 1894; *L'Intransigeant,* Feb. 17, 1894.

149 The bomb thrown on February 12: Ba 141, testimony; *L'Intransigeant* and *L'Éclair*, Feb. 14–15, 1894; *Le Matin*, Feb. 13, 1894; *Le XIXe Siècle*, Feb. 14, 1894; *L'Événement*, May 21, 1894; Ba 1115, police reports, Feb. 13 and Mar. 27, 1894; Varennes, *De Ravachol*, pp. 213–43.

152 His clothes had been torn: Ba 1115, reports of guards, Feb. 18, 1894; *L'Éclair*, Feb. 15, 1894.

154 notified the prefect: *L'Éclair*, Feb. 15, 1894.

155 the Café Terminus had been blocked: *Le XIXe Siècle*, *L'Intransigeant*, *L'Éclair*, Feb. 14, 1894.

   taken into the receiving room: Ba 1113, police report, Feb. 13, 1894.

157 the "anthropomorphic" department: Ba 141, Feb. 13, 1894, 2:30 a.m.; *Observations anthropométriques* in Ba 1115, noting various small scars, and giving his height at five feet, three inches.

   to see Judge Meyer: F7 12517; *Le Matin*, Feb. 13, 1894.

   He invoked "legitimate defense": Ba 1115, *fichier*, and reports of Feb. 13, 1894; *L'Éclair*, Feb. 15, 1894.

   Two of the guards: Ba 1115, report of Feb. 14, 1894, and *chef de service* of the Conciergerie, Feb. 14, 1894, 2:30 a.m.

159 striking similarities: Ba 1115, "Léon," Feb. 13, 1894, and report of Feb. 14, 2:00 a.m.

   Vaillant, whose execution: *Le Matin*, Feb. 13, 1894.

   a "ridiculous bomb": *Le 19e Siècle*, Feb. 16, 1894.

   Émile's bomb: Ba 1115, Feb. 13, 1894, *chef de service*; *Le Journal*, Feb. 22, 1894.

160 The door had been forced: *Le Figaro*, Feb. 16, 1894; *L'Intransigeant*, Feb. 17 and 18, 1894; Ba 1215, police, "Léon," Apr. 27, 1894; Ba 1115, Mar. 22–23, 28, Apr. 1 and 27, 1894; F7 13053, Moreau, commissaire spécial, "L'anarchisme en France," 1897.

   a photo of Émile: *Le Figaro*, Feb. 16, 1894.

   material for making more bombs: *L'Intransigeant*, Feb. 18, 1894; *Le Gaulois*, Feb. 15, 1894; *Le Gil Blas*, Feb. 16, 1894.

161 "scandalous scenes": *Belle France*, Feb. 13, and *Le 19e Siècle*, Feb. 15, 1894.

   The press immediately seized: *La Lanterne* and *L'Événement*, Feb. 14, 1894.

7. The Trial

163 "our so troubling and complex": *Le Matin*, Feb. 15, 1894.

   The Anarchist Peril: Félix Dubois, *Le péril anarchiste* (Paris, 1894).

   When part of the scenery: Ernest A. Vizetelly, *The Anarchists: Their Faith and Their Record* (London, 1911), p. 164.

164 "a new Poland": *L'Intransigeant,* Feb. 14, 1894.

offering insurance policies: Sonn, "Marginality and Transgression," p. 130.

more searches of residences: *Le Gaulois,* Mar. 3, 1894; *L'Intransigeant,* Feb. 26, 1894; Guillaume Loubat, *Code de la législation contre les anarchistes* (Paris, 1895), p. 188.

Martial Bourdin: *La Patrie,* Feb. 19, 1894.

"moneyed bourgeois": DiPaola, *Italian Anarchists,* p. 47; Oliver, *International Anarchist Movement,* p. 101.

The police showed up: Ba 1115, police report, Feb. 15, 1894.

165 Three journalists made their way: *Le Petit Temps,* Feb. 16, 1894.

merely vulgar insults: *Le 19e Siècle,* Feb. 20, 1894.

166 "I am transfigured!": *Le 19e Siècle,* Feb. 23, 1894; Ba 1115, Feb. 16, 1894.

the marquise de Chamborant: Ba 1115, Feb. 15 and 17, 1894; *Le 19e Siècle,* Feb. 24, 1894.

"his easy gusto": *Débats* and *République Française,* Feb. 15, 1894.

On February 17, a magistrate: Ba 1115, telegram, Feb. 17, 1894; *L'Intransigeant,* Feb. 19, 1894; *Le 19e Siècle,* Feb. 20, 1894; *L'Éclair,* Feb. 20, 1894.

167 he had left the bomb: Ba 1115, Feb. 21, 1894; Ba 77, Apr. 2, 1892.

My dear little Mother: Ba 1115, Feb. 19, 1894.

168 "He has avenged his father!": Martin A. Miller, "Ordinary Terrorism in Historical Perspective," *Journal for the Study of Radicalism,* 2, 2 (2008), p. 140.

moved by seeing her: Ba 1115, Feb. 21, 1894; *L'Éclair,* Feb. 22, 1894.

"Don't speak to me about it": Ba 1115, Feb. 21, 1894; *L'Éclair,* Feb. 22, 1894.

169 piece number 462: *La Libre Parole,* Mar. 20, 1894.

Hornbostel initially insisted: *L'Éclair,* Feb. 22, 1894; Ba 1115, Feb. 23 and Mar. 13–14, 1894.

During a reconstruction: Ba 1115, Feb. 26 and 28, 1894, commissaire de police; telegram, Feb. 28, 1894.

"always threatens exhausted brains": *La Petite République* and *L'Éclair,* Apr. 26, 1894.

170 The relative comfort: Ba 1115, police reports, Feb. 22 and 25, Mar. 7–12, 15–16, 20, 30, and Apr. 5, 1894; *Le 19e Siècle,* Mar. 31, 1894; *Le Gaulois,* Apr. 14, 1894; Reg Carr, *Anarchism in France: The Case of Octave Mirbeau* (Montreal, 1977), pp. 65–66.

"absolute equality": Henry, *Coup pour coup,* p. 33; Guérin, ed., *No Gods, No Masters,* p. 397; Ba 1115, Émile Henry, Feb. 22, 1894.

Sometimes Émile walked: Ba 1115, Mar. 28–30, Apr. 1, 4, 12–14, 16–17, and 20, 1894; *Le 19e Siècle,* Mar. 31, 1894; Longoni, *Four Patients,* p. 154; *La Lanterne,* Mar. 5, 1894; *L'Intransigeant,* Feb. 19, 1894.

171 newspapers debated the significance: Henri Ribeyre, "Chronique poli-tique," *La Revue Blanche*, 6, Mar. 1894; Sonn, *Anarchism and Cultural Politics*, p. 252; *Le Figaro*, Mar. 27; *La Patrie*, Feb. 22; *Le Soleil*, May 6, 1894, which added that Henry was "a materialist and atheist . . . the natural product of our Judeo-Freemason society, of our frivolous and corrupt society, without beliefs, ideals, and faith."

172 bomb exploded in Lyon: *Le Figaro*, Feb. 25; *L'Intransigeant*, Mar. 31, 1894. "What do the waves": Herbert, *The Artist*, p. 124.

The explosion at the Foyot: Halperin, *Félix Fénéon*, pp. 3–4, 275–76; Ba 142, reports, Mar. 26, Apr. 4, 5, 11, 13, 25, and June 25, 1894; *L'Écho*, Apr. 7, 1894; Herbert, *The Artist*, p. 124; *La Libre Parole*, Apr. 17, 1894; Sonn, *Anarchism and Cultural Politics*, p. 234.

173 "Once more, the idea": *La Libre Parole*, Apr. 17, 1894.

Girard, the chemist: Ba 1115, Mar. 13–14, 1894.

174 covered by a woman's wig: Ba 1115, Feb. 23, 1894.

"had never had relations": Ba 1115, Mar. 8, 1894.

Ten francs arrived: Ba 1115, Mar. 9, 1894.

anarchist Philibert Pauwels: Ba 1215, Jan. 14, 1885; Oct. 14 and 27, 1887; Mar. 21, Nov. 17, and Dec. 9, 1890; Mar. 9, Apr. 25–26, May 1, 3, 5, 7, July 15, 17, 21, 22, 27, Aug. 1, 8, 25, 28, and Dec. 31, 1891; act of expulsion, Apr. 28, 1891; minister of the interior, Dec. 19, 1891, and Jan. 28, 1892; Jan. 11, 19, 23, 28, Feb. 10, 13, Mar. 26, May 10, 17, and Dec. 9, 13, 29, 1892; Oct. 6, 1893 (report of X.2); Feb. 27 and Mar. 11, 16, 17, 18, 20–21, 24, 27, 28, 1894; *procès-verbal*, Aug. 7; Pauwels, Aug. 8; prefect of police, Apr. 23, 1892; *Le Matin*, Mar. 17, 1894, *Le Temps*, Sept. 18, 1894; prefect of Gironde, Mar. 21, 1894; *Le Gil Blas*, Mar. 18, 1894; minister of the interior, Dec. 19, 1891; prefect of police, Apr. 23, 1892; *Le Matin*, Mar. 17, 1894, *Le Temps*, Sept. 18, 1894; *Le Journal*, Mar. 18, 1894; Ba 142, Feb. 21; *Le Matin* and *France*, Feb. 21; *L'Éclair*, Feb. 22; *La Patrie*, Feb. 27, 1894; Ba 142; *L'Éclair*, Mar. 17, 1894; *Le Journal*, May 10, 1894; letter of "Étienne Rabardy," 69, rue Saint-Jacques, n.d.; *Le Matin* and *Le Figaro*, Mar. 16, 1894; *La Patrie* and *Greffier*, May 11, 1894; *Le Figaro*, Mar. 21, 1894.

179 each side of the courtroom: See Katherine Fischer Taylor, *In the Theater of Criminal Justice: The Palais de Justice in Second Empire Paris* (Princeton, 1993), especially pp. 31–33, 43–48, 65ff; *Le Matin*, Apr. 16, 1894; Association de la Presse Judiciaire, *The Paris Law Courts: Sketches of Men and Manners* (New York, 1894), pp. 180–201.

The jury sat: Varennes, *De Ravachol*, pp. 312–43; Albert Bataille, *Causes criminelles et mondaines de 1894: Les procès anarchistes* (Paris, 1895), pp. 50–93; *L'Intransigeant*, Apr. 29, 1894; *Le Figaro*, Apr. 28 and 29, 1894; Ba 141, minister of the interior, Feb. 24, 1894; *L'Éclair*, Apr. 3, 1894; *La Patrie*, Apr. 25, 1894.

182 thereby identifying accomplices: Ba 1115, Feb. 23 and 26, Mar. 7, 11–16, 24, 1894; *L'Éclair,* Feb. 21, 1894; *Le Matin,* Feb. 23, 1893; Ba 140, police reports, Feb. 14, and prefect of police, Feb. 15, 1894; *L'Intransigeant,* Feb. 16, 1894: *Le 19e Siècle,* Feb. 16, 1894.

183 Girard, the omnipresent director: Ba 1115, Émile Henry, Feb. 27, 1894, Conciergerie.

188 Hornbostel's defense was disastrous: Gérard A. Jaeger, *Anatole Deibler, carnets d'exécutions, 1885–1939* (Paris, 2004), p. 121; Maitron, *Histoire du mouvement,* note 1, p. 226; *Le Figaro,* Apr. 29, 1894; Ba 1115, Apr. 28, 1894.
"his loss of the instinct": *La Petite République,* May 6, 1894.

189 "is the life of anarchism": *La Petite République,* May 7, 1894.
"this final test . . . a thousand kisses": Ba 1115.
On May 1, Émile wrote: Ba 1115, Apr. 24, 1894; Ba 1115, Apr. 24, 1894; *Le 19e Siècle,* Apr. 27, 1894, with Émile's letter; Émile Henry, *Déclaration* (Paris, 1894); Varennes, *De Ravachol,* pp. 233–34; Bataille, *Causes criminelles,* pp. 50–93, carried by *Le Figaro,* Apr. 28, 1894. On April 25, the police, who had searched in April the residence Fénéon shared with his mother, Marie-Louise, turned up again. As they neared the door, his mother got rid of the copy of the work Henry was preparing for his trial (Halperin, *Félix Fénéon,* pp. 276–79).

190 "miraculous image": *Le Journal,* May 12, 1894.
"I don't want to see her!": *Le Figaro,* May 6, 1894.
Élisa Gauthey had become a star: *Le Journal,* May 17, 1894.

191 By tradition, no one: *L'Événement,* May 22, 1894.
"If they cut off his head": *L'Intransigeant,* May 22, 1894.
the "national razor": Daniel Arasse, *The Guillotine and the Terror* (London, 1989), pp. 2–75, quote from p. 13.

192 guillotined per year: Georges Grison, *Souvenirs de la place de la Roquette* (Paris, 1883), p. 18.
to Anatole Deibler: *Le Matin,* May 21, 1894; *19e Siècle,* May 22, 1894; *Justice,* May 22, 1894; *L'Événement,* May 22, 1894.

193 "to put on a play": Bernard, *Les deux Paris,* pp. 137–38.

194 "a solemnity of horror and majesty": *Le Journal,* May 22, 1894, "Un témoin de la guillotine"; *L'Écho de Paris,* May 22, 1894.
a mere "aristocrat of crime": *La Libre Parole,* May 22, 1894.
"Don't talk to me about anarchists": *Le Gaulois,* May 21, 1894.

196 "as miserable as his machine": Gérard A. Jaeger, *Anatole Deibler (1863–1939): L'homme qui trancha 400 têtes* (Paris, 2001), pp. 74, 128.
Some of the workmen: *Le Journal,* May 21 and 22, 1894; *Le Matin,* May 21, 1894; *L'Événement,* May 21, 1894.

197 Louis Deibler, with one or two: Jaeger, *Anatole Deibler, carnets,* pp. 15–25; Jaeger, *Anatole Deibler (1863–1939),* pp. 131, 274.

198 The small procession: *Le Journal*, May 21 and 22, 1894; *La Libre Parole*, May 22, 1894.

199 "Long live the Commune!": *Le Matin*, May 21, 1894.
"a humanization of customs": *Le Journal*, May 23, 1894.
Émile's body: *19e Siècle*, May 22, 1894; *Le Journal*, May 21, 1894; *Le Figaro*, *La Libre Parole*, *L'Éclair*, *La Petit République*, and *Le Journal*, May 22, 1894; office of the prefect of police to the dean of the medical school, May 21, 1894; Goupil, May 21, 1894; Ba 1115, dean of the medical school, May 21 and 23.

200 departed for Brévannes: *L'Écho de Paris*, May 22, 1894; *19e Siècle*, May 22, 1894; *L'Intransigeant*, May 22, 1894.

201 On May 24, Émile was buried: Ba 1115, reports of Descaves, May 24, and commissaire spécial to the prefect of the Seine-et-Oise, May 25, 1894.
"Who is next?": Leyret, *En plein faubourg*, p. 161.

8. Reaction

203 "To those who say: hate": *La Renaissance*, May 20, 1896.
"A mortal enemy": *Le Journal*, Feb. 19, 1894, cited in Maitron, ed., *Dictionnaire biographique*.
"not that which lashes out": Ibid., "Malato, Charles."
embarrassment to the anarchist cause: James Joll, "Singing, Dancing, and Dynamite," *Times Literary Supplement*, Sept. 10, 1976.

204 self-proclaimed "resolute avenger": Leyrat, *En plein faubourg*, pp. 161–65.
Émile entered history: *L'Écho de Paris*, May 22, 1894.

205 "monstrous hatred": *L'Événement*, May 22, 1894.
Items related to Émile: Sonn, *Anarchism and Cultural Politics*, p. 247; Ba 1115, May 11, 1894; DiPaola, "Italian Anarchists," p. 57. The Belgian newspaper was *La Débâcle Sociale*.
"his sensitivities so full of love": Ba 1115, Nov. 22, 1893, commissaire special of Boissy St. Léger to prefect and to his counterpart in Versailles, Nov. 22, 1894; *La Renaissance* (G. Pérot), May 20, 1896.

206 Émilienne-Henriette: Léger, *Journal*, pp. 250, 302, saluting Caserio, "he pulled off the greatest coup. To wipe out a president of the Republic, *c'est princier* ..."
"the great human family": Kedward, *The Anarchists*, p. 42; Levy, "The Anarchist Assassin," p. 13.

207 "dynamite psychosis": Eisenzweig, *Fictions*, chapter II/3, esp. pp. 300–303, 325; R. Garraud, *L'anarchie et la répression* (Paris, 1895), pp. 11, 19–23, 114–15, 133.
"acts of violence": M. P. Fabreguettes, *De la complicité*, pp. 39–41; Machelon, *La République*, pp. 409–45; Varennes, *De Ravachol*, pp. 246–72; R.

Garraud, *L'anarchie*, p. 53, citing article 2, law of 28–7–94; F7 12508, "considérations générales," Jan. 1894; Loubat, *Code de la législation*, pp. 177–78.

208 "Trial of the Thirty": Préposiet, *Histoire*, p. 400; Manevy, *Sous le plis*, p. 75; E. V. Zenker, *Anarchism: A Criticism and History of the Anarchist Theory* (New York, 1897), pp. 320–23; Varennes, *De Ravachol*, pp. 286–349.

209 Deibler's "accessories": *Le Journal*, May 22, 1894. In any case, the "scoundrelly laws" remained in place for decades; the third one, that of July 1894, remained on the books until 1992.

Marie-François Goron: Marie-François Goron, *Les mémoires de Goron, ancient chef de la Sûreté* (Paris, 1897–98), pp. 7–8, 12–16.

pilgrimage to the auberge: Ba 1115, police reports, Feb. 12 and May 16, 1896; May 31, 1897; and May 31, 1898; *La Renaissance*, May 20 and 23, 1896; *Foureur*, May 5, 1901; *Liberté*, May 26, 1896; prefect of police, May 21, 23, 25, and n.d., and Int., May 20, 1896; police reports, May 9, 18, 22, 26, and 29, 1896; May 21, 23, 25, 26, and 27, 1901; May 14, 1902, and telegram, Mar. 5, 1905, indicating that about two hundred anarchists showed up at the auberge; *La Petite République*, May 26, 1896; *L'Événement*, May 25, 1896; *Les Temps Nouveaux*, May 31, 1901.

210 "ridiculous deprivations": Maitron, *Histoire*, I, p. 367.

As for Jules: Zévaès, "Sous le signe," *Vendémiaire*, Dec. 30, 1935 and Jan. 6, 1937.

211 toward syndicalism: Sonn, *Anarchism and Cultural Politics*, p. 25; Guérin, *Anarchism*, p. 78; Jean-Marie Mayeur and Madeleine Rebérioux, *The Third Republic, from Its Origins to the Great War, 1871–1914* (New York, 1987), p. 144; Joll, *The Anarchists*, pp. 180–81, 187; Woodcock, *Anarchism*, pp. 321–22.

212 a character much like Émile: Zola, *Paris*, p. 466.

In London, the anarchists: Ba 1509; Oliver, *The International*, pp. 104–5, 141; Ba 1509.

213 the number of militant anarchists: *Le Matin*, Mar. 5, 1894. The number fell from about 10,000 to 8,000, and in Paris from about 2,800 to 2,300, still a considerable number, along with 1,500 to 2,000 in Lyon and its region, and about 1,000 in Marseille. F7 13053, Moreau, commissaire special, "L'anarchisme en France," 1897.

Bonnot's band terrorized: Maitron, *Histoire du mouvement*, I, pp. 396–406; Joll, "Singing, Dancing, and Dynamite."

Elsewhere anarchism continued: Jensen, "The International Campaign," pp. 18–21; Joll, *The Anarchists*, pp. 207–23.

214 In the United States, anarchist attacks: Jensen, "The International Campaign," pp. 23–24.

215 "They have shown how": Joll, *The Anarchists*, pp. 158 and 163.

"there weren't any": F7 13053, Moreau, commissaire spécial, "L'anarchisme en France," 1897.

"a great bandit": *L'Intransigeant,* Apr. 29, 1894.

216 "cowardly" and ignorant: Maitron, *Histoire du mouvement,* p. 222, n. 5 (quoting R. Gressent, *L'Humanité Nouvelle,* I, 1, Paris 1897, p. 631), from Jean Grave, *Le mouvement libertaire sous la Troisième République* (Paris, 1930), p. 139.

"In contrast to Vaillant": Malato, "Some Anarchist Portraits," p. 331.

"I love all people": Henry, *Coup pour coup,* p. 184.

a nineteenth-century Hamlet: Marius Boisson, *Les attentats anarchistes sous la Troisième République* (Paris, 1931), pp. 158–59, n. 1. Another interpretation, one shared by Fortuné, was that Émile's acts constituted an "indirect suicide" because he never recovered from having fallen in love with Élisa Gauthey (R. Gressent, *L'Humanité Nouvelle,* first year, Paris 1897, t. I, vol. 1, p. 631). Yet Émile struggled to get away after the Café Terminus bombing, in order to kill again.

"a pacified capital": Bernard, *Les deux Paris,* p. 240.

Bibliography

PRIMARY SOURCES

Archives Nationales
BB24 853
F7 12504, 12506–09, 12518, 12830–32, 12835, 13053
14 AS 25, 14 AS 136

Archives de la Préfecture de Police
Ba 66, 75–79, 103, 140–42, 303, 508–10, 894, 1085, 1115, 1132, 1170, 1215, 1237, 1289,
1500, 1502–04, 1507–09

Archives Départementales de la Loire
1M 528, 529, 533,
4M 153, 173, 569, 582
(4)U 299

National Archives of Great Britain
HO 45/10254/X36450
HO 144/587/B2840C
HO 144/545/A55176

L'Endehors, La Révolte, La Petite République, L'Éclair, Le 19e Siècle, La Libre Parole, Le Figaro, L'Intransigeant, Le Matin, La Patrie, Le Gaulois, Débats, Le Rap-

pel, *Le Temps, La Cocarde, Le Jour, Le Petit Journal, Le Gil Blas, L'Écho de Paris, L'Événement, Le Soleil, Paris, Gazette des Tribunaux, Le Petit Temps, Justice, Le Journal, La Renaissance*

SECONDARY LITERATURE

Adamic, Louis. *Dynamite: The Story of Class Violence in America.* New York, 1931.

Almanach du Père Peinard, 1894–1896–1897–1898–1899. Paris, 1984. Preface by Pierre Drachline.

Andrieux, Louis. *Souvenirs d'un préfet de police.* Paris, 1885.

Arasse, Daniel. *The Guillotine and the Terror.* London, 1989.

Association de la Presse Judiciaire. *The Paris Law Courts: Sketches of Men and Manners.* Translated by Gerald P. Moriarty. New York, 1894.

Avrich, Paul. *Anarchist Portraits.* Princeton, 1988.

Baedeker, Karl. *Paris and Environs, with Route from London to Paris,* Paris, 1896.

Bantman, Constance. "French Anarchist Exiles in London Before 1914." Unpublished doctoral dissertation, University of Paris, 2007.

Bataille, Albert. *Causes criminelles et mondaines de 1894: Les procès anarchistes.* Paris, 1895.

Benjamin, Walter. "Paris: Capital of the Nineteenth Century," in *Reflections: Essays, Aphorisms, Autobiographical Writings,* ed. Peter Demetz. New York, 1978.

Bérard, Alexandre. *Sur l'anarchie.* Lyon, 1897.

Berlanstein, Lenard R. *The Working People of Paris, 1871–1914.* Baltimore, 1984.

Bernard, Jean-Pierre A. *Les deux Paris: Les représentations de Paris dans le seconde moitié du XIXe siècle.* Champ Vallon, 2001.

Bertrand, Louis. *Histoire de la démocratie et du socialisme en Belgique depuis 1830.* Vol. 2. Brussels, 1907.

Besant, Walter. *London North of the Thames.* London, 1911.

Blond, Georges. *Grande armée du drapeau noir.* Paris, 1972.

Boisson, Marius. *Les attentats anarchistes sous la Troisième République.* Paris, 1931.

Bongar, Bruce, Lisa M. Brown, Larry E. Beutler, James N. Breckenridge, and Philip G. Zimbardo, eds. *Psychology of Terrorism.* New York, 2007.

Bookchin, Murray. *The Spanish Anarchists: The Heroic Years, 1868–1936.* San Francisco, 1998.

Bouchardon, Pierre. *Ravachol et compagnie.* Paris, 1931.

Boussinot, Roger. *Les mots de l'anarchie.* Paris, 1982.

Brunet, Jean-Paul. *Saint-Denis, la ville rouge, 1890–1939.* Paris, 1980.

Bunyan, Tony. *The History and Practice of the Political Police in Britain.* London, 1976.

Carr, Reg. *Anarchism in France: The Case of Octave Mirbeau.* Montreal, 1977.

Chesterton, G. K. *The Man Who Was Thursday: A Nightmare.* New York, 1975 (1908).

Chevalier, Louis. *Montmartre: Du plaisir et du crime.* Paris, 1980.

Clark, T. J. *The Painting of Modern Life: Paris in the Art of Manet and His Followers.* New York, 1984.

Cobb, Richard. *The Police and the People: French Popular Protest, 1789–1820.* New York, 1972.

Collyer, Michael. "Secret Agents: Anarchists, Islamists, and Responses to Politically Active Refugees in London," *Ethnic and Racial Studies,* 28, 2 (March 2005), 278–303.

Conrad, Joseph. *The Secret Agent.* New York, 1998 (1907).

Coutry, Jean-Pierre. *Endehors.* Paris, 1974.

David, Hugh. *The Fitzrovians: A Portrait of Bohemian Society, 1900–1955.* London, 1988.

Delacour, Albert. *Les lettres de noblesse de l'anarchie.* Paris, 1899.

Destrée, Jules, and Émile Vandervelde. *Le socialisme en Belgique.* Brussels, 1903.

DiPaola, Pietro. "Italian Anarchists in London (1870–1914)." Unpublished doctoral dissertation, Goldsmiths College, University of London, 2004.

——. "The Spies Who Came in from the Heat: The International Surveillance of the Anarchists in London," *European History Quarterly,* 37 (2), 189–215.

Dostoyevsky, Fyodor. *Crime and Punishment.* New York, 2003 (1866).

Dubois, Félix. *Le péril anarchiste.* Paris, 1894.

Dumas, René. *Ravachol: L'homme rouge de l'anarchie.* Saint-Étienne, 1981.

Eisenwein, George. "Sources of Anarchist Terrorism in Late-Nineteenth-Century Spain." Unpublished paper.

Eisenzweig, Uri. *Fictions de l'anarchisme.* Paris, 2001.

Evenson, Norma. *Paris: A Century of Change, 1878–1978.* New Haven, 1979.

Fabreguettes, M. P. *De la complicité intellectuelle et des délits d'opinion: De la provocation et de l'apologie criminelle de la propaganda anarchiste.* Paris, 1894–95.

Faure, Sébastien, L. Barbedette, Victor Méric, and Voline. *La véritable révolution sociale.* Limoges, 1933.

Fitzgerald, Edward Peter. "Emile Pouget, the Anarchist Movement, and the Origins of Revolutionary Trade-Unionism in France (1880–1901). Unpublished doctoral dissertation, Yale University, 1973.

Fleming, Marie. *The Anarchist Way to Socialism: Élisée Reclus and Nineteenth-Century European Anarchism.* Totowa, New Jersey, 1979.

——. "Propaganda by the Deed: Terrorism and Anarchist Theory in Late-Nineteenth-Century Europe," in *Terrorism in Europe,* ed. Yonah Alexander and Kenneth A. Myers. New York, 1982.

Gage, Beverly. *The Day Wall Street Exploded: A Story of America.* New York, 2009.

Garçon, Maurice. *Histoire de la justice sous la IIIe République.* Vol. 1. Paris, 1957.

Garraud, R. *L'anarchie et la repression.* Paris, 1895.

Gerould, Daniel. *Guillotine: Its Legend and Lore.* New York, 1992.

Goron, Marie-François. *Les mémoires de Goron, ancien chef de la Sûreté,* Paris, 1897–98.

Grave, Jean. *Le mouvement libertaire sous la Troisième République: Souvenirs d'un révolté.* Paris, 1930.

———. *Quarante ans de propagande anarchiste.* Paris, 1973.

———. *La société mourante et l'anarchie.* Paris, 1893.

Green, James. *Death in the Haymarket: A Story of Chicago, the First Labor Movement, and the Bombing That Divided Gilded-Age America.* New York, 2006.

Grison, Georges. *Souvenirs de la place de la Roquette.* Paris, 1883.

Guérin, Daniel. *Anarchism: From Theory to Practice.* New York, 1970.

Guérin, Daniel, ed. *No Gods, No Masters.* Oakland, 2005.

Halperin, Joan. *Félix Fénéon, Aesthete and Anarchist in Fin-de-Siècle Paris.* New Haven, 1988.

Hamon, Augustin. *Psychologie de l'anarchiste-socialiste,* Paris, 1895.

———. *Socialisme et anarchisme: Études sociologiques, définitions.* Paris, 1905.

Harmel, Claude. *Histoire de l'anarchie: Des origines à 1880.* Paris, 1984.

Harvey, David. *Consciousness and the Urban Experience: Studies in the History and the Theory of Capitalist Urbanization.* Baltimore, 1985.

(Henry, Émile.) *Coup pour coup.* Paris, 1977.

Henry, Émile. *Déclaration.* Paris, 1894.

Henry, Fortuné. *Les chants de l'enfance.* Paris, 1881.

Herbert, Eugenia. *The Artist and Social Reform: France and Belgium, 1885–1898.* New Haven, 1980 (1961).

———. "Les artistes et l'anarchisme," *Mouvement Social,* 36, July–September 1961.

Herbert, Robert L. *Impressionism: Art, Leisure, and Parisian Society.* New Haven, 1988.

Higonnet, Patrice. *Paris: Capital of the World.* Cambridge, Massachusetts, 2002.

Hobsbawm, E. J. "Political Violence and Political Murder," in *Social Protest, Violence, and Terror,* ed. Wolfgang Mommsen and Gerhard Hirschfeld. New York, 1982.

———. *Primitive Rebels: Studies in Archaic Forms of Social Movements in the Nineteenth and Twentieth Centuries.* New York, 1959.

Horowitz, Irving L. *The Anarchists.* New York, 1964.

Iviansky, Ze'ev. "Individual Terror," *Journal of Contemporary History,* 12 (1977), 43–63.

Jacquement, Gérard. "Belleville ouvrier à la belle époque," *Le Mouvement Social,* 118 (January 1982), 61–77.

Jaeger, Gérard A. *Anatole Deibler, carnets d'exécutions (1885–1939)*. Paris, 2004.

———. *Anatole Deibler (1863–1939): L'homme qui a tranché 400 têtes*. Paris, 2001.

Jensen, Richard Bach. "Daggers, Rifles, and Dynamite: Anarchist Terrorism in Nineteenth-Century Europe," *Terrorism and Political Violence*, 16, 1 (Spring 2004), 116–53.

———. "The International Campaign Against Anarchist Terrorism, 1880–1914/1930s." Unpublished paper, 2007.

Joanne, Paul. *Paris*. Paris, 1889.

———. *Paris-Diamant*. Paris, 1894.

Joll, James. *The Anarchists*. London, 1979.

———. "Singing, Dancing, and Dynamite," *Times Literary Supplement*, Sept. 10, 1976.

Jonas, Raymond A. *France and the Cult of the Sacred Heart: An Epic Tale for Modern Times*. Berkeley, 2000.

———. "Sacred Mysteries and Holy Memories: Counter-Revolutionary France and the Sacré-Coeur," in *Symbols, Myths and Images of the French Revolution*, ed. Ian Germani and Robin Swales. Regina, 1998.

———. "Sacred Tourism and Secular Pilgrimage: Montmartre and the Basilica of Sacré-Coeur," in *Montmartre and the Making of Mass Culture*, Gabriel P. Weisberg, ed. New Brunswick, 2001.

Jordan, David P. *Transforming Paris: The Life and Labors of Baron Haussmann*. New York, 1995.

Kalifa, Dominique. *Crimes et culture au XIXe siècle*. Paris, 2005.

———. *L'encre et le sang*. Paris, 1995.

Kalken, Franz van. *Commotions populaires en Belgique (1834–1902)*. Brussels, 1936.

Kedward, Roderick. *The Anarchists: The Men Who Shocked an Era*. London, 1971.

Kossmann, E. H. *The Low Countries, 1780–1940*. Oxford, 1995.

Kropotkin, Peter. *The Conquest of Bread*. New York, 1927.

Langlais, Roger, ed. *Père Peinard*. Poitiers, 1976.

Laqueur, Walter. *The Age of Terrorism*. Boston, 1987.

———. *A History of Terrorism*. New Brunswick, 2006.

Lefrère, Jean-Jacques, and Philippe Oriol. *Zo d'Axa: Un patrician de l'anarchie*. Paris, 2002.

Léger, Augustin. *Journal d'un anarchiste*. Paris, 1895.

Levy, Carl. "The Anarchist Assassin and Italian History: 1870s to 1930s." Unpublished paper.

———. "Anarchism, Internationalism, and Nationalism in Europe, 1860–1939," *Australian Journal of Politics and History*, 50:3 (2004), 330–42.

Leyret, Henry. *En plein faubourg*. Paris, 2000 (1895).

Longoni, J. C. *Four Patients of Dr. Deibler: A Study in Anarchy.* London, 1970.

Loubat, Guillaume. *Code de la législation contre les anarchistes (commentaire des lois du 28 juillet 1894, 12 décembre 1893, et 18 décembre 1893).* Paris, 1895.

Loyer, François. "Le Sacré-Coeur de Montmartre" in *Les lieux de mémoire,* III, ed. Pierre Nora. Paris, 1992.

Machelon, Jean-Pierre. *La République contre les libertés? Les restrictions aux libertés publiques de 1879 à 1914.* Paris, 1976.

Maitron, Jean. "Un 'anar,' qu'est-ce que c'est?" *Le Mouvement Social,* 83, April–June 1973.

———. *De la Commune à l'anarchie.* Paris, 1894.

———. *Dictionnaire biographique de mouvement ouvrier français: 1871–1914.* Paris, 1973.

———. *Histoire du mouvement anarchiste en France, 1880–1914.* Paris, 1951.

———. *Le mouvement anarchiste en France* (2 volumes). Paris, 1975.

———. *Paul Delesalle, an "anar" de la belle époque.* Paris, 1985.

Maitron, J., and A. Droguet. "La presse anarchiste française de ses origines à nos jours," *Le Mouvement Social,* 83 (April–June 1973).

———. *Ravachol et les anarchistes.* Paris 1964.

Malato, Charles. *Les joyeusetés de l'exile.* Ossas-Suhare, 1985.

———. "Some Anarchist Portraits." *Fortnightly Review,* 333, Sept. 1, 1894.

Manevy, Raymond. *Sous les plis du drapeau noir.* Paris, 1949.

Martin, F. *Notice historique et archéologique sur Limeil-Brévannes.* Corbeil, 1880.

Mayeur, Jean-Marie, and Madeleine Rebérioux. *The Third Republic from Its Origins to the Great War, 1871–1914.* New York, 1987.

Merriman, John. *Aux marges de la ville: Faubourgs et banlieues en France, 1815–1870.* Paris, 1994.

Miller, Martin A. "Dance Macabre: Problems in the History of Terrorism," forthcoming, *Journal for the Study of Radicalism.*

———. "The Intellectual Origins of Modern Terrorism in Europe," in *Terrorism in Context,* ed. Martha Crenshaw. University Park, 1995.

———. *Kropotkin.* Chicago, 1976.

———. "Ordinary Terrorism in Historical Perspective," *Journal for the Study of Radicalism,* 2, 2 (2008).

Miquel, Pierre. *Les anarchistes.* Paris, 2003.

Monroe, John Warner. *Laboratories of Faith: Mesmerism, Spiritism, and Occultism in Modern France.* Ithaca, 2008.

Mulatière, Marie F. de la. *Regards sur Limeil-Brévannes.* Saint-Georges-de-Luzençon, 1988.

Nadal, Jordi, and Xavier Tafunell, *Sant Martí de Provençals, pulmó industrial de Barcelona, 1847–1992.* Barcelona, 1992.

Nataf, André. *La vie quotidienne des anarchistes en France, 1880–1910.* Paris, 1986.

Nord, Philip. *Parisian Shopkeepers and the Politics of Resentment*. Princeton, 1986.

Oliver, H. *The International Anarchist Movement in Late Victorian London*. London, 1983.

Ory, Pascal. *L'Expo Universelle*. Paris, 1989.

O'Squarr, Flor. *Les coulisses de l'anarchie*. Paris, 1990 (1892).

Patsouras, Louis. *Jean Grave and French Anarchism*. Middletown, New Jersey, 1995.

Pentalow, Mike, and Marsha Row. *Characters of Fitzrovia*. London, 2001.

Polasky, Janet. *The Democratic Socialism of Emile Vandervelde: Between Reform and Revolution*. Oxford, 1995.

Post, Jerrold M. *Leaders and Their Followers in a Dangerous World: The Psychology of Political Terror*. Ithaca, 2004.

Préposiet, Jean. *Histoire de l'anarchisme*. Paris, 2002.

Quillard, Pierre. "Entretien sur la vie et la mort de Ravachol," *Mercure de France*, September 1892.

Rapoport, David C. "The Four Waves of Modern Terrorism," in *Attacking Terrorism: Elements of a Grand Strategy*, ed. Audrey Cronin and James Ludes. Washington, 2004.

Raynaud, Ernest. *Souvenirs de police (au temps de Ravachol)*. Paris, 1923.

Reclus, Paul. *Les frères Élie et Élisée Reclus*. Paris, 1964.

Reich, Walter, ed. *Origins of Terrorism: Psychologies, Ideologies, Theologies, States of Mind*. Cambridge, England, 1990.

Rewald, John. "Félix Fénéon," *Gazette des Beaux-Arts*, 31, series 6, 1947, and 32–33, 1948.

Ribeyre, Henri. "Chronique politique," *La Revue Blanche*, 6 (March 1894).

Rochefort, Henri. *The Adventures of My Life*. Vol. 2. London, 1896.

Salmon, André. *La terreur noire*. Paris, 1959.

Schwartz, Vanessa R. *Spectacular Realities: Early Mass Culture in Fin-de-Siècle Paris*. Berkeley, 1998.

Scott, Joan Wallach. *The Glassmakers of Carmaux: French Craftsmen and Political Action in a Nineteenth-Century City*. Cambridge, Mass., 1974.

Seigel, Jerrold. *Bohemian Paris: Culture, Politics, and the Boundaries of Bourgeois Life, 1830–1930*. New York, 1986.

Shattuck, Roger. *The Banquet Years: The Origins of the Avant-Garde in France, 1885 to World War I*. New York, 1968.

Sonn, Richard D. *Anarchism and Cultural Politics in Fin-de-Siècle France*. Lincoln, Neb., 1989.

———. "Marginality and Transgression: Anarchy's Subversive Allure," in *Montmartre and the Making of Mass Culture*, Gabriel P. Weisberg, ed. New Brunswick, 2001.

Stafford, David. *From Anarchism to Reformism: A Study of the Political Activities of Paul Brousse*. Toronto, 1971.

Sweeney, John. *At Scotland Yard: Being the Experiences During Twenty-Seven Years of Service of John Sweeney.* London, 1904.

Taylor, Katherine Fischer. *In the Theater of Criminal Justice: The Palais de Justice in Second Empire Paris.* Princeton, 1993.

Tilly, Charles, Louise Tilly, and Richard Tilly. *The Rebellious Century: 1830–1930.* Cambridge, Mass., 1975.

Trempé, Rolande. *Les mineurs de Carmaux, 1848–1914.* Paris, 1971.

Tuchman, Barbara W. *The Proud Tower: A Portrait of the World Before the War, 1890–1914.* New York, 1967.

Van Kalken, Franz. *Commotions populaires en Belgique, 1834–1902.* Brussels, 1936.

Varennes, Henri. *De Ravachol à Caserio.* Paris, 1895.

Varias, Alexander. *Paris and the Anarchists: Aesthetes and Subversives During the Fin-de-Siècle.* New York, 1996.

Vincent, K. Steven. *Pierre-Joseph Proudhon and the Rise of French Republican Socialism.* New York, 1984.

Vizetelly, Ernest A. *The Anarchists: Their Faith and Their Record.* London, 1911.

Williams, Rosalind H. *Dream Worlds: Mass Consumpion in Late-Nineteenth-Century France.* Berkeley, 1982.

Winock, Michel. *La Belle Époque.* Paris, 2002.

Winter, Jay. *Dreams of Peace and Freedom.* New Haven, 2006.

Wolgensinger, Jacques. *L'histoire à l'une: La grande aventure de la presse.* Paris, 1989.

Woodcock, George. *Anarchism: A History of Libertarian Ideas and Movements.* New York, 1962.

Wright, Gordon. *Between the Guillotine and Liberty: Two Centuries of the Crime Problem in France.* New York, 1983.

Zenker, E. V. *Anarchism: A Criticism and History of the Anarchist Theory.* New York, 1897.

Zévaès, Anne-Léa. "Sous le signe de la dynamite: Émile Henry," *Vendémiaire,* Dec. 30, 1936, and Jan. 6, 1937.

Zola, Émile. *Germinal.* Paris, 1895.

———. *Paris.* Paris, 1898.

Index